GIRLS CAN DO ANYTHING

FROM SPORTS TO INNOVATION, ART TO POLITICS, MEET OVER 200 WOMEN WHO GOT THERE FIRST

Dedicated to Bump

This title comes from a sign my encouraging
parents hung in my room when I was small.
This book is dedicated to the women and
men in my life who taught me from a young
age that, truly, girls can do anything.—C.D.

HarperCollins*Publishers*
1 London Bridge Street
London SE1 9GF

www.harpercollins.co.uk

First published by HarperCollins*Publishers* in 2016

1 3 5 7 9 10 8 6 4 2

Copyright © HarperCollins*Publishers*

Cover design © HarperCollins*Publishers*
Caitlin Doyle asserts her moral rights as author of the text.
Cover and interior illustrations by Chuck Gonzales
Cover and interior design by Pete Clayman

Library of Congress Cataloging-in-Data has been applied for.

ISBN: 978-0-00-795503-9

Printed and bound in China

DISCLAIMER: The Author and the Publishers are committed to respecting
the intellectual property rights of others and have made all reasonable efforts
to trace the copyright owners of the images reproduced, and to provide an
appropriate acknowledgement within this book. In the event that any copyright
holders come forward after the publication of this book, the Author and the
Publishers will use all reasonable endeavors to rectify the position accordingly.

GIRLS CAN DO ANYTHING

FROM SPORTS TO INNOVATION, ART TO POLITICS, MEET OVER 200 WOMEN WHO GOT THERE FIRST

BY CAITLIN DOYLE

Harper
Collins

CONTENTS

Introduction

Hello ladies and gentlemen, boys and girls, and welcome to the adventure that is *Girls Can Do Anything!*

Within these colorful and informative pages, there is something for everyone—a little bit of round-the-world record-breaking here, some major history changers there . . . But mostly, this book is a wonderful opportunity for each of us to hear about the making of the world around us, and to listen to the female voices—so often silenced by history books and social norms—that spoke so much of the world's wisdom.

I sometimes think about a fridge magnet I once saw, which said, "For most of history, Anonymous was a woman." I wanted to give this inanimate magnet the power of speech, because its message was the same as the one that I hoped to deliver through this book: for much of history, a majority of the silent voices were those of girls and women. I know that some of you are thinking, "but it's the 21st century, and everyone from Beyoncé to Taylor Swift, Joseph Gordon Levitt to Chimamanda Ngozie Adichie, is leaning in, standing up, and shouting loud in support of women." That's true, so you *might* also say that feminism's no longer a dirty word and women have made it—and that this book is simply an attractive, educational, historical, and "politically correct" artefact about a time and place where women found themselves to be the supporting acts on an otherwise masculine stage... Right? *Wrong*.

If history has taught us anything, it is that those great thinkers and doers of the past must stand as inspiring examples for us to learn from—and do better. For every woman who has chipped away at the glass ceiling of business, or outperformed every other runner on the track, there are still millions of others who never even make it to the starting line. My wish is for you, dear readers, the creators of the future, to ensure that we all learn from the greatness that came before, in order to make the future even greater—for all.

Within these pages, I have included more than 200 incredible women who I believe to have been at the top of their game within their chosen fields. However, there are simply not enough pages to include every great individual, and the selection I have made is limited by my own research and subjectivity. I invite you to include your own "greats" within the pages of this book. You will find blank pages at the end of each chapter, where you can add the names and details of the women who really mean something to you—be they big names from history, or current affairs, or people from your own life who have inspired and amazed you. Make this book your own.

Caitlin Doyle

June 2016

Arts & literature

 CONTENTS

CONTENTS

SAPPHO
ONE OF THE GREATEST POETS OF ANTIQUITY

FULL NAME: Sappho
BORN: C. 620 B.C., LESBOS, GREECE
DIED: 550 B.C., LESBOS, GREECE
NATIONALITY: ANCIENT GREEK

> 66 Beauty endures only for as long as it can be seen; goodness, beautiful today, will remain so tomorrow. 99
> SAPPHO

A poetess, believed to be Sappho, from an ancient Roman fresco

THE POETESS

Sappho, or Psappha, is often simply referred to as "the Poetess"—so great was her talent. Her fame is considerable, especially as very little is known about the woman herself.

Sappho spent most of her life on the Greek island of Lesbos and is believed to have been born to an aristocratic family. She is said to have married and had a daughter, but any details of this are scarce. Sappho wrote many songs and poems and is considered to be one of the greatest of the ancient poets.

BEAUTY ENDURES

Little remains of Sappho's work, but scholars continue to be fascinated by her. Newly discovered poems have been published as recently as 2014. Her poetry and songs were written in a unique style, now called "Sapphic" meter. The language was simple and direct, but full of melody.

Often Sappho wrote about beauty and love—sometimes addressing her poems to men but more often to women. In fact, her name (as an adjective, "Sapphic") is used to describe romantic love between women, as is the island where she was born ("lesbian" comes from "Lesbos"). She wrote odes to the goddesses and retellings of Greek myths. She also wrote about her community and, it is believed, herself. This was different from the male poets of the time, who tended to focus on politics.

In spite of the fact that Sappho lived over 2,000 years ago, and that much of her work has been lost, her words are still read and studied today. Sappho remains known as one of the greatest ancient poets, and her memory lives on through her work.

MURASAKI SHIKIBU
FIRST MODERN NOVELIST

FULL NAME: Murasaki Shikibu
BORN: C. 978, HEIAN-KYŌ, JAPAN
DIED: C. 1014, POSSIBLY BIWA, JAPAN
NATIONALITY: JAPANESE

LADY MURASAKI

Murasaki Shikibu, also known as "Lady Murasaki," was an 11th-century poet and novelist in Japan. She wrote during Japan's "Heian" period, a golden age of peace, harmony, and the arts. Heian women did not typically learn written Chinese (the language of government in Japan), but Murasaki was anything but typical. She excelled and quickly became a prolific writer of poems and novels in Japanese and is believed to be the world's first novelist. Her novel, *The Tale of Genji*, was written in 1007. Many consider it the greatest work of Japanese literature and the oldest full novel in the world. Among other works, she also wrote a volume of poetry entitled *The Diary of Lady Murasaki*.

Murasaki was married and had a daughter, but her husband died within two years of their marriage. It is believed that because of her incredible writing talent and intelligence, she was brought to live at the royal court. There, she became a lady-in-waiting to Empress Akiko. Murasaki kept a diary about her views on life at court. She used these observations for her novel about daily life among upper class society. *The Tale of Genji* was immediately successful. It has since been translated into several languages and illustrated editions. To this day, it continues to be studied as the main source of knowledge about life in ancient Japanese society.

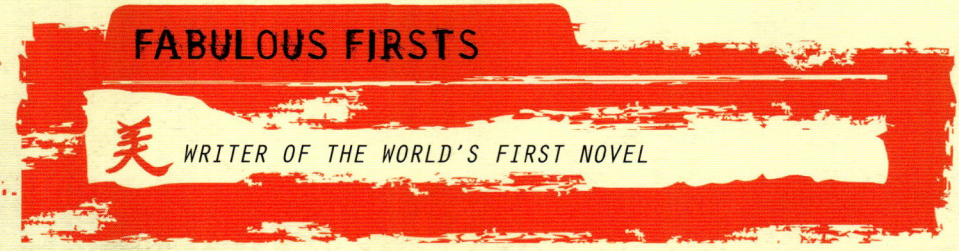

FABULOUS FIRSTS

美 *WRITER OF THE WORLD'S FIRST NOVEL*

SAINT HILDEGARD OF BINGEN
IMPORTANT MEDIEVAL COMPOSER AND "INVENTOR" OF OPERA

FULL NAME: Hildegard von Bingen (A.K.A. Sibyl of the Rhine)
BORN: C. 1098, BEMERSHEIM, WEST FRANCONIA (NOW GERMANY)
DIED: 1179, RUPERTSBERG, WEST FRANCONIA (NOW GERMANY)
NATIONALITY: GERMAN

Sv. Hilde garda

Illustration of Saint Hildegard (date unknown)

INSTRUCTIONS FROM GOD

Hildegard von Bingen achieved many things through devotion to her faith. She became a nun, but she was also a composer, author, preacher, visionary healer-doctor—later a saint. She is also credited as being the inventor of opera. From a young age, Hildegard felt a connection to God. She experienced visions and heard voices. Her parents sent her, aged eight, to live in a convent. As a student of the mother superior, Jutta, Hildegard read and studied widely. When Jutta died, 38-year-old Hildegard was unanimously elected by her fellow nuns to replace her. Her writings became well known, and many nuns came to learn from her. Hildegard knew about medicine and was a great healer. Crowds gathered to have her "miracles" worked on them. She preached widely, even though this was illegal for women. She often challenged senior Church officials and fought for independence. Some of her views on the Church, and on women in society, were progressive. She corresponded with several important figures of the time, many of whom sought her advice, including the German emperor and the English monarchs.

THE CULT OF HILDEGARD

Hildegard was one of the most prolific writers of her time. She documented her religious visions, as well as writing poetry, plays, and books on medicine and women's health. As well as for her role as a visionary, she is best known today as a composer of popular songs, which are still being performed. Around 70 of her compositions have survived—a huge number for a medieval composer.

After she died, the process of making her a saint was started—but it wasn't until 2012 that she was declared a saint. She was also named a "Doctor of the Church"—a title held by very few saints—to emphasize the importance of her teachings. A "Cult of Hildegard" exists today, followed by those who live by those teachings. Hildegard was a determined leader. She is still celebrated as a feminist who both promoted and celebrated the virtues of female community and intellect.

THE MONA LISA
THE WORLD'S MOST FAMOUS PAINTING

FULL NAME: *La Gioconda* (or, more commonly, *The Mona Lisa*)

CREATED: C. 1503, FLORENCE, ITALY

NATIONALITY: ITALIAN/FRENCH

THE WORLD'S MOST FAMOUS SMILE

La Gioconda, the painting better known as *The Mona Lisa*, is one of the most visited and best-known paintings in the entire world. Its painter, Leonardo da Vinci, was not only an artist, but also an inventor, sculptor, architect, and engineer. He painted the work in Florence some time between 1503 and 1506, and the painting now hangs in the Musée de Louvre in Paris, France. Leonardo's composition and style set the standard and revolutionized portrait painting.

Just who is the woman in the painting? No one is certain. All we do know is that The Mona Lisa was painted in oil paints on wood around 1503.

WHO IS *MONA LISA*?

In spite of its claim to be the world's most famous painting, a lot of mystery surrounds the half-smiling woman in the picture. Many historians believe her to be Lisa Gherardini del Giocondo, the wife of a silk merchant from Florence. Others believe the model could have been Leonardo's mother, Caterina, or an Italian princess named Isabella d'Este. A more unusual suggestion is that the painting is actually meant to be a riddle: a self-portrait of Leonardo himself. The question remains unanswered to this day, over 500 years later.

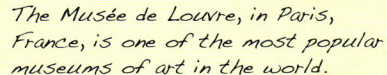

The Musée de Louvre, in Paris, France, is one of the most popular museums of art in the world.

The Mona Lisa remains one of the most replicated artworks, imitated by artists such as Marcel Duchamp and Andy Warhol. Operas and ballads have been written about her, as well as movies, novels, and plays. Her mysterious smile remains the most recognized in the world.

ARTEMISIA GENTILESCHI
IMPORTANT PAINTER OF THE ITALIAN RENAISSANCE

FULL NAME: Artemisia Gentileschi
BORN: JULY 8, 1593, ROME, ITALY
DIED: C. 1652, NAPLES, ITALY
NATIONALITY: ITALIAN

"Birth of St. John the Baptist,"
1635 oil-on-canvas painting by
Artemisia Gentileschi

Artemisia Gentileschi was the daughter of Orazio Gentileschi, an accomplished Italian painter of the Baroque period. (Baroque design was grand and full of movement and a major artistic style in Renaissance Europe.) Orazio encouraged his daughter's artistic skills, and they worked together on several paintings. Artemisia eventually moved to Florence, where she worked for wealthy art patrons, including the Medici family and the King of Spain.

STRONG WOMEN

Artemisia's most famous works include "Madonna and Child," "Susanna and the Elders," "Judith Slaying Holofernes," and "Cleopatra," as well as several self-portraits. Her paintings often focus on active female characters who are equal to men. This was unusual at a time when women were usually painted as beautiful and passive. Very few women made it as Renaissance painters. However, Artemisia was successful during her lifetime, which is uncommon for any painter, but even more so for a woman in that period. She was also the first woman to become a member of the famous Academy of Fine Arts in Florence. She is now considered one of the best and most progressive painters of the time and a feminist icon.

FABULOUS FIRSTS

FIRST WOMAN TO BECOME A MEMBER OF THE
ACADEMY OF FINE ARTS, FLORENCE, ITALY

OROONOKO:
OR, THE
Royal Slave.
A TRUE
HISTORY.
By Mrs. A. BEHN.

LONDON,
Printed for Will. Canning, at his Shop in
the Temple Cloisters. 1688.

FULL NAME: Aphra Behn
BORN: C. 1640, U.K.
DIED: APRIL 16, 1689, LONDON, U.K.
NATIONALITY: ENGLISH

Original 1688 first
edition cover of Aphra
Behn's novel, Oroonoko

UNLADYLIKE?

Aphra Behn was many things: novelist, playwright, poet, translator, and spy. She lived in the mid-1600s, at a time when women were very firmly under the control of their fathers and husbands. Nevertheless, Aphra became a celebrity. She was a paid author, financially independent, and this made her very unusual. She also fought for the equality of the sexes. For all of this, she was accused of being "unladylike"—but she did not let this stand in her way.

CELEBRITY, SPY, WRITER

Little is known of Aphra's early years, other than that she spent some time in South America. In 1666, Aphra is known to have acted as an English spy in Antwerp, Holland on behalf of the royal family. She collected intelligence about military threats during the Second Dutch War. Not long after, she began writing plays, followed by novels and poetry, as a means of earning an income and paying off her debts. Being a professional (paid) writer was almost unheard of for a woman at the time. Her most successful play was called "The Rover" and was written in 1681. She wrote several plays and was considered one of the most prolific playwrights of her time. Her speciality was comedy, but through her plays she was able to question the contemporary treatment of women. Her 1688 novel, *Oroonoko*, is today recognized as iconic in the development of the novel in the English language. The novel told the story of an enslaved prince and the harsh treatment of the local people by the colonists.

Aphra was also unusual in that she never used a male pen name or pretended to be a man when she wrote or competed against male playwrights. She was radical in her belief that women should be educated. Aphra Behn's work was overlooked for roughly 300 years, until the 20th century. Now, she is recognized as an important writer, novelist, and feminist icon.

COUNTESS D'AULNOY
NOVELIST WHO COINED THE TERM "FAIRY TALE"

FULL NAME: Marie-Catherine Le Jumel de Barneville
BORN: (EXACT DATE UNKNOWN) 1650, NEAR HONFLEUR, FRANCE
DIED: JANUARY 14, 1705, PARIS, FRANCE
NATIONALITY: FRENCH

FAIRY TALES FOR GROWN-UPS

Marie-Catherine Le Jumel de Barneville, also known as the Countess d'Aulnoy or Madame d'Aulnoy, was a 17th-century novelist and fairy-tale writer. Many of her works told of intrigue and scandal, just like her own personal life. As a young wife, Marie is rumored to have conspired with her mother to make up false accusations about her husband. When the plot backfired, Marie had to leave France for 15 years. During this time, she traveled in Spain, England, and Holland. Her adventures fed into her stories, and when she returned to France in 1685, she began her literary career. At the time, literary salons (where writers would share stories out loud) were fashionable. Marie hosted her own popular salon, and her work was soon published.

Countess d'Aulnoy, in an 18th-century engraving

Marie's novels were very popular across Europe. They told fictionalized accounts of history in the royal European courts. However, it was her fairy tales (*contes de fées*), first published in 1707, for which she is best known. Marie coined the term "fairy tales" for the popular folk tales featuring fantasy characters and magic. The Brothers Grimm would become famous for their own collections of such tales over 100 years later. While Marie's tales are less well known today, she made a huge contribution to the genre that helped create the tales we love today.

FAIRY TALE CHARACTERS

Fairy tales are fantasy stories—often, but not always, for children—that feature magic and include creatures such as fairies, elves, and dragons. Countess d'Aulnoy coined the term *contes de fées* (fairy tales) in the 17th century, grouping together this style of story. Traditionally, these tales were told out loud and passed down from generation to generation. The Grimm Brothers, Charles Perrault, Countess d'Aulnoy, and Hans Christian Anderson all collected these stories, and they have become the tales we know and love today.

Many fairy tales have a girl or woman at the center of them, such as *Cinderella*, *Sleeping Beauty*, and *Rapunzel*. In some cases, these women are able to make their own choices and rescue themselves. However, in several retellings that are now common today, these women often need to be rescued by someone else. There is a modern trend to give women in these stories a sense of their own control once again, as can be seen in current versions of these stories on the big screen, such as *Tangled* and *Enchanted*.

CLOCKWISE FROM TOP LEFT:
RAPUNZEL, AURORA (FROM SLEEPING
BEAUTY), SNOW WHITE, CINDERELLA,
AND LITTLE RED RIDING HOOD

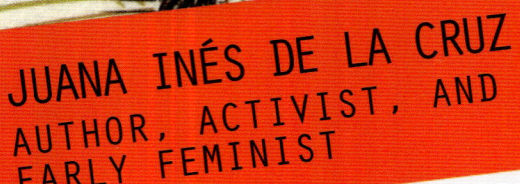

JUANA INÉS DE LA CRUZ
AUTHOR, ACTIVIST, AND EARLY FEMINIST

FULL NAME: Juana Inés de la Cruz
BORN: NOVEMBER 12, 1651, SAN MIGUEL NEPANTLA (NOW TEPETLIXPA), MEXICO
DIED: APRIL 17, 1695, MEXICO CITY, MEXICO
NATIONALITY: MEXICAN

> " I don't study to know more, but to ignore less. "
>
> JUANA INÉS DE LA CRUZ

TEENAGE WONDER

Almost 400 years ago, Juana Inés de la Cruz was her generation's Malala (*see pages* 150–151). An outspoken activist for women's right to an education, Juana's scholarly work became known throughout Mexico—and as far as Spain—when she was still a teenager. Aged 16, Juana decided to become a nun in Mexico City, as it would give her the freedom to study and write. At the time, living as a nun was one of the only options for a girl who wanted to pursue these activities. As a nun, Sor (Sister) Juana wrote poetry, plays, and essays, challenging social norms and defending women's rights. Juana found her own access to education— as she was entirely self-taught. From 1669 until the end of her life, Juana lived at the Convent of Santa Paula, where she wrote, taught music and drama, composed music, and worked as the convent's accountant and archivist. She built up one of the largest private libraries in the New World. (The "New World" was an early European name for the Americas.)

THE TENTH MUSE

Unlike many writers and artists throughout history, Juana was successful in her lifetime, during the Golden Age of Spanish arts. Her nickname was the "Tenth Muse." She was a very talented writer and set her hand to many different genres and styles. She was also the unofficial royal court poet in the 1680s. The characters in her plays included women who were both brave and clever, and her religious works praised the learned female saints. Eventually, the Church disapproved of her writing and her beliefs, instructing her to focus on religious studies. However, Juana defended herself admirably, while also asserting all women's right to knowledge: "One can perfectly well philosophize while cooking supper."

Juana has lived on as a lasting icon of many things: Mexican identity, early feminism, and independence. In the 20th century—thanks, in part, to the work of Mexican artists Diego Rivera and Frida Kahlo (*see pages* 46–47) and contemporary artists—Juana became famous again. (She can be seen in Rivera's 1947 mural, *Dream of a Sunday Afternoon in the Alameda Central* in Mexico City, Mexico.) Her ideas and accomplishments were ahead of their time, but the world has finally caught up. She is credited as the first published feminist of the New World and an outstanding writer of her period. Today, Juana's portrait is on Mexican currency and she remains an inspiration to modern artists, scholars, and feminists.

A statue of Sister Juana Inés de la Cruz, given from Mexico to Madrid, Spain in 1981

FABULOUS FIRSTS

FIRST PUBLISHED FEMINIST OF THE "NEW WORLD"

19·OCTVBRE·1981

EL PVEBLO DE
MEXICO
A TRAVES DEL CLAVSTRO DE
SOR JVANA INES
DE LA CRVZ. A. C.

DEDICA ESTA ESTATVA DE LA INSIGNE
MISTICA Y POETISA MEXICANA
AL PVEBLO DE
MADRID

JULIA MARGARET CAMERON
EARLY PIONEER OF PHOTOGRAPHY

FULL NAME: Julia Margaret Cameron
BORN: JUNE 11, 1815, CALCUTTA, INDIA
DIED: JANUARY 26, 1879, KALUTARA, SRI LANKA
NATIONALITY: BRITISH

FROM SCIENCE TO ART

One of the most influential and innovative photographers of the 1800s, Julia Margaret Cameron was also a visionary. In the 19th century, photography was a new and developing science —a cutting-edge way to record a person or scene. Julia, however, used her portraits to elevate photography to an art form.

Portrait of Julia Margaret Cameron from 1870, by Henry Herschel Hay Cameron

A camera similar to the type Margaret would have used late in her career

A LATE BLOOMER

The fourth of seven daughters, Julia could have disappeared as the middle child of a large family. But instead, she stood out as the most artistic and eccentric. Julia had an international upbringing: while her family was British, she was born in India, educated in France, and spent time in India, Sri Lanka, and Africa.

While in South Africa in 1836, Julia met John Herschel, the famous British astronomer. They became life-long friends, and a few years later he introduced her to photography. He would continue to advise her on technical matters until he died. (Remember, at the time, photography was still a very manual process involving chemistry and darkrooms.) Julia started her photography career relatively late in life, at the age of 48, when her daughter gave her a camera as a present.

Julia's 1870 photograph, "Vivian and Merlin"—an illustration for poet Alfred Lord Tennyson's work, "Idylls of Spring"

CAPTURING BEAUTY

Julia experimented with artistic uses for photography and was one of the first ever to do so. She is best known for her portraits, often close-ups of family, friends, and the celebrities from her social circle. Julia used her photographs to re-tell stories from myths and legends, including those of King Arthur. She wanted to capture beauty, and even the sitter's soul, rather than simple reality. Julia's style was very unusual: her photographs were intentionally out of focus, and she kept, or even added, scratches and marks in her work. Fellow photographers often thought her work was sloppy, but painters loved her style. Perhaps her work was simply ahead of its time, as she remains a huge inspiration to many modern photographers and other artists. Today, Julia's work continues to be shown in exhibitions around the world, from New York's Metropolitan Museum of Art to London's Victoria and Albert Museum.

BEATRIX POTTER
ONE OF THE BEST-LOVED CHILDREN'S AUTHORS OF ALL TIME

FULL NAME: Helen Beatrix Potter

BORN: JULY 28, 1866, LONDON, U.K.

DIED: DECEMBER 22, 1943, NEAR SAWREY, CUMBRIA, U.K.

NATIONALITY: BRITISH

PETER RABBIT'S CREATOR

Despite writing 100 years ago, Beatrix Potter remains one of the best-loved and best-selling children's authors in history. The mischievous Peter Rabbit is recognized by children all over the world.

Beatrix came from a wealthy English family, and her parents were very artistic. At the time, it was common for children to be looked after by nannies. The Potter nannies spent a lot of time outside with the children and allowed them to set up homes for all sorts of creatures in their nursery. From a young age, Beatrix was fascinated. She sketched animals and insects very carefully and accurately. Eventually, she studied at the National Art Training School. Even though her animal characters wear clothes and engage in human activities, they still look remarkably realistic.

A British postage stamp, circa 1979, showing The Tale of Peter Rabbit

Beatrix first had success making greeting cards, but she also wrote and illustrated stories for friends. One such story was *The Tale of Peter Rabbit*. In 1902, the publisher Frederick Warne & Co. published *Peter Rabbit*, and it quickly became popular with young readers. Several tales followed, including *The Tale of Squirrel Nutkin*, *The Tale of Tom Kitten*, and *The Tale of Jemima Puddle-Duck*. In total, Beatrix wrote 28 books in her lifetime, many of which became instant children's classics.

A portrait of Beatrix outside of her home in the Lake District, by Charles G.Y. King

WRITING IN NATURE

Throughout her life, Beatrix remained fascinated by nature and animals. Beatrix moved from being a writer in London to a farmer in the countryside of the English Lake District (see top left). Later in life, she wrote less and spent a lot of her time tending her farms and sheep. In particular, she raised a local breed of sheep, the Herdwick, for which she won many prizes. Her commitment to nature and the environment was ahead of its time, and today she would be called a conservationist. She actively campaigned about nature and was a smart businesswoman. When she died, she left 4,000 acres of land and farms to the National Trust, a nature preservation organization in England.

Beatrix Potter's work remains just as popular today as it was in her lifetime. Her works have been translated into 35 languages and have sold over 100 million copies. And 110 years after the publication of her first book, Beatrix's fans have a new surprise in store. A long-lost and previously unpublished story, *The Tale of Kitty-in-Boots*, was found in 2014. The text, illustrated by prize-winning artist Quentin Blake, is available September 2016!

Beatrix's home in the English Lake District was Yew Tree Farm, pictured here. It can still be visited today.

VIRGINIA WOOLF
LITERARY PIONEER

FULL NAME: Adeline Virginia Stephen Woolf
BORN: JANUARY 25, 1882, LONDON, U.K.
DIED: MARCH 28, 1941, NEAR LEWES, EAST SUSSEX, U.K.
NATIONALITY: BRITISH

> " A woman must have money
> and a room of her own . . . "
>
> VIRGINIA WOOLF

A FAMILY OF ARTISTS

Virginia Woolf is considered to be one of the most influential writers of the 20th century. She helped kick-start modernism—a major art movement that rejected traditional ideas and instead focused on brand-new concepts that fit better in the modern, industrial world. Modernism included every art form—from painting to novels, music to architecture—and continues to influence styles of art today.

Adeline Virginia Stephen was born into a very artistic family (including her great aunt, the famous portrait photographer Julia Margaret Cameron—*see pages* 24–25). One of eight children, young Virginia was especially close to her sister Vanessa (later the famous painter Vanessa Bell). Writerly from childhood, at the age of nine Virginia founded the family newspaper, the *Hyde Park News*. The family suffered a series of tragedies, with the death of Virginia's mother, followed by that of two of her siblings and her father. These sadnesses contributed to Virginia's depression, but they would also later be channeled into her writing.

The Bloomsbury Group of like-minded artists and writers lived in this square in Bloomsbury, London. The area was a hive of creativity for a number of years.

THE BLOOMSBURY BOHEMIANS

Around 1907, Virginia and Vanessa moved to Bloomsbury, in London, where they held informal gatherings of bohemian artists and thinkers. Virginia met Leonard Woolf, who would become her husband and chief supporter for the rest of her life. The group quickly became the "Bloomsbury Group"—a talented group of artists, writers, and philosophers with a strong influence over the London art scene. Virginia and her writing were in the middle of it all.

Virginia had unique thoughts on how to construct a novel. She liked the idea of not plotting a story from A to B, but instead following her natural flow of thoughts (a technique known as "stream-of-consciousness"). She also wrote about everyday, domestic happenings rather than great, dramatic events. Her first novels, including *The Voyage Out*, were more traditional, but the more she wrote, the more she experimented. In the course of her life, Virginia wrote reviews, essays, diaries, letters, and novels and became one of the most influential and respected writers of the era.

A ROOM OF ONE'S OWN

In 1917, Virginia and Leonard started a publishing company, called the Hogarth Press. It soon became a major publisher of modernist works and published over 500 books. In addition to being a writer, Virginia was a social activist and later feminist icon, exploring themes of class, war, women's rights, and politics in her writing. The 1929 essay *A Room of One's Own* contains Virginia's most famous feminist remark, which became a slogan for later feminists aiming to achieve success in all areas: "A woman must have money and a room of her own if she is to write fiction."

Virginia's mental health grew worse over the years, and in 1941 she committed suicide. In spite of such a tragic end, at the age of only 59, the great writer's works live on larger than life. Her most famous novels, *Mrs. Dalloway*, *To the Lighthouse*, *Orlando*, and *Jacob's Room*, remain classics of modern literature. Virginia's voice was unique and ahead of its time. Her style has influenced generations of writers, as well as artists and film-makers.

COCO CHANEL
FASHION ICON AND ONE OF THE MOST INFLUENTIAL DESIGNERS OF ALL TIME

FULL NAME: Gabrielle "Coco" Bonheur Chanel
BORN: AUGUST 19, 1883, SAUMUR, FRANCE
DIED: JANUARY 10, 1971, PARIS, FRANCE
NATIONALITY: FRENCH

More than 100 years after Coco Chanel hit the fashion scene, her stylish designs and recognizable logo remain iconic all over the world.

FAREWELL TO THE CORSET

Voted one of the top fashion icons of all time by *Time* magazine, Coco Chanel was a game-changer in the world of women's fashion. Before she made an impact with her designs, women squeezed themselves into corsets and super-feminine dresses. Coco was seen as revolutionary—bringing looser, more "masculine" clothes to women. She was one of the first women to wear pants, and the first to design pajamas and lightweight sportswear for women. Coco introduced the now-iconic "little black dress," and her tweed skirt suits, costume jewelry, and simple yet elegant designs have become staples in the world of women's apparel.

Gabrielle "Coco" Chanel, stylishly posed, in 1920

AMAZING ACHIEVEMENTS

- GAME-CHANGER IN WOMEN'S FASHION
- INTRODUCED THE LITTLE BLACK DRESS, PAJAMAS, AND BELL-BOTTOM PANTS

Coco was the very first fashion designer to launch her own perfume.

ENDURING STYLE ICON

Born Gabrielle Bonheur Chanel, Coco had a difficult early life. She was born into poverty in France and was raised in a girls' home at a convent, where she was taught to sew. As a young woman, she made her way briefly into the entertainment industry as a cabaret singer, where she picked up the nickname of "Coco." In 1910, she was funded to open her own hat shop, before moving on to women's clothing and, eventually, perfume—the first fashion designer to do so. She felt that in order for clothes to be luxurious, they ultimately needed to be comfortable. This included her large role in bringing pants into women's fashion. Coco's designs were loved by Hollywood royalty, including actresses such as Audrey Hepburn and Grace Kelly. Coco Chanel quickly earned a position at the height of contemporary fashion, and her place as a revered fashion icon holds firm to this day.

With the Great Depression, followed by World War II, even wealthy people's ability to buy high fashion was in decline. Coco closed the Chanel stores in 1939. However, in 1954, at the age of 70, she made a grand return to the world of clothing—with the introduction of bell-bottom pants. Coco opened her first fashion store over 100 years ago, yet her name continues to be a byword for iconic style. Her designs and philosophy of fashion have greatly influenced generations of designers that followed. Her "CC" logo is now one of the world's most recognizable trademarks.

Coco's fashion house remains as popular today as it was during her lifetime. This boutique window, in Milan, Italy, displays some of the 2012 Chanel designs.

MA RAINEY
MOTHER OF THE BLUES

FULL NAME: Gertrude Malissa "Ma" Nix Pridgett Rainey
BORN: C. APRIL 26, 1886, COLUMBUS, GEORGIA, U.S.A.
DIED: DECEMBER 22, 1939, ROME, GEORGIA, U.S.A.
NATIONALITY: AMERICAN

MADAM GERTRUDE MA RAINEY

Gertrude Malissa Nix Pridgett began performing when she was around 13, first through her Baptist church and later on tour. In 1904, Gertrude married William Rainey, and the pair began touring as "Ma" and "Pa" Rainey soon after. By 1905, Ma had heard blues music and began to work it into her performance list. She quickly developed her own "raw" singing style, using her booming voice and unusual phrasing. She became the first popular entertainer to perform the blues on stage and came to be known as the "Mother of the Blues."

FROM GERTRUDE TO MA

She would go on to perform live music for over 30 years, including during the blues heyday of the 1920s. Her stage presence was captivating. Ma became the first great female blues vocalist and brought blues to a wider audience. After the Raineys separated in 1916, Ma began touring with her own band, Madam Gertrude Ma Rainey and her Georgia Smart Sets.

> *They don't understand that's [the blues is] life's way of talking. You don't sing to feel better. You sing 'cause that's a way of understanding life.*
>
> MA RAINEY

A collection of her songs from 1924 to 1928, "Ma Rainey's Black Bottom" album remains a classic of the blues genre.

FABULOUS FIRSTS

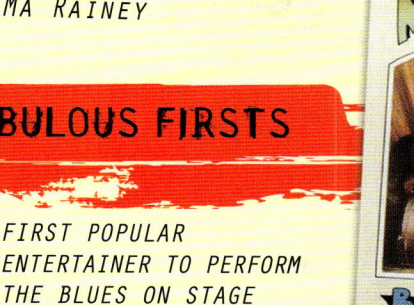

FIRST POPULAR ENTERTAINER TO PERFORM THE BLUES ON STAGE

BLUESY BUSINESSWOMAN

In 1923, Ma made her first record for Paramount Records. This was to be part of the first wave of blues records. (Mamie Smith was the first black woman to record an album, in 1920.) Ma's songs dealt with love and work, and the everyday lives of Southern African-Americans. Ma worked with many famous musicians and singers of her day, including Louis Armstrong and Coleman Hawkins. Ma was known as a savvy businesswoman, and she also owned two entertainment venues: the Lyric Theater and the Airdome.

Not only was Ma Rainey important to the evolution of blues music, her work inspired a wide range of musicians, as well as poets and novelists, such as Langston Hughes, Sterling Brown, and Alice Walker. Ma has been inducted into both the Blues Foundation's Hall of Fame (in 1983) and the Rock and Roll Hall of Fame (in 1990) for her tremendous contributions to music of all genres.

GEORGIA O'KEEFFE
MOTHER OF AMERICAN MODERNISM

FULL NAME: Georgia Totto O'Keeffe
BORN: NOVEMBER 15, 1887, SUN PRAIRIE, WISCONSIN, U.S.A.
DIED: MARCH 6, 1986, SANTA FE, NEW MEXICO, U.S.A.
NATIONALITY: AMERICAN

Cow skulls and colorful flowers featured heavily in Georgia's work.

MODERN AMERICA ON CANVAS

Even if you don't know the name "Georgia O'Keeffe," chances are you've seen her work. Georgia is one of the most well-known American painters of all time. Her paintings are bold and brightly colored and grace the walls of museums around the world, as well as greeting cards and posters. She painted huge canvases with iconic images of America, including New York skyscrapers, Southwestern deserts and cow skulls, and huge flowers and clouds.

FROM SKYSCRAPERS TO COW SKULLS

Georgia came from a family of Wisconsin dairy farmers, and she was the second of seven children. As a young girl, she was taught watercolor painting. By age ten, she knew she would be an artist. She went on to study at the Art Institute of Chicago (which now houses the majority of her works) and the Art Students League in New York. There, she was taught revolutionary ideas of composition. The charcoal drawings she did as a result made Georgia one of the very first American artists to produce abstract art—this was her first exhibited work, in 1916. The art dealer and photographer responsible for this exhibition was Alfred Stieglitz. Alfred and Georgia would eventually marry, and Alfred would spend the rest of his life as Georgia's supporter. By the 1920s, Georgia was becoming famous for her now-trademark themes of skyscrapers and flowers. Soon after, she began traveling to New Mexico. The desert landscapes made their way into her work, as a beautiful contrast to her skyscraper pieces. Her desire for new ideas led her to travel internationally, and she produced incredible paintings of the mountains of Peru and Japan.

Georgia painted the deserts and rock formations of New Mexico.

A U.S. postage stamp from 2013 commemorating Georgia's work

Georgia O'Keeffe | *forever* | usa

FAMOUS PAINTER AND FEMINIST ICON

Later in life, Georgia suffered from an eye condition called macular degeneration that caused her to lose her sight. But she refused to be defeated. Georgia painted her last work without help at the age of 85. After that, she had the help of several assistants and continued to create beautiful art that she pictured in her imagination. Georgia was painting at a time when most famous artists were men, but she continued with her unique style and found great success. Her work is described as distinctly "female" for its curvy, "feminine" lines and close-ups, as well as her focus on nature. She has become a feminist icon, both for her distinct style and determination. Georgia was awarded the National Medal of Arts, in 1977, and the Presidential Medal of Freedom, in 1985, for her huge contribution to the arts. She remains one of the most important and influential American painters of all time and is known as the Mother of American Modernism.

DOROTHEA LANGE
INFLUENTIAL DOCUMENTARIAN AND PHOTOJOURNALIST

FULL NAME: Dorothea Margaretta Nutzhorn Lange
BORN: MAY 26, 1895, HOBOKEN, NEW JERSEY, U.S.A
DIED: OCTOBER 11, 1965, SAN FRANCISCO, CALIFORNIA, U.S.A.
NATIONALITY: AMERICAN

"America Survives the Depression," a 1998 U.S. postage stamp, features Dorothea's iconic 1936 "Migrant Mother" photograph.

TOP OF HER GAME

Among famous photographers, Dorothea Lange ranks right at the top, alongside Ansel Adams, Henri Cartier-Bresson, and Annie Leibovitz. Dorothea's black-and-white photographs of America's Great Depression and Dust Bowl of the 1930s helped create the genre of documentary photography we know today.

At the age of seven, Dorothea contracted polio, a potentially fatal infectious disease that affects the muscles. Dorothea survived, but her right leg was badly affected, which left her with a permanent limp. However, she believed this condition helped form the person she would become. Dorothea studied photography at Colombia University, and in her early 20s she set out to travel the world. She only got as far as San Francisco—but her thwarted plans would result in some of the most iconic images of America in history. For a time, Dorothea ran a portrait studio in San Francisco, but then the Great Depression hit. This was a time of severe economic depression, with hardship, high unemployment, and widespread poverty. The Depression started in the U.S.A. after a fall in prices on the stock market, before reaching around the globe.

THE STORY BEHIND THE PHOTOGRAPH

Dorothea saw what was happening around her and decided to take her camera to the streets. She began documenting the struggles around her: soup kitchens, unemployed workers, and starving families. She was hired by the U.S. government's Resettlement Administration (later the Farm Security Administration) to capture daily life in America. Dorothea's most iconic photo—and arguably the most famous photo of American life—is called "Migrant Mother," taken in 1936. It shows children huddled around their young mother, a portrait of complete despair. This photo made the public realize the Depression's very real impact and also raised the bar of documentary photography. The photograph prompted the U.S. government to rush aid to its people. In 1940, Dorothea won the very prestigious Guggenheim fellowship—the first woman to do so. She was gifted at making the people she photographed feel respected and listened to. Her work made a significant difference to the lives of many.

With the start of World War II, Dorothea was again hired by the U.S. government. This time it was to take photos of Japanese Americans who had been put into "detention camps" (prisons for whole groups of people for "security" during wartime). These photographs were so critical of the government, the Army kept them hidden from view for decades. Dorothea traveled widely for the rest of her life, and she went on to document the lives of people from as far afield as Utah to Vietnam, Ireland to Pakistan.

Dorothea Lange's work forever changed the course of photojournalism: she was able to give her stories heart. Her work continues to influence the work of photographers around the globe to this day.

Dorothea documented the hardships faced by the American people. In this 1937 photograph, she shows cotton sharecroppers toiling on the land in Greene County, Georgia.

ANNI ALBERS
MOST INFLUENTIAL TEXTILE ARTIST OF THE 20TH CENTURY

FULL NAME: Annelise Elsa Frieda Fleischmann Albers
BORN: JUNE 12, 1899, BERLIN, GERMANY
DIED: MAY 9, 1994, ORANGE, CONNECTICUT, U.S.A.
NATIONALITY: GERMAN/AMERICAN

The German Bauhaus art movement included everything from architecture to object design, furniture to textiles.

THE ART OF WEAVING

Anni Albers was the most significant textile designer of the 20th century. Technically, "textiles" refer to any woven objects, such as items made from yarn, fibers, or any other material, that can be used for practical or decorative purposes. This includes anything from a quilt or clothing to wall hanging or sculpture. Textiles have been around since the earliest civilizations, but textile arts had a surge in popularity at the start of the 20th century. Anni played a pivotal part in this; she helped re-establish textiles as an art form.

Anni and her husband, Josef Albers, were members of the Bauhaus movement—a German art movement that celebrated the connection between architecture and crafts. Anni's distinctive textile works had a very architectural and industrial feel to them. This was a completely new take on the traditional world of textiles as a very delicate and feminine craft. Anni used everything to create her pieces, including metal, plastic, and even horse hair. Anni and Josef moved to the U.S.A. after the outbreak of World War II, when the Nazi Party closed the Bauhaus School. In 1949, Anni had a solo exhibition at New York's prestigious Museum of Modern Art (MoMA)—she was the first textile artist ever to do so. Anni was also a very talented printmaker, but it was for her textile work that she made the biggest mark on the history of art. For Anni and Joseph Albers, art was part of everyday life. Anni's groundbreaking work, combined with the Albers' shared artistic vision, remains the single biggest contribution to textile art of the 20th century.

WOMEN IN PHOTOGRAPHY

Female photographers have had a considerable role to play in the advancement of photography, both as an important art form and a hard-hitting social commentary that can make us change the way we perceive our very existence.

Julia Margaret Cameron saw photography as an opportunity to tell a story, and even to see into a person's very soul. Diane Arbus and Sarah Moon had great talent and unique style, while Annie Leibowitz is famous across the globe for her gorgeous contemporary portraits. Dorothea Lange, Margaret Bourke-White, and Lee Miller had great courage as well as an incredible eye, and each brought something unique: Dorothea gave heart to the genre of photojournalism; Margaret epitomized bravery as a pioneering combat zone photographer; and Lee Miller, model-turned-war correspondent/photographer, delivered honest accounts of life in war. Their remarkable work can be seen online and in galleries and museums all over the world.

CLOCKWISE FROM TOP LEFT:
DOROTHEA LANGE, MARGARET
BOURKE-WHITE, ANNIE LEIBOWITZ,
AND LEE MILLER

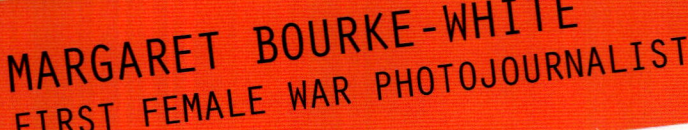

MARGARET BOURKE-WHITE
FIRST FEMALE WAR PHOTOJOURNALIST

FULL NAME: Margaret Bourke-White
BORN: JUNE 14, 1904, NEW YORK CITY, NEW YORK, U.S.A.
DIED: AUGUST 27, 1971, STAMFORD, CONNECTICUT, U.S.A.
NATIONALITY: AMERICAN

Camera from the 1930s, similar to the model Margaret would have used for her early work

A SERIES OF FIRSTS

Margaret Bourke-White stood out as many things: the first U.S. female war photojournalist, the first Western photographer allowed to take pictures of Soviet industry, the first female photographer to work with the U.S. Armed Forces, and one of the first photographers of the hugely famous *Life* magazine. Her incredible photographs—of everything from the Great Depression and Mahatma Gandhi to the German concentration camps of Nazi Germany—remain iconic to this day.

Photography began as a hobby for Margaret, but she quickly realized that it was what she wanted to do with her life. Her early work was in architectural and industrial photography, and she became known for her originality. From there, Margaret's career began to take shape. In 1930, she was hired to photograph an iron works factory in Soviet Germany, which quickly grew to a longer-term project documenting the industry and people of the Soviet Union. At this time, she also photographed the Dust Bowl and Great Depression in the American Midwest, as well as racial and class divides. In both of these projects, she had a great eye for capturing personal and social

FABULOUS FIRSTS

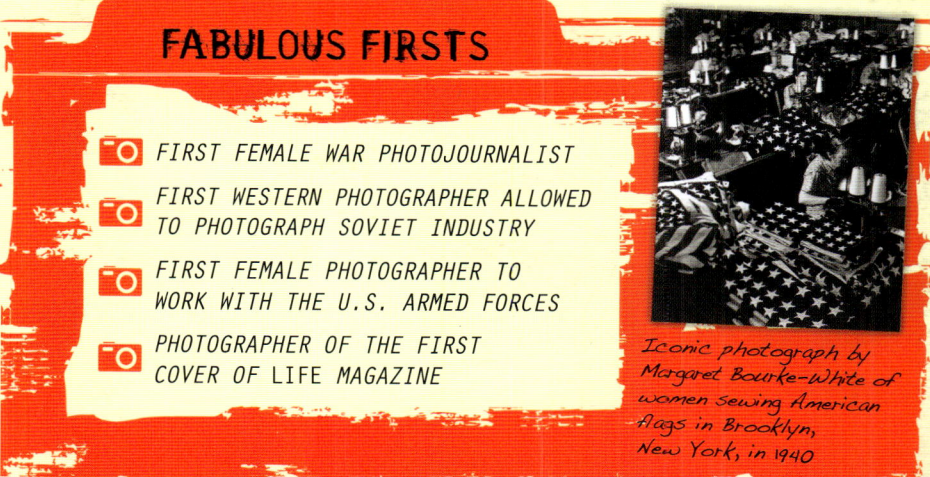

- 📷 FIRST FEMALE WAR PHOTOJOURNALIST
- 📷 FIRST WESTERN PHOTOGRAPHER ALLOWED TO PHOTOGRAPH SOVIET INDUSTRY
- 📷 FIRST FEMALE PHOTOGRAPHER TO WORK WITH THE U.S. ARMED FORCES
- 📷 PHOTOGRAPHER OF THE FIRST COVER OF LIFE MAGAZINE

Iconic photograph by Margaret Bourke-White of women sewing American flags in Brooklyn, New York, in 1940

situations. Her work helped explain and share these difficult stories from around the globe. Her photograph of Montana's Fort Peck Dam became the cover photograph of the very first issue of *Life* magazine, where she worked as its first female photojournalist (and one of only four staff photographers). Margaret documented World War II for *Life* magazine, as the first female photographer to work directly with the U.S. Armed Forces. She was the only foreign photographer in Moscow when German forces invaded. Her shocking photographs of the inmates of Nazi concentration camps were some of the first ever seen. After World War II, Margaret traveled to India and documented the work of the peace activist Mahatma Gandhi (incredibly, capturing an iconic portrait of him only hours before his assassination). She also recorded the extreme violence that broke out over the mass migration between India and Pakistan, known as the Partition. Her work was direct, and she was not afraid to show the horrors of war.

FEARLESS PHOTOGRAPHER

Margaret was not only an incredibly talented photographer, she was also fiercely brave. She knew that the stories around her needed to be told and shared with an audience, and she was never afraid to throw herself into any situation, however dangerous it might have been for her. Margaret's influences on photography and photojournalism are monumental. Her iconic photographs are on public display around the world, such as at the Library of Congress, New York's Museum of Modern Art, and Amsterdam's Rijksmuseum.

JOSEPHINE BAKER
PIONEERING PERFORMER AND CIVIL RIGHTS ACTIVIST

FULL NAME: Freda Josephine McDonald Baker
BORN: JUNE 3, 1906, ST. LOUIS, MISSOURI, U.S.A.
DIED: APRIL 12, 1975, PARIS, FRANCE
NATIONALITY: AMERICAN/FRENCH

HURRICANE JOSEPHINE

The world may not have been ready for Josephine Baker, but from the start she was ready to take on the world. Her impact was huge, from dance, music, and film to civil rights and war resistance. Josephine was the first black woman to become a world-famous entertainer, as well as an international entertainment and political icon.

Freda Josephine McDonald was born in St. Louis, Missouri, to a washerwoman and a drummer. The family was poor, and Josephine grew up cleaning houses, babysitting, and waitressing to make ends meet. At the age of 15, she joined a variety show and soon moved to New York City. It was the early days of the Harlem Renaissance, an incredible artistic and social explosion of African-American arts in 1920s New York. Josephine was in the right place at the right time, and she quickly joined Broadway revues. However, she was rejected for larger roles for being "too skinny and too dark." Undeterred, Josephine worked backstage and learned the routines. When a dancer left, Josephine was cast as the chorus line's "last dancer," a comic role in which the dancer "forgets" the routine before performing it perfectly at the end. With her impeccable comic timing, dancing talent, and stylish flair, Josephine was a hit.

A SUPER SPY IN A BANANA SKIRT

A move to Europe is really what allowed Josephine to shine. In Paris she became an overnight sensation for her now-famous *Danse Sauvage*. Wearing a feather skirt for that performance and an all-banana one for the next, Josephine performed with confidence and style, displaying movements that had never been seen before. Her career blossomed. She became one of the most photographed women in the world, and by 1927 she was the highest-paid entertainer in Europe. In the late 1930s, she starred in a number of movies and became the first black woman to star in a major film.

Josephine's European success was incredible—but 1930s America was not ready for a black female celebrity with talent, success, and confidence. A brief 1936 U.S. tour was disastrous; the press called her terrible names. She quickly returned to Europe, just in the nick of time to make another massive contribution. World War II was starting, and Josephine supported France's war effort in many ways. She raised morale by performing for troops, as well as smuggling secret messages on song sheets and acting as sub-lieutenant in the women's air force. For her courage and contribution, Josephine was awarded the Medal of Resistance and named a Chevalier of the Legion of Honor—very high praise from the French government.

MAKING THE WORLD A BETTER PLACE

A political icon, Josephine returned to the U.S.A. in the 1950s and 1960s to support the Civil Rights Movement. While Europe was more cosmopolitan, racism was still rampant in mid-century America. Josephine toured the country, writing articles and performing. She refused to perform for segregated audiences, and this helped integrate many venues across the country. The National Association for the Advancement of Colored People (NAACP) declared May 20 "Josephine Baker Day" for her contributions. In 1963, Josephine spoke beside Dr. Martin Luther King, Jr., at the March on Washington for Jobs and Freedom, one of the largest political rallies in U.S. history. After Dr. King's death, she was even asked to take over his leadership. Josephine adopted 12 children from around the world, creating what she called the "Rainbow Tribe," showing that children of different religions and ethnicities could be brothers and sisters.

In 1973, Josephine agreed to perform at New York's prestigious Carnegie Hall. She received a standing ovation before the show even started—she had finally got her great American showbiz success. In 1975, the 68-year-old Josephine performed her last show, a medley of her hits, and received some of the best reviews of her career. Sadly, she died a few days later. More than 20,000 people attended her funeral procession on the streets of Paris. She was given a 21-gun salute by the French military in recognition of her incredible contribution to French life.

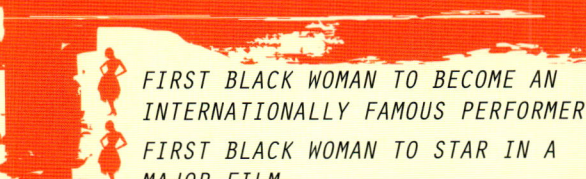

FABULOUS FIRSTS

FIRST BLACK WOMAN TO BECOME AN INTERNATIONALLY FAMOUS PERFORMER

FIRST BLACK WOMAN TO STAR IN A MAJOR FILM

Carnegie Hall, New York City

KATHARINE HEPBURN
MOST OSCAR WINS OF ANY ACTOR

FULL NAME: Katharine Houghton Hepburn
BORN: MAY 12, 1907, HARTFORD, CONNECTICUT, U.S.A.
DIED: JUNE 29, 2003, FENWICK, CONNECTICUT, U.S.A.
NATIONALITY: AMERICAN

During her 60-plus-year career of four Oscar wins, Katharine Hepburn attended the ceremony only once— to give an award to someone else!

SPARKLING 60-YEAR CAREER

With her first public performance at the age eight as part of a rally for women's right to vote, Katharine Hepburn embarked on a sparkling career that lasted more than 60 years. In that time, she acted in 52 feature films and was nominated for 12 Academy Awards (Oscars). Katharine is the winner of the most Oscars—four—of any actor in history. The first she won in 1933, at the age of 25, for *Morning Glory*; her final three were won after she had turned 60.

FABULOUS FIRSTS

FIRST (AND ONLY) ACTOR TO WIN FOUR OSCARS

A.M.P.A.S.

Katharine's parents supported the women's suffrage (right to vote) movement and instilled in Katharine the belief that she could do anything.

U.S. postage stamp, circa 2010, commemorating the great Hollywood actress

GREATEST SCREEN LEGEND

One of Hollywood's great screen beauties, Katharine was considered a tomboy from an early age. She is even known to have referred to herself as "Jimmy" in her childhood. Katharine's parents were very progressive and fought hard for women's rights. They filled the young Katharine with determination and fierce independence. In the difficult world of Hollywood, this sense of self-assurance would serve her well in managing her career exactly as she chose. She was known for refusing to conform to Hollywood's expectations of women. She was a modern woman: she wore pants at a time when it was hugely unfashionable for women to do so, and she was assertive and lived her life to her own design.

Katharine's first movie was the 1932 hit drama *A Bill of Divorcement*, and it made her an overnight star. She was adept at everything from literary drama to comedy. Her performance as Jo March in *Little Women* (1933) is considered one of her finest, and her role in *The Philadelphia Story* (1940) is the one for which she is best known. Katharine is considered by many, including the American Film Institute, to be the greatest female screen legend of all time.

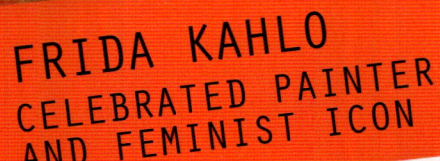

FRIDA KAHLO
CELEBRATED PAINTER AND FEMINIST ICON

FULL NAME: Magdalena Carmen Frida Kahlo y Calderon
BORN: JULY 6, 1907, COYOACÁN, MEXICO
DIED: JULY 13, 1954, COYOACÁN, MEXICO
NATIONALITY: MEXICAN

FRIDA THE FIGHTER

Frida Kahlo was born in Mexico City to a German father and Mexican mother. The third of four daughters (with two older stepsisters), Frida grew up in a world surrounded by women. When she was only three years old, the Mexican Revolution broke out. Her family and these revolutionary politics helped to shape the person young Frida would become.

At the age of six, Frida caught polio, which affected the use of her legs. She didn't let this get in her way and continued playing sports, including boxing. Her early lessons in persevering through difficulty would serve Frida well in later life. As a teenager, Frida attended one of the top schools in Mexico, dreaming of becoming a doctor. But that dream was soon to change.

At the age of 18, Frida was riding a bus that was suddenly struck by a tram. She survived but was very seriously injured. Afterward, Frida spent three months in bed in a full-body cast. Even after this recovery, the teenage Frida had to relearn to walk and remained in

Mexico takes great pride in Frida Kahlo the painter. She appears on the Mexican 500-peso bill, alongside an image of her work.

constant pain for the rest of her life. But Frida was a fighter. During her recuperation, Frida's mother had a special easel built that allowed her to paint from bed. She changed her dream from medicine to art. (Much of Frida's work continued to include her knowledge of anatomy and medicine.) Frida was entirely self-taught, but her artistic talent was impressive. She was soon attracting attention from some of the great artists of the day, including Diego Rivera, whom she later married—twice. Frida and Diego influenced each other's work for the rest of their lives. Frida remained ill for much of her life, and she died at the young age of 47.

I PAINTED MY OWN REALITY

Frida Kahlo remains known for her use of bright colors, self-portraits, and images of Mexican culture. Her work is sometimes described as dreamlike. But as Frida explained, "I never painted dreams. I painted my own reality." She was very political and had a strong, independent spirit.

It wasn't until after her death that Frida became known as an incredible artist and feminist icon. Her paintings can now be found in museums all over the world, from Detroit to Japan, as well as at Caza Azul in Mexico— the house where Frida was born, painted, lived, and died. Several movies, books, and plays have been written about Frida's life and work. She remains an inspiration of what can be achieved through dedication and spirit.

FULL NAME: Virginia "Ginger" Katherine McMath
BORN: JULY 16, 1911, INDEPENDENCE, MISSOURI, U.S.A.
DIED: APRIL 25, 1995, RANCHO MIRAGE, CALIFORNIA, U.S.A.
NATIONALITY: AMERICAN

THE MAKING OF A STAR

Born Virginia McMath, the young star-to-be began using her nickname of "Ginger" early, because a cousin couldn't pronounce "Virginia." As a child, Ginger acted on stage. She won a Charleston dance contest and was awarded her own vaudeville tour, with her mother as manager. From there, she landed her first Broadway production.

Ginger did film work during the day and live stage work at night, before moving to Hollywood in 1931. Her first big movie was the 1933 musical classic, *42nd Street*. The same year, she was cast in *Flying Down to Rio*—her first movie with Fred Astaire, with whom she would be forever linked. Their amazing dance chemistry dazzled studio bosses, and as the ultimate dance partnership of movie history, they went on to be cast together in a total of nine films, including *Top Hat* and *Swing Time*. Ginger starred in non-dancing roles, too, alongside such screen icons as Marilyn Monroe (*see pages* 66–67), Cary Grant, and Katharine Hepburn (*see pages* 44–45).

BACKWARDS IN HIGH HEELS

Ginger starred in more than 70 movies and won a leading actress Oscar for her role in the 1941 movie *Kitty Foyle*. For a time, she was the highest-paid woman in America. But it was for her incredible footwork with Fred Astaire for which she remains best known. Both Fred and Ginger looked stunning, but in any photographs you'll see that Ginger is often wearing flowing, trip-hazard dresses and high heels—often dancing backwards. While each of the pair was a phenomenal dancer, Ginger is said to have made the comment that she did everything Astaire did, but "backwards in high heels." The expression became famous and has come to describe the extra work women often need to put in to make their way in a male-dominated world just to achieve the same success as men. In 2007, a play called *Backwards in High Heels*, representing the life of Ginger Rogers, premiered in West Palm Beach, Florida.

FUNNY WOMEN

Phyllis Diller became the first female stand-up, and Lucille Ball the first female creator of a TV comedy—and today, the world of female comedians is wonderfully rich and varied.

With a career spanning six decades, Carol Burnett is one of the most respected TV humorists in history, alongside the incredible and audacious Gilda Radner, a *Saturday Night Live* stalwart. Joan Rivers became a household name for her biting humor and self-deprecating style. At the other end of the spectrum, Ellen DeGeneres is loved for a more kind-hearted brand of comedy. Wacky impressionist Maria Bamford ranks top among fellow comedians. Star of stage and screen, Lily Tomlin is renowned for her outrageous personas, which have already influenced several generations of comedians. Best known today for the talk show *The View*, Whoopi Goldberg is a tremendous comedian who has enjoyed crossover success in stand-up, film, TV, and on the stage. Another TV great, the beloved Betty White has had the longest TV career of any female entertainer. Contemporary stars such as Sarah Silverman, Amy Poehler, Tina Fey, and Kristen Wiig are not afraid to use their humor to speak their mind on subjects including sexism and ageism. One such comedian, Amy Schumer, has used her comic platform to highlight gender inequality and social injustice. In recognition of this, *Time* magazine named her as one of their "100 Most Influential People."

CLOCKWISE
FROM TOP LEFT:
JOAN RIVERS,
WHOOPI GOLDBERG,
LILY TOMLIN,
AND BETTY WHITE

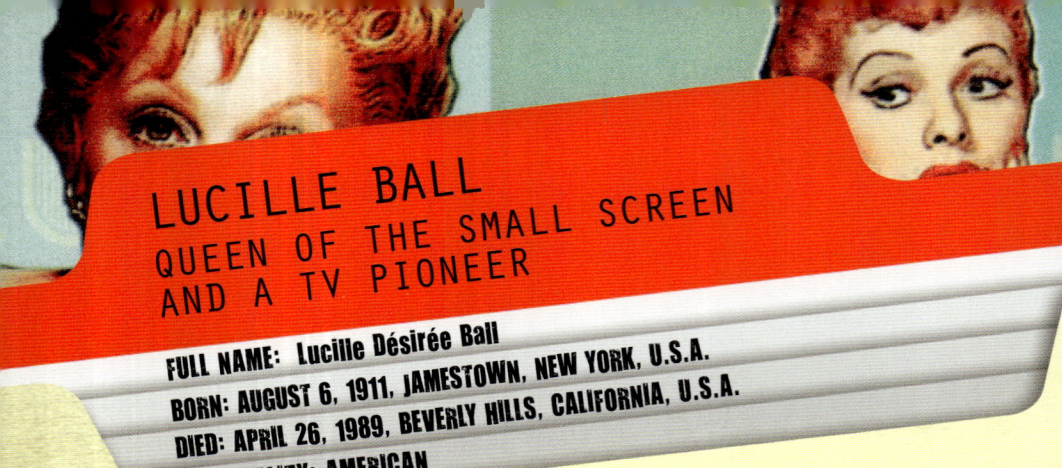

FULL NAME: Lucille Désirée Ball
BORN: AUGUST 6, 1911, JAMESTOWN, NEW YORK, U.S.A.
DIED: APRIL 26, 1989, BEVERLY HILLS, CALIFORNIA, U.S.A.
NATIONALITY: AMERICAN

QUEEN OF COMEDY

Lucille Désirée Ball had many nicknames: Queen of the B Movie, First Lady of Television, Queen of Comedy, and, simply, "Lucy." In a packed career, Lucille was a model, comedian, actress, producer—and the first woman to run a major television studio. Her larger-than-life screen presence ensured that, in spite of the black-and-white TV sets of the time, her vibrant red hair and incredible talent shone through. Lucille had an impressively long career in television, lasting over 65 years.

U.S. postage stamp, circa 2009, to commemorate the much-loved T.V. series, I Love Lucy

FROM STAGE TO SCREENS, BOTH BIG AND SMALL

After starting work as a model under the name Diane Belmont, Lucille began performing on Broadway. This was followed by bit parts for RKO Radio Pictures, where she was a "contract player" (a step up from an extra). During that time, Lucille earned the nickname of "Queen of the B Movie" for the sheer number of films she appeared in—72 in all. In spite of her beauty and incredible screen presence, her big break came in the unexpected form of a radio show called *My Favorite Husband*. It was there that Lucille, soon to be known as one of America's best-loved comedians, would find her niche. She had a contract from CBS and the world of TV laid out at her feet.

AMAZING ACHIEVEMENTS

- FIRST WOMAN TO RUN A MAJOR TV STUDIO
- CREATOR OF ONE OF MOST ICONIC SHOWS IN TV HISTORY

In everything from content to cinematography, Desilu Productions was groundbreaking.

MODERN LIFE

In 1940, Lucille married Desi Arnaz, a Cuban bandleader she met on set. Together, the pair would go on to create and co-own both the Desilu Production Company and the *I Love Lucy* show: one of the most iconic shows in television history. *I Love Lucy* debuted in 1951 and was an instant success. Ahead of its time, the show dealt with modern issues: women in the workplace, marital strife, troubled suburbia—all through the lens of Lucille's incredible gift for humor and outlandish mischief. The show also broke new ground by showing Lucy and Desi as an interracial couple, as well as Lucy's onscreen pregnancy. Generations of comedians have been inspired by her work, including Carol Burnett and Robin Williams. For the majority of its run, *I Love Lucy* was the number-one show in the country, receiving incredible viewer ratings. In 1962, Lucille took sole control of Desilu Productions—the first time a woman had been in charge of a major TV studio. Desilu was also a pioneer of the live studio audience and the use of multiple cameras.

THE LEGACY OF LUCY

Lucille won four Emmys and was inducted into the Television Hall of Fame in 1984. After her death, she was awarded the Presidential Medal of Freedom, in 1989, and in 1990 *Newsweek* selected her as the top female entertainer of the 20th century. Lucille's passion, ambition, and clear vision created an unforgettable showbiz success and one of the most influential actresses of her time. Her perfect comic timing and slapstick perfection continue to inspire generations of comedians and actors.

Lucille, circa 1988, attending a celebrity charity event

SISTER ROSETTA THARPE
GOSPEL LEGEND AND GODMOTHER OF ROCK AND ROLL

FULL NAME: Sister Rosetta Nubin Tharpe
BORN: MARCH 20, 1915, COTTON PLANT, ARKANSAS, U.S.A.
DIED: OCTOBER 9, 1973, PHILADELPHIA, PENNSYLVANIA, U.S.A.
NATIONALITY: AMERICAN

> *She would sing until you cried and then she would sing until you danced for joy.*
>
> FROM SISTER ROSETTA THARPE'S GRAVESTONE

MUSICAL PRODIGY

By all accounts, Rosetta Tharpe (born Rosetta Nubin) was a musical prodigy. Her mother was a talented singer, mandolin player, and preacher for the Church of God in Christ. This predominantly African-American Church encouraged music and the work of female preachers.

At the age of four, Rosetta started playing guitar and singing on stage with her mother. Two years later, little Rosetta was a regular performer with her mother's group, traveling across the South before settling in Chicago. Rosetta gained fame as a musical prodigy, as well as for being a rarity as a black female guitarist. She would go on to become one of the greatest gospel singers of all time.

FABULOUS FIRSTS

FIRST COMMERCIALLY SUCCESSFUL GOSPEL SINGER

ROCK STAR BEFORE THERE WAS ROCK AND ROLL

USA 32

GOSPEL SINGER

SISTER ROSETTA

1998

A 1998 U.S. postage stamp featuring the godmother of rock and roll, Sister Rosetta Tharpe

GODMOTHER ROSETTA OF ROCK

In 1938, at the age of 23, Rosetta became the first commercially successful gospel singer. She signed with the now-legendary Decca Records label and recorded four songs. These were the first gospel songs ever recorded for the label. The songs were instant hits and brought gospel to a wider audience. That same year, Rosetta was asked to perform with a group at the illustrious Carnegie Hall, New York City. Later, she also performed with such icons as Cab Calloway, Benny Goodman, and Muddy Waters. At the time, it was new and incredible (and controversial) to see gospel music performed for a non-religious audience, especially by a female guitarist. Over the next decade, Rosetta continued to record and perform both gospel and secular (non-religious) music. Due to her upbringing, her style was unique, mixing together gospel, blues, folk, and jazz—and even using an early electric guitar. One of those first four hit songs, "That's All," is believed to have had a strong impact on later music legends Chuck Berry and Elvis Presley. Decades ahead of her time, the little black girl with a gospel voice and guitar in hand had created the earliest rock and roll. Rosetta's appeal was wide: religious and non-religious, black and white, young and old. Search YouTube for videos of her tremendous performances. In 2015, Rosetta was inducted into the Grammy Hall of Fame.

Rosetta sang, recorded, strummed, and performed for over 50 years. Today, she remains one of the most influential musicians of all time. Quite simply, she was a rock star before there was rock. So, regardless of which bands are currently on your playlist, chances are they owe a big "thank you" to Sister Rosetta Tharpe, the godmother of rock and roll.

Rosetta was famous for playing a 1961 Gibson Les Paul Custom guitar, similar to this one.

BILLIE HOLIDAY
LEGENDARY JAZZ SINGER AND ICON

FULL NAME: Eleanora Fagan
BORN: APRIL 7, 1915, PHILADELPHIA, PENNSYLVANIA, U.S.A.
DIED: JULY 17, 1959, NEW YORK CITY, NEW YORK, U.S.A.
NATIONALITY: AMERICAN

Billie's signature flower: a white gardenia blossom

LADY SINGS THE BLUES

If you've ever heard a classic jazz ballad with a female vocalist, chances are you've heard Billie Holiday. Billie, also known as Lady Day, was a pioneer of American jazz and blues. Her distinctive, soulful voice is one of the greatest jazz sounds of all time.

In 1915, Eleanora Fagan was born in Philadelphia, Pennsylvania. She grew up around neighboring Baltimore, a jazz-rich hotspot at the time. Eleanora had a tumultuous childhood, living with distant relatives and finding herself in reform school by the age of nine. She dropped out of school before she reached high school and spent time as a prostitute, as well as time in jail.

Throughout all this, Eleanora always found comfort in music. She was entirely self-taught, with no technical training. As a teenager, she sang in after-hours jazz clubs, eventually moving to New York City with her mother. It was there that Eleanora was hired for shows in a series of unknown Harlem nightclubs, and became Billie Holiday ("Billie" after the actress Billie Dove and "Holiday" using the last name of the father she never knew). At only 18, Billie was talent-spotted and cut a record with a group led by the soon-to-be-famous Benny Goodman.

BECOMING LADY DAY

As she continued to perform, Billie's popularity grew. In 1935, she recorded four big hits, including the now-famous "What a Little Moonlight Can Do." From there, she earned her own recording contract with Columbia Records. Soon, Billie was performing with big-name musicians and band leaders, including Lester Young, Count Basie, and Artie Shaw, making her one of the first black singers to perform with a white orchestra. In 1930s America, this was a huge achievement. Billie recorded with a number of major record labels, including Columbia, Decca, Commodore, and Verve, where she found mainstream success. Billie recorded and toured extensively throughout her short life, including a hugely successful 1954 European tour and star-studded shows at Carnegie Hall, in New York City.

JAZZ SINGER, 1915-1959

U.S. postage stamp, circa 1994, commemorating the great songstress

ANGEL OF HARLEM

By her thirties and forties, Billie was struggling with drug and alcohol addiction and with abusive relationships, and she even found herself in prison for drugs offences. She continued to perform to sold-out venues, but her reputation began to deteriorate, as did her voice from all the strain. Sadly, Billie died at the young age of 44. However, the voice of Lady Day lives on. After her death, Billie was awarded four Grammy awards for Best Historical Album. In 1973, she was inducted into the Grammy Hall of Fame, and in 2002 into the Rock and Roll Hall of Fame. U2 recorded "Angel of Harlem" in tribute to her, and there is a statue of her in the center of Baltimore. Hailed as one of the greatest and most influential singers of all time, Lady Day remains an inspiration to musicians of all genres around the globe.

Billie was amazing at improvising. Now classics of jazz and blues, Billie's powerful songs told of love, struggle, and everyday life for African-Americans living during the age of segregation. Her unique phrasing, powerful voice, and raw emotion were all important parts of her trademark style—as were the white gardenias she wore in her hair. The most famous of her masterpieces remain "Summertime," "Strange Fruit," "God Bless the Child," and "Lover Man," still played around the world today.

Baltimore was full of popular jazz clubs during Billie's early years.

WELCOME TO BALTIMORE

ÉDITH PIAF
THE GREATEST FRENCH SINGER OF ALL TIME

FULL NAME: Édith Giovanna Gassion
BORN: DECEMBER 19, 1915, PARIS, FRANCE
DIED: OCTOBER 10, 1963, GRASSE, FRANCE
NATIONALITY: FRENCH

Édith's nickname was Little Sparrow.

THE LITTLE SPARROW

French national icon Édith Piaf is considered the greatest and most popular French singer in history. The much-loved singer-songwriter remains one of France's greatest international stars.

While little is known for certain about her early years, Édith Giovanna Gassion led a difficult life of health problems and family troubles, and her songs are often autobiographical. Édith's mother left after Édith was born, and the young girl lived with various family members. Eventually, she joined her father and became a street singer and acrobat. As a teenager, Édith gave birth to a daughter, Marcelle, who died of an illness at the age of two.

Édith's street performances took her all over Paris, but her big break would come in 1935, when she was discovered by a nightclub owner. That year, two significant things happened: she had her stage debut at the popular Le Gerny club and recorded two albums. Her songs told of her life on the streets, and her voice was raw, powerful, and full of emotion. Her most iconic songs, including "*La Vie en rose*," "*Mon Dieu*," and "*Non, je ne regrette rien*" tell stories of love and sorrow and have become anthems in France and across the globe. The name "Piaf" is the French slang for "sparrow," and Édith was dubbed the "Little Sparrow" for her tiny frame and nervous energy. (She was only 4 foot 8 inches.)

Édith was an incredible performer, considered to be one of the best of the 20th century. She became one of the most popular performers in France during World War II, and she eventually toured the globe, including performances at New York's Carnegie Hall and Paris' Olympia Theater. There was criticism of her wartime performances for the occupying German Nazi army. However, after the Liberation of Paris, it was revealed that Édith had likely been working in secret for the French Resistance and helping Jews flee the invading Nazis.

A 2012 French postage stamp honoring the incredible singer and national icon

As a teenager, the young Édith was an acrobat and singer around the streets of Paris, France (seen here circa 1920).

I REGRET NOTHING

Sadly, despite her triumphal rags-to-riches story, Édith's misfortunes continued. Her life was full of sadness, including the death of a lover, addictions, health problems, serious car accidents, and scandal—but she refused to give up. When she died at the age of only 47, tens of thousands of people attended her funeral. One of her later songs, *"Non, je ne regrette rien"* ("No, I Regret Nothing") perfectly sums up Édith's difficult life and determination. Her life was beset by struggle, but this only made the Little Sparrow work harder. To this day, her songs continue to touch people—in France and across the globe. In 2007, a movie was made of her life, called *La Vie en Rose*, which won an Academy Award. So widespread is her influence, a small planet, 3772 Piaf, has been named after her. More than 50 years after hear death, Édith is still an icon and inspiration for writers, artists, and musicians for her passion and determination.

ELLA FITZGERALD
FIRST LADY OF SONG AND QUEEN OF JAZZ

FULL NAME: Ella Jane Fitzgerald
BORN: APRIL 25, 1917, NEWPORT NEWS, VIRGINIA, U.S.A.
DIED: JUNE 15, 1996, BEVERLY HILLS, CALIFORNIA, U.S.A.
NATIONALITY: AMERICAN

Ella Fitzgerald, captured in a 1946 photograph by William P. Gottlieb

THE EARLY DAYS OF JAZZ

To this day, Ella Fitzgerald holds the crown as the Queen of Jazz. Lady Ella, as she was known, had one of the most recognizable voices in music and is considered to be one of the most important jazz and blues artists of all time. In addition, she was the most popular female jazz singer for more than 50 years and helped create the musical genre we know today.

Ella was born in Virginia, but she and her mother soon moved to New York. Ella had a happy childhood, playing baseball, dancing, and singing with her friends. She grew up in a mixed-race neighborhood, removed from the segregation experienced in other parts of the U.S.A. When Ella was 15, her life changed. Her mother died in a car accident. Ella moved in with her aunt, but never settled in. She was often in trouble with the police, spent time in reform school, and—during the Great Depression—was alone and broke. She would later say these experiences helped her music greatly.

ELLA'S BIG BREAK

In 1934, Ella got her break, when her name was picked at random to perform in Amateur Night at the Apollo Theater, in Manhattan. She had planned to dance, but at the last minute she decided to sing. The crowd booed young Ella as she came onto the stage—but as soon as she started singing, the crowd was hooked. They even asked for an encore. Ella, and her adoring audiences, never looked back. She went on to win numerous talent shows and was eventually hired to travel with Chick Webb's band. As the big band sound moved into "bebop" jazz, Ella was at the forefront. She was the master of the new jazz sounds of bebop and scat. In 1938, Ella found fame through recording *A-Tisket, A-Tasket*. The album sold one million copies and hit the number-one spot.

UNITING AUDIENCES

A star in her own right, Ella performed with top jazz singers and musicians of the day, including Dizzie Gillespie, Louis Armstrong, Frank Sinatra, and Count Basie. Ella became a regular on popular TV variety shows, including *The Frank Sinatra Show*, *The Tonight Show*, and *The Ed Sullivan Show*. At a time of troubled race relations, Ella was popular with both black and white audiences. Her voice brought together people of all backgrounds, religions, and nationalities; the fans loved her. Ella's manager felt strongly that his musicians should be treated equally, regardless of their skin color, and his tours ensured there was no discrimination at hotels, restaurants, or venues. However, discrimination still reared its ugly head. The Mocambo was a very popular nightclub in West Hollywood in the 1950s, in spite of the fact it would not book non-white acts. Superstar Marilyn Monroe (*see pages* 66–67) was a big fan of Ella's and a supporter of civil rights. In 1955, Marilyn called the owner of the Mocambo, requesting that he book Ella immediately. For this, she said she would book a front-row table every night and the press would go wild. Marilyn stayed true to her word. Ella was able to sell out large venues, and her popularity rose. Ella went on to tour all over the world and played multiple shows at Carnegie Hall, in New York City.

THE QUEEN OF JAZZ

In total, Ella recorded more than 200 albums and sold more than 40 million records. She won hundreds of awards in her lifetime, including 13 Grammy Awards, plus the Grammy Lifetime Achievement Award, in 1967. She was inducted into the Jazz Hall of Fame in 1979. U.S. President Ronald Reagan gave her the National Medal of Arts, and France awarded her the Commander of Arts and Letters Award. She was given a star on the Hollywood Walk of Fame. In 1992, Ella was awarded the Presidential Medal of Freedom.

In spite of a difficult childhood and severe ill health in her later years, Lady Ella remained strong and positive. Her talent was incredible, but so was her genuine drive to make the world a better place. One hundred years after her birth, Ella remains the Queen of Jazz and a monumental figure for everything she gave to the arts—and to the world.

PHYLLIS DILLER
FIRST SOLO FEMALE STAND-UP COMEDIAN

FULL NAME: Phyllis Ada Driver Diller
BORN: JULY 17, 1917, LIMA, OHIO, U.S.A.
DIED: AUGUST 20, 2012, LOS ANGELES, CALIFORNIA, U.S.A.
NATIONALITY: AMERICAN

Phyllis Diller, 2010

LARGER THAN LIFE

Phyllis Diller's big break, in 1955, was as unique as the woman herself. As a contestant on comedian Groucho Marx's game show, *You Bet Your Life*, Phyllis was memorable. So memorable, in fact, that she was offered a comedy debut at a San Francisco comedy club. Phyllis was already 37 and the mother of five children. Phyllis exaggerated her already larger-than-life makeup, costumes, expressions, and cackle and quickly created her unique comic persona.

Phyllis became known for her one-liners and monologues, and she played up her role as a typical American housewife with everyday problems. Audiences loved her—and by 1961, she had found her way into film and theater. But her talents still didn't end there: Phyllis was also an accomplished pianist and the author of five best-selling books.

FABULOUS FIRSTS

★ *FIRST FEMALE STAND-UP COMEDIAN*

PAVING THE WAY

Phyllis earned a star on the Hollywood Walk of Fame in 1975. In 1992, she received the American Comedy Award for Lifetime Achievement. Her trailblazing role in the entertainment industry, as well as her caricature of life as a suburban housewife, led to her place as a feminist icon. Phyllis paved the way for the funny women who would follow in her footsteps and onto the stage. Comedians as diverse as Zooey Deschanel, Amy Poehler, and Joan Rivers credit Phyllis for their place at the mic.

Honoring fellow comedian Bob Hope in 2003, Phyllis Diller celebrates with members of Hope's family and fellow actors, including Kelsey Grammer.

MARGOT FONTEYN
ONE OF GREATEST BALLET DANCERS OF ALL TIME

FULL NAME: Margaret Evelyn Hookham
BORN: MAY 18, 1919, REIGATE, SURREY, U.K.
DIED: FEBRUARY 21, 1991, PANAMA CITY, PANAMA
NATIONALITY: BRITISH

TRUE GRACE

Born Margaret Evelyn Hookham in Surrey, England, to a British father and an Irish-Brazilian mother, Margaret came from a very artistic family.

At the age of four, she began ballet classes. At eight, her family moved to China, where she began studying ballet with a Russian teacher. At 14, Margaret returned to London to concentrate on her dancing. Not yet a teenager, the young Margot had already invested a lot into the study of ballet around the world. Margaret's stage name, Margot Fonteyn, was a play on her own mixed-race roots.

A NATIONAL TREASURE

In 1934, at the age of 15, Margot made her professional debut with the Vic-Wells Ballet in London (later to be called the Royal Ballet—with whom she would spend the rest of her career). The following year, she became one of the troupe's leading dancers. Margot was renowned for her outstanding interpretations of the classics. Her portrayal of Aurora in *Sleeping Beauty,* in 1939, is still considered to be the best ever. In addition, she was loved for her creation of contemporary roles in more modern productions. Margot was said to be technically perfect, but she also had great style and musicality. Her charm and charisma also opened up ballet to a wider audience.

FABULOUS FIRSTS

FIRST BRITISH DANCER TO BE AN INTERNATIONAL BALLET STAR

For several years, Margot's dance partner was Rudolf Nureyev. The two of them are seen here at the Stockholm Opera, in 1969.

Ballet sensation Margot Fonteyn, pictured in 1969

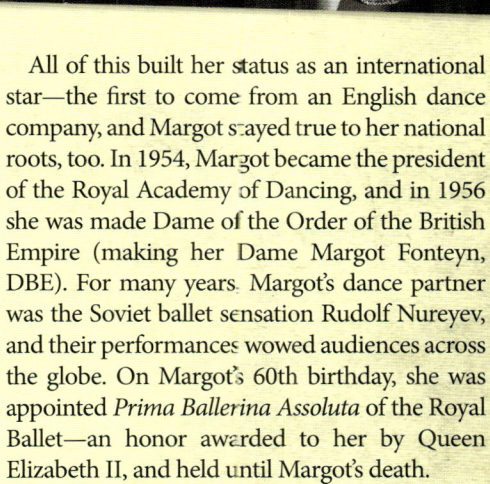

All of this built her status as an international star—the first to come from an English dance company, and Margot stayed true to her national roots, too. In 1954, Margot became the president of the Royal Academy of Dancing, and in 1956 she was made Dame of the Order of the British Empire (making her Dame Margot Fonteyn, DBE). For many years, Margot's dance partner was the Soviet ballet sensation Rudolf Nureyev, and their performances wowed audiences across the globe. On Margot's 60th birthday, she was appointed *Prima Ballerina Assoluta* of the Royal Ballet—an honor awarded to her by Queen Elizabeth II, and held until Margot's death.

MARIA CALLAS
MOST INFLUENTIAL FEMALE OPERA SINGER OF THE 20TH CENTURY

FULL NAME: Anna Maria Sofia Cecelia Kalos
BORN: DECEMBER 2, 1923, NEW YORK CITY, NEW YORK, U.S.A.
DIED: SEPTEMBER 16, 1977, PARIS, FRANCE
NATIONALITY: GREEK-AMERICAN

LA DIVINA

Think "Diva" and you most likely picture a modern-day celebrity strutting her stuff on stage. But the original diva was actually an opera singer, born almost 100 years ago. Maria Callas was a Greek-American soprano singer, nicknamed "*La Divina*" (the Divine) and "The Tigress." Maria was one of the most important opera singers of the 20th century. Her vocal range was huge, and her performances were incredibly dramatic, whether in traditional operas or musical dramas.

A Greek postage stamp, circa 1997, honors the great diva.

AN ALL-AROUND PERFORMER

Maria was born in New York, but her parents were Greek and moved to the U.S.A. when Maria's mother was pregnant with her. When Maria was a young teenager, she moved back to Greece again. Maria's Greek heritage remained important to her throughout her life. From the age of three, Maria's singing talent was obvious. Her mother often made her sing, and Maria did not enjoy singing to begin with. But by her teenage years, Maria was receiving proper voice training. She took it very seriously and began to "devour" anything musical. Her stage debut was in 1939 in a school production. In 1941, she had a professional debut with the Royal Opera of Athens. Only a year later, Maria had the lead role in the famous opera *Tosca*. From Greece, she spent her time between the U.S.A. and Italy, with successful debuts in both countries. Her American debut, in 1956, gave her

Maria performed the role of Violetta in La Traviata, in 1958. Photograph by Houston Rogers

the opportunity to sing with the Metropolitan Opera in her original home city of New York. Maria's life was often caught up in scandal, which heightened her "diva-esque" persona. She continued to sing all over the world, and her performances wowed critics and audiences alike. Her voice was well loved, but it was her stage presence and personality that truly created an incredible all-around performer.

Maria Callas continues to rank as one of the highest-selling classical vocalists of all time, and her performances helped popularize opera as an art form. She is famous across the globe and considered to be one of the greats of modern opera. Sadly, Maria died of a heart attack at only 53, but her mighty influence lives on.

MARILYN MONROE
INFLUENTIAL ACTRESS AND TIMELESS POP CULTURE ICON

FULL NAME: Norma Jean Baker Mortenson
BORN: JUNE 1, 1926, LOS ANGELES, CALIFORNIA, U.S.A.
DIED: AUGUST 5, 1962, LOS ANGELES, CALIFORNIA, U.S.A.
NATIONALITY: AMERICAN

Andy Warhol-inspired street art of Marilyn, in Montreal, Canada, 2015

BEYOND THE FAÇADE

Marilyn Monroe's beauty, charm, and talent were jewels to behold. On the surface, Marilyn was known for her appearance and "dumb" bombshell movie roles. But Marilyn was also a fearless activist, determined businesswoman, studious master of her craft, and tireless humanitarian. Those lucky enough to work with her called her a genius and a master of the screen. Despite the "dumb blonde" image, she had an inquisitive mind, fascinated by everything from religion to psychology, literature to poetry, and she counted slavery abolitionist Abraham Lincoln among her heroes. One of her favorite possessions was a photo of Albert Einstein, signed with the words: "To Marilyn, with respect and love and thanks."

THE BIRTH OF MARILYN MONROE

Marilyn Monroe was born Norma Jean Mortenson (and was occasionally called Norma Jean Baker). Her single mother was unable to look after her, so Norma spent her childhood alternating between foster care and an orphanage. By the age of 16, she had dropped out of school and married her boyfriend, to get her out of the cycle of foster homes. When her husband left for the merchant marines, Norma began work at a weapons factory. It was during this time that she was discovered by a photographer and started work as a model. Her star quality radiated in ads and pinups from the start, but Norma dreamed of becoming an actress. In 1946, she came up with the name of "Marilyn Monroe"—by combining the family name of "Monroe" with that of "Marilyn Miller," a popular 1920s performer.

With her new name (and newly dyed blonde hair), Marilyn signed her first movie contract, in 1946. She quickly gained attention for her beauty and stage presence, but it wasn't until her performance in *All About Eve*, starring Bette Davis, that audiences sat up and took notice. From there, Marilyn would go on to star in a string of hits, mostly light-hearted comedies and musicals, such as the 1953 movie *Gentlemen Prefer Blondes*. She won a Golden Globe for Best Actress in a Comedy for her starring role in 1959's *Some Like it Hot*, and the American Film Institute later named this film the greatest American comedy of all time.

ICON OF STYLE AND CULTURE

Marilyn was an all-around icon: a style icon for her clothes, curvaceous figure, and hair; a cultural icon for the roles she played. The white halterneck dress she famously wore in *The Seven Year Itch* sold for $5.6 million, making it the most valuable costume in movie history, and countless designers have been trying to copy her look ever since. It is less known that she was also a political icon for her activism. In 1955, Marilyn made a stand for civil rights when she persuaded the famous Mocambo Club to book black jazz singer Ella Fitzgerald (*see pages* 58–59) and become an integrated venue. For this, Ella called her "ahead of her times." But at the time, Marilyn was much more famous for scandals and headlines. In addition to her teenage marriage, Marilyn was married to baseball legend Joe DiMaggio and playwright Arthur Miller and had several other high-profile relationships. She suffered from insecurities and anxiety and was constantly in the press.

On August 5, 1962, at the age of only 36, Marilyn was found dead at her home. The cause of death was listed as suicide, but controversy continues to surround the star's demise. Marilyn famously said that it was the people, not the studios, who made her a star, for which she was grateful. However, it is believed that it was the fame and scrutiny that killed her.

Marilyn's films made more than $200 million during her career, and her appeal has not diminished—more than 50 years after her death. Influencing stars from Madonna (*see pages* 82–83) to Lady Gaga, today she remains one of the world's most popular cultural icons and celebrated actresses.

MAIJA ISOLA
INFLUENTIAL TEXTILE DESIGNER

FULL NAME: Maija Isola
BORN: MARCH 15, 1927, RIIHIMÄKI, FINLAND
DIED: MARCH 3, 2001, FINLAND
NATIONALITY: FINNISH

FLOWER POWER

While you may not know the name Maija Isola, chances are you know her designs. Her simple, colorful poppy pattern is one of the most recognized prints on Earth! Maija was an artist who became one of the most influential designers in the world. Her work is very popular today. The Finnish textile company, Marimekko, was founded in 1951, selling bold fabric patterns and stylish clothing. Maija was one of the company's first designers. With a background in painting and visual arts, she was able to create bright, colorful patterns, inspired by nature, folk art, and by her trips around the world. These patterns brought fame to Marimekko in the 1960s, when the company exploded onto the international scene. Marimekko was hugely popular in Europe, and it catapulted to U.S. success when First Lady Jacqueline Kennedy wore a Marimekko dress on a 1960 cover of *Sports Illustrated*.

DESIGN REBEL

During her 38 years at Marimekko, Maija created over 500 prints. Her most popular patterns include *Lokki* (seagull) and *Luonto* (nature)—created using real plants. But of stand-alone fame was her poppy print, *Unikko*, nicknamed the "rebel flower." Maija created *Unikko* in 1964 in protest, after Marimekko's founder banned floral patterns. Maija refused to be told what to draw, so she responded by creating several floral prints. Unikko quickly became Marimekko's most popular design and is still in production today—over 50 years later.

Maija's daughter, Kristina, also became a textile artist at Marimekko. From 1987 until her death, in 2001, Maija focused on painting rather than textiles. She left behind an incredible design legacy. While Maija's designs never faded from popularity, they have seen a resurgence in the 2000s. Her patterns perfectly capture a mid-20th-century style, and they are also characteristically Scandinavian. Maija made a great impact on modern design globally, and she remains an international icon.

YAYOI KUSAMA
WORLD'S MOST POPULAR ARTIST

FULL NAME: Yayoi Kusama
BORN: MARCH 22, 1929, MATSUMOTO, JAPAN
NATIONALITY: JAPANESE

Yayoi's work is popular among all ages around the world. Here, a young girl visits the Yayoi Kusama Exposition in France's Centre Pompidou, in 2012.

POLKA-DOT PRINCESS

The trademark of Yayoi Kusama's art is brightly colored polka dots, but her work encompasses so much more: painting, sculpture, performance art, fashion, writing, film—the list goes on. Yayoi is recognized as one of the most important living Japanese artists, as well as one of the top living artists around the world.

Yayoi has dealt with mental health issues since childhood. Since 1977, she has chosen to live in a psychiatric hospital in Tokyo, Japan, across the street from which she has an artist studio. Yayoi's work helps her process the world she sees and to share her experiences. She has won a number of international awards and has influenced artists and musicians from around the globe.

Yayoi is believed to have influenced such artistic giants as Andy Warhol (of Marilyn Monroe screen-print fame) and Claes Oldenburg (known for giant everyday objects). Her early work set the scene for significant art movements that followed, including pop art and minimalism. However, the incredibly talented Yayoi was widely forgotten between the 1970s and 2000, when she left the New York art scene and moved back to her native Japan. Fortunately, love for her art was rekindled, and she has had major exhibitions of her work in New York's Museum of Modern Art (MoMA), London's Tate Modern, and the Centre Pompidou in Paris. Her star is on the rise again, and in 2008, one of her pieces sold for an incredible $5.1 million—a record for a living female artist. Spectacularly, in 2014, at the age of 86, Yayoi was labeled the world's most popular artist, as ranked by museum attendance. This was for the touring retrospective of her work, which attracted over two million visitors at galleries all around the globe.

AUDREY HEPBURN
ACTRESS, HUMANITARIAN, CULTURAL ICON

FULL NAME: AUDREY KATHLEEN VAN HEEMSTRA RUSTON
BORN: MAY 4, 1929, BRUSSELS, BELGIUM
DIED: JANUARY 20, 1993, TOLCHENAZ, SWITZERLAND
NATIONALITY: BRITISH

U.S. postage stamp, circa 2003, memorializing Audrey Hepburn

Known for her love of animals, Audrey adopted a fawn from one of her films and named him Ip.

GRACE, BEAUTY, AND HEART

It is fitting that Audrey Hepburn should follow so closely behind Marilyn Monroe (*see pages 66–67*) in this book. Audrey's most famous movie role was Holly Golightly in *Breakfast at Tiffany's*. The part was originally written for Marilyn Monroe, already a huge screen star, but the petite rising star—with aristocratic chic—wowed the crew and won the part.

Born in Belgium to an English banker father and a Dutch baroness, Audrey Kathleen van Heemstra Ruston spent her childhood alternating between the Netherlands and England. "Hepburn" was a name she added later. During World War II, Audrey and her mother lived in the Nazi-occupied Netherlands, where they experienced the brutality of war. Young Audrey saw Jewish people all around her taken from their homes, and she herself suffered malnutrition and other hardships. Audrey reportedly helped the resistance movement by delivering messages and raised funds by dancing in secret ballet performances. These experiences would have a profound impact on her lifelong dedication to humanitarianism.

CINDERELLA OF THE SILVER SCREEN

After the war, Audrey continued to study ballet. She made her debut on the London stage in 1948. In 1951, she won a bit part in her first feature film, *One Wild Oat*, before starring in the Broadway production of *Gigi* in the same year. Her success was building fast. In 1953, aged just 22, Audrey starred opposite Gregory Peck in *Roman Holiday* as a free-spirited princess. For the role, she won an Academy Award for Best Actress. Often, Audrey's roles centered on Cinderella-like transitions, such as those in *Sabrina* and *Funny Face*, and she starred in everything from light-hearted comedies to epic tragedies. One of her two most famous transformation movies was *Breakfast at Tiffany's* (1961), based on a novella by Truman Capote. The film earned her millions of fans, and to this day it remains a much-loved cult classic. The other was the beloved musical classic *My Fair Lady* (1964). Star of stage and Hollywood's Golden Age, Audrey is one of only a handful of actresses to win an Emmy (for TV), Tony (for theater), Grammy (for music), and Academy Award (for film). The American Film Institute ranked Audrey third among the greatest female stars of all time. She won one Oscar and was nominated for five, as well as winning three Golden Globes.

Audrey quickly became a style icon, on the opposite end of the spectrum from curvy, glamorous Marilyn. Audrey had short hair, a slim body, and minimalistic fashion sense. Her look was more attainable to the average woman at the time, and she is often named among the greatest style icons of the 20th century.

MAKING A DIFFERENCE

By the 1970s and 1980s, Audrey appeared in fewer films. She still made the occasional onscreen appearance, but humanitarian work was now her priority. In around 1988, Audrey began to serve as a UNICEF Goodwill Ambassador. Fluent in six languages, she traveled the world with UNICEF, raising awareness about poverty, hunger, and healthcare. From her own childhood experiences, Audrey knew what it felt like to suffer hardships, and she was renowned for her incredible ability to connect with people— especially children. In spite of the atrocities she witnessed, Audrey remained hopeful for the future. In return for her contributions, she was awarded the Presidential Medal of Freedom in 1992, as well as a special Academy Award for her humanitarian work in 1993. Just after her death, her sons and partner established the Audrey Hepburn Society at UNICEF.

DELIA DERBYSHIRE
PIONEER OF ELECTRONIC MUSIC, WHO ALSO PRODUCED THE DISTINCTIVE SOUND OF *DOCTOR WHO*

FULL NAME: Delia Derbyshire
BORN: MAY 5, 1937, COVENTRY, U.K
DIED: JULY 3, 2001, NORTHAMPTON, U.K.
NATIONALITY: BRITISH

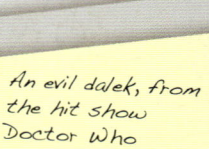

An evil dalek, from the hit show Doctor Who

FOR THE LOVE OF SOUND

Delia loved math and music, especially the overlaps between the two—the patterns of "acoustics." Even the sound of air-raid sirens and running feet had a musical impact upon her during World War II (which she lived through). After graduating in math and music from Cambridge University, she followed her passion and applied to Decca Records. She was told flat out that women were not employed in the recording studio there. Eventually, she got a job as a trainee studio manager at the British Broadcasting Corporation (BBC). She then moved to the BBC's Radiophonic Workshop, where she did some of her best work. One of her first works, and the one for which she became most famous, was the *Doctor Who* theme song. TV composer Ron Grainer had put together a score, but it was Delia who made it work as the iconic sound audiences loved. When it was done, Ron barely recognized it, but he loved it. It was the first TV theme entirely created by electronic means—and probably the first time the public had heard electronic music.

Before the days of synthesizers and tape recorders, sound engineers had to improvize. Delia was known for using keys, bits of tape, and a cheese grater—and in the soundtrack for a nature documentary, she used the sounds of her own voice, combined with a green lampshade, to great effect. Delia composed a huge number of pieces for the BBC, but it did not credit individual engineers. Much of her work was ahead of its time. As well as at the BBC, she worked with a wide range of musicians, including Jimi Hendrix and Yoko Ono. With the rise of new technology in the 1970s, Delia became disillusioned with music and stopped making any. However, by the 1990s, a new generation of musicians recognized her massive influence. Electronic music had taken off, and the likes of Aphex Twin and Sonic Boom were fans. She got excited about music again and began creating. Sadly, the comeback was short. She died in 2001, at the age of 64. Today, Delia Derbyshire is credited as a pioneer of electronic music.

WOMEN IN MUSIC

Every music genre has been influenced by the talent and creativity of a wide range of women. Their impact has been so great, in fact, that it would be impossible to fit them all into the pages of this book!

Saint Hildegard is credited with inventing opera; Maria Callas personified the genre. In the world of gospel, jazz, and blues, Mamie Smith, Ma Rainey, Billie Holiday, Ella Fitzgerald, and Nina Simone set the world ablaze—with Sister Rosetta Tharpe crowned the Godmother of Rock. In spite of her short life, Janis Joplin remains a bastion of blues and rock, epitomizing the sound of the 1960s. Another 1960s icon, Carole King, is the most successful female songwriter of the 20th century, while Joni Mitchell's song-writing and distinctive vocals have arguably made her the most influential female recording artist of the last 50 years. Queen of Pop Madonna and genre-spanning Beyoncé reign supreme as live performers. As the Godmother of Soul, Aretha Franklin—with her powerful voice and chart-topping success—remains a living legend. Patsy Cline endures as one of the most influential voices in country music, and Taylor Swift and Dolly Parton have both found continued success as country and crossover singers— Dolly with a career that has spanned more than 50 years. Ani DiFranco was one of the first independent artists to start her own label (Righteous Babe), which she did at the impressive age of 18! Genre-defying musicians Björk and Laurie Anderson continue to expand the boundaries of music and art across the globe. Listen out for the sounds of all of these women to learn more!

CLOCKWISE FROM TOP LEFT: JANIS JOPLIN, NINA SIMONE, MADONNA, AND MA RAINEY

DOLLY PARTON
QUEEN OF COUNTRY MUSIC

FULL NAME: Dolly Rebecca Parton Dean
BORN: JANUARY 19, 1946, SEVIER COUNTY, TENNESSEE, U.S.A.
NATIONALITY: AMERICAN

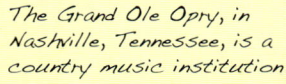

The Grand Ole Opry, in Nashville, Tennessee, is a country music institution.

RAGS TO RHINESTONES

The fourth of 12 children, Dolly was born near the Great Smoky Mountains of Tennessee. In her own words, Dolly has had a "rags-to-rhinestones" life story. Her family didn't have much money, but what they lacked financially, they made up for in music. Dolly's mother was a singer, and the family sang church songs together. As a little girl, Dolly was given a guitar as a present and started writing her own songs. At age eight, she recalls knowing her life path, and by the age of ten, she was already performing on radio and TV. At 13, she made her stage debut at the iconic Grand Ole Opry. Barely 48 hours after high school graduation, Dolly moved to Nashville, the country music hotspot, to focus on her career.

Dolly soon signed with the label RCA Records. The early 1970s brought a wave of successes, starting with her first number-one country hit "Joshua," in 1971. Country music—and karaoke—favorites "Jolene" and "I Will Always Love You" (later covered by Whitney Houston) followed. Soon, Dolly had crossover hits on both the country and pop charts and began winning awards. She became known as an impressive solo singer and engaging performer, but her duets with a number of fellow music legends also won her major acclaim. While Dolly's musical roots began in gospel and country, she is an accomplished pop and bluegrass performer, winning a Grammy for best bluegrass album in 1999.

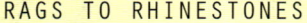

Loved for her music as well as her unique style, Dolly continues to attract new fans wherever she goes.

PERFORMER AND PHILANTHROPIST

Never one to turn down a challenge, Dolly tried out acting, too, including in the hit 1980 movie, *9 to 5*, and the much-loved 1989 *Steel Magnolias*. In addition to singing, song-writing, performing, and acting, Dolly is also a successful businesswoman. In 1986, she opened her own theme park, called Dollywood, close to where she grew up. The theme park attracts three million visitors a year. Her aim is to increase jobs and revenue for her old stomping ground. Dolly has also published a cookbook and co-owned a production company. While she has become just as famous for her big hair, bright, rhinestone-laden clothes, and curvy figure as for her songs, she also has a tremendously big heart. Dolly does a huge amount of charity work and philanthropy, mostly through her Dollywood Foundation. She has a literacy program called Dolly Parton's Imagination Library. The program sends one book per month to each enrolled child from birth until kindergarten, and over 920,000 children participate. Dolly also raises money for animal rights, the American Red Cross, and HIV charities.

Dolly Parton is a singer, songwriter, actress, philanthropist, businesswoman, activist, cultural icon—the list goes on. But at the heart of it all, she is one of the most revered, longest-performing country music singers of all time. She remains one of a very small group of people to have received nominations from all four major American entertainment awards: Emmy, Grammy, Oscar, and Tony. Dolly has won eight Grammy awards (including a Lifetime Achievement Award, in 2011) and 46 Grammy Award nominations—tied only with Beyoncé (*see pages* 90–91) for the most of any female artist in history. In 2000, she was inducted into the Country Music Hall of Fame, and in 2006, she received the Kennedy Center Honors. She has her own star on the Hollywood Walk of Fame and was given both a Living Legend Medal by the U.S. Library of Congress (in 2004) and a National Medal of Arts (in 2005). Dolly has been writing and performing for 60 years, but her talent—and success—continue to soar. In 2014, Dolly played the landmark British music festival Glastonbury, with an estimated 180,000 fans—the largest crowd in the festival's history. Dolly remains a country music icon and an inspiration.

FULL NAME: Mary Louise "Meryl" Streep
BORN: JUNE 22, 1949, SUMMIT, NEW JERSEY, U.S.A.
NATIONALITY: AMERICAN

Meryl at the 82nd Annual Academy Awards, in Hollywood, California, in 2012

FROM OPERA TO ACTING

Considered by many critics to be the best actress of her generation, Meryl Streep has performed in 77 movies in less than 40 years. Meryl is an acting legend of the stage, TV, and the big screen. Despite an early interest in becoming an opera singer, Meryl started out in New York theater in the late 1960s. Her first film role was in the movie *Julia*, in 1977. The very next year, she won her first Oscar for the movie *The Deer Hunter*. Not bad for a "rookie" big screen actress!

Meryl has won eight Golden Globe Awards and three Academy Awards, as well as two Emmys. Katharine Hepburn, with four Oscar wins (*see pages* 44–45), is at the top of the Academy Award list, and Meryl is in second place with three Oscars (tied with Ingrid Bergman, Walter Brennan, Daniel Day-Lewis, and Jack Nicholson). However, it is for her nominations that Meryl outshines all others. Meryl has racked up an incredible 19 Oscar nominations (15 for Best Actress and four for Best Supporting Actress) and 29 Golden Globe nominations—on both counts, higher than any other actor in history.

The year after she started making movies, Meryl won an Oscar for the Vietnam movie The Deer Hunter.

AMAZINGLY ADAPTABLE ACTOR

Meryl is known for her incredible, chameleon like range of characters. She has played real-life figures, such as Margaret Thatcher and Emmeline Pankhurst, has been a voice on *The Simpsons*, and has sung her way through the feel-good musical *Mamma Mia!* She is known for her perfectionism in every role she takes on, many of which are among the most challenging in Hollywood. In 1998, she earned a star on the Hollywood Walk of Fame.

In 2010, U.S. President Barack Obama awarded Meryl the National Medal of Arts, and, in 2014, the Presidential Medal of Freedom. Meryl describes herself as a humanist—humanism being a philosophy that emphasizes reason and dignity in the natural world. On International Women's Day (March 8) of 2016, Meryl Streep, alongside a handful of other celebrities, wrote an open letter to world leaders, calling for global gender equality. Meryl believes in the value of trying to make the world a better place. She has worked to support the Equal Rights Amendment in the U.S.A. and has set up scholarships for female screenwriters and struggling students.

In addition to her Oscars success, Meryl has won eight Golden Globes. She is pictured here at the 69th Golden Globe Awards in Beverly Hills, California, in 2012.

ANNA WINTOUR
ONE OF THE MOST INFLUENTIAL AND POWERFUL PEOPLE IN FASHION

FULL NAME: Anna Wintour
BORN: NOVEMBER 3, 1949, LONDON, U.K.
NATIONALITY: BRITISH

SENSE OF STYLE

With her bobbed haircut and near-permanent large sunglasses, Anna Wintour is unmistakable. But she's so much more than that. For several decades, Anna has been one of the most influential people in fashion.

Anna in Milan, Italy, during Fashion Week, 2016

Anna came from a publishing family, but she became hugely successful in her own right. She had a clear direction and sharp sense of style. From a young age, Anna knew that she wanted to go into fashion. She dropped out of finishing school and spent her time in the clubs and designer shops of 1960s London. After working for *Harper's*, she eventually moved to New York and got the job of editor-in-chief of *American Vogue* in 1988. At the helm for almost 30 years, Anna has made *Vogue* a huge success. In 2013, she also became the overall artistic director of *Condé Nast*, the publisher of *Vogue*.

FIERY FASHIONISTA

Even people with no interest in fashion know of the powerhouse that is Anna Wintour. She is known for being direct, and even cold, but she has no problem with that critique. She feels her perfectionism can help others succeed. The movie *The Devil Wears Prada*, starring Meryl Streep (*see pages* 76–77) and Anne Hathaway, is based on the experience of working with Anna. Along the way, Anna has helped launch the careers of designers, editors, and photographers. In spite of her intimidating persona, Anna does a lot of charity work. She has helped to create a fund to support up-and-coming designers and does a lot of fundraising for the arts, politics, and AIDS charities. In 2008, Anna was awarded an OBE from Queen Elizabeth II for her services to both British journalism and fashion. She remains an unstoppable force in fashion across the globe.

FEMALE FASHION-SETTERS

Even the most ancient artefacts can reveal how different cultures throughout history have used fashion as an expression of status and identity. These days, the world of fashion is as varied as the designers themselves.

Coco Chanel revolutionized women's clothing and set it free from the confines of the corset, with her "little black dress" and pants for women. Mary Quant took it a step further, epitomizing 1960s chic with the invention of the miniskirt. Fellow Brit Vivienne Westwood brought punk into mainstream fashion, in a career that continues to shock and innovate. High fashion has traditionally included elaborate designs full of high-end style, as seen in the work of of Donatella Versace and Vera Wang, for example. But the stylists at the other end of the spectrum have made their mark, too. The simple, deconstructed, "anti-fashion" designs of Rei Kawakubo, for instance, are both bold and thought-provoking. Carolina Herrera and Diane von Furstenberg are renowned for their elegant styles, as is Donna Karan for the sheer accessibility of her designs. Fashion does not have to be exclusive and "high end," as Stella McCartney's line—in everything from T-shirts to sportswear—clearly shows.

CLOCKWISE FROM TOP LEFT:
ANNA WINTOUR, VIVIENNE WESTWOOD,
DONATELLA VERSACE, AND VERA WANG

OPRAH WINFREY
"THE QUEEN OF ALL MEDIA"

FULL NAME: Oprah Gail Winfrey
BORN: JANUARY 29, 1954, KOSCIUSKO, MISSISSIPPI, U.S.A.
NATIONALITY: AMERICAN

Oprah acted alongside Whoopi Goldberg in the 1985 movie, The Color Purple, written by Alice Walker.

MASSIVE MEDIA INFLUENCE

The multi-talented Oprah Winfrey is a superstar of all things media: she is an actress, producer, entrepreneur, publisher, philanthropist—and, most famously, the host of the highest-rated talk show in history, *The Oprah Winfrey Show*. The show ran for an impressive 25 years, from 1986 to 2011. The year it ended, Oprah launched her own TV channel, The Oprah Winfrey Network.

Oprah is famous for her warm, open conversations with interviewees, and this gift of putting people at ease allowed her to take top place in the competitive talk-show market. She avoided the gossipy topics of other talk shows, and for this she outlived them all. *The Oprah Winfrey Show* was shown on 120 channels globally, with an audience of ten million, and Oprah took control of the production company in charge of her show, making her a producer. Additionally, in 1985, Oprah was cast in Steven Spielberg's heart-wrenching movie *The Color Purple*. She was nominated for an Academy Award for her performance. Oprah is also responsible for "Oprah's Book Club," helping give a huge boost to the activity of reading across the U.S.A. To add to her media empire, she co-founded a company that produces cable and Internet programming for women, and she launched *O: The Oprah Magazine* in 2000. Oprah is one of the most influential people in show business and much loved by her legion of fans.

FABULOUS FIRSTS

🎤 *FIRST WOMAN TO OWN AND PRODUCE HER OWN TALK SHOW*

🎤 *FIRST AFRICAN-AMERICAN WOMAN TO BECOME A BILLIONAIRE*

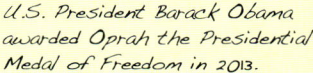

U.S. President Barack Obama awarded Oprah the Presidential Medal of Freedom in 2013.

Oprah at the 30th Annual People's Choice Awards in Pasadena, California, in 2004

THE "OPRAH EFFECT"

So beloved and influential is Oprah, her opinions and endorsement have been nicknamed the "Oprah Effect." *Life* magazine calls Oprah the most influential woman of her generation. According to *Forbes* magazine, she was the world's only black billionaire for three years running, from 2004 through 2006, as well as the richest African-American of the 20th century. Oprah is a committed activist and fundraiser: her Angel Network has reportedly raised more than $50 million for education and emergency charities. Support for children's rights is particularly close to Oprah's heart, and she campaigns tirelessly for this cause. Through her talk show, Oprah is credited with helping gain support within mainstream media for lesbian, gay, bisexual, and transgendered (LGBT) people from as far back as the 1980s. Oprah continues to be one of the most respected and influential voices in television today.

MADONNA
QUEEN OF POP

FULL NAME: Madonna Louise Veronica Ciccone

BORN: AUGUST 16, 1958, DETROIT, MICHIGAN, U.S.A.

NATIONALITY: AMERICAN

THE MATERIAL GIRL

Madonna Louise Veronica Ciccone was born in suburban Detroit, Michigan, the same year as fellow pop legends Michael Jackson and Prince. From a young age, Madonna was an enthusiastic dancer, and she earned a dance scholarship to go to college. But in 1978, Madonna dropped out of college and moved to New York City. She later said it was the bravest thing she'd ever done. In New York, Madonna performed as a backup dancer and singer, before focusing her attention on becoming a solo act. Her debut album, *Madonna*, was released in 1983.

Madonna quickly became an icon of both the music and fashion worlds—her style influenced a generation of youngsters to copy her fishnet tights, large crucifixes, and lace. Her second album, *Like a Virgin*, released in 1984, won her international acclaim, topping billboard charts all around the world. Overall, she has released 13 albums. She has also starred in a number of films, including *Desperately Seeking Susan* and *A League of Their Own* (see pages 242–243). She has never failed to court controversy for her outlandish performances onstage, which have further fueled her popularity.

POWERFUL PERFORMER

Madonna has been cited by several musicians and singers as hugely influential to their work. She has been nicknamed the "Queen of Pop," and is one of the longest-enduring stars to remain in the limelight. Her lyrics push boundaries, and her stage performances set the bar for the live show spectacle. Madonna was one of only two singers to be included in *Time* magazine's "25 Most Powerful Women of the 20th Century" (the other was Aretha Franklin), and she also topped VH1's list of the greatest women in music. Madonna has reputedly sold more than 300 million records worldwide and has won seven Grammys. *The Guinness Book of World Records* cites Madonna as the best-selling female recording artist of all time, and *Billboard 100* named her as the top solo artist ever.

As well as an influential musician and iconic performer, Madonna is also an impressive businesswoman. She has remained in tight control of her own career and has kept herself at the top in a tough industry by constantly reinventing herself. With determination, passion, and a unique style, she has opened doors for female performers who followed in her wake.

Madonna's tours are known for their high energy and outrageous outfits. Madonna and her dancers are seen here during the 2012 MDNA tour in Cleveland, Ohio, U.S.A.

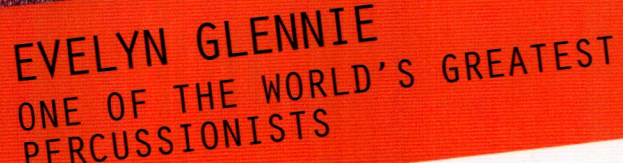

EVELYN GLENNIE
ONE OF THE WORLD'S GREATEST PERCUSSIONISTS

FULL NAME: Evelyn Elizabeth Anne Glennie
BORN: JULY 19, 1965, ABERDEENSHIRE, U.K.
NATIONALITY: BRITISH

> *Losing my hearing meant learning to listen differently, to discover features of sound I hadn't realized existed. Losing my hearing made me a better listener.*

EVELYN GLENNIE
©WWW.EVELYN.CO.UK

DRUM LOVE AT FIRST SIGHT

Evelyn Glennie is an incredible composer, performer, and percussionist, playing every kind of drum, xylophone, marimba, bell, rattle, and more, as well as non-percussion instruments, such as the bagpipes. She is also the first person in history to have a full-time career as a solo percussionist.

Evelyn was born in Scotland to a family steeped in Scottish folk music. From a young age, she played the harmonica, clarinet, and piano. At the age of eight, Evelyn began losing her hearing. Since the age of 12, she has been "profoundly deaf" (almost completely without hearing). This never deterred the young Evelyn. Instead, she taught herself to hear with the rest of her body. Evelyn performs barefoot to feel the sound vibrations created by the music. When she was 12, Evelyn came across the drums—and she was instantly hooked.

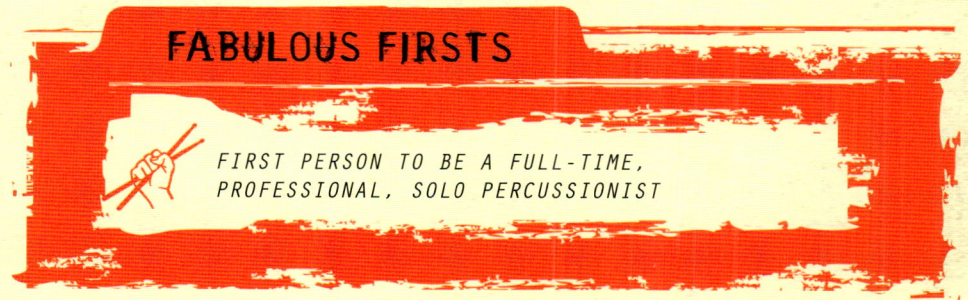

FABULOUS FIRSTS

FIRST PERSON TO BE A FULL-TIME,
PROFESSIONAL, SOLO PERCUSSIONIST

THE RHYTHMS
OF EVELYN GLENNIE

Evelyn has built up an incredible career playing an instrument normally hidden at the back of the stage, behind a band. But so amazing is her talent, she has now recorded more than 30 albums and continues to perform solo, and in collaboration, around the world. She has worked with a wide range of artists, including Björk and Béla Fleck. At the 2012 London Olympic Games' Opening Ceremony, Evelyn led a group of nearly 1,000 drummers on stage. Evelyn gives about 100 concerts a year around the world, as well as teaching and speaking in schools. She is also a jewelry maker, and active in music education and youth initiatives across the U.K. Her mission: to teach the world to listen.

In 2001, Evelyn appeared on *Sesame Street*, playing the drums with Oscar the Grouch's band. She has been given a DBE (Dame Commander of the Order of the British Empire) by Queen Elizabeth II and won an incredible number of other awards, including three Grammies and the 2015 Polar Music Prize. Evelyn collects percussion instruments and now has an amazing collection of over 2,000. A true Scot, she also has her own registered tartan: the Rhythms of Evelyn Glennie.

Evelyn is a master of everything, from bagpipes to xylophones. She is pictured here with a snare drum.

J.K. ROWLING
AUTHOR OF THE BEST-SELLING BOOK SERIES OF ALL TIME

FULL NAME: Joanne "Jo" Rowling
BORN: JULY 31, 1965, YATE, U.K.
NATIONALITY: BRITISH

J.K. Rowling, 2006

BELIEVING IN YOURSELF

It's now a famous story: aspiring author Joanne Rowling was struggling to make ends meet when she came up with the idea for Harry Potter on a delayed train journey. Finding rare snippets of spare time to write, Joanne wrote the children's fantasy story in coffee shops around Edinburgh, Scotland. Now picture yourself trying to focus on your homework, night after night, in loud, busy restaurants, while taking care of a small child—that's exactly the backdrop to the creation of the now-famous Harry Potter! The first instalment of the Harry Potter series was rejected countless times. However, Joanne always knew she wanted to be a writer, so she persevered—and the rest is truly remarkable history! She is clearly a testament to believing in yourself and pursuing your dreams.

THE ULTIMATE WIZARD

The Harry Potter series has become the best-selling book series of all time. Since publication of the first novel, *Harry Potter and the Sorcerer's Stone*, in 1997, the seven-book series has gone on to sell 450 million copies in 69 languages. The fourth instalment, *Harry Potter and the Goblet of Fire*, was the fastest-selling book in history. An eighth instalment, *Harry Potter and the Cursed Child*, will join the series more than nine years after the seventh book. Joanne's Potter stories have already been made into a series of smash-hit films—the most successful movie franchise in history, which launched the careers of now-international stars Emma Watson and Daniel Radcliffe, among others. According to *Atlantic* magazine, the series created a reported $21 billion dollar industry, including the books, movies, merchandise, video games, soundtrack, theme park, and more.

In addition to the Harry Potter series, Joanne has written a number of other books, including *The Casual Vacancy* (a novel for adults) and the screenplay to a film called *Fantastic Beasts and Where to Find Them*. Joanne is the winner of several awards, including the British Book Awards' Lifetime Achievement Awardand an OBE (Officer of the Order of the British Empire) from Queen Elizabeth II. On the back of her tremendous success, she works to promote aspiring writers, like herself, who find themselves overlooked by the publishing industry. J.K. Rowling is living proof that hard work and self-belief can overcome the most difficult obstacles to achieving success.

The Harry Potter series is wildly popular all over the world. Japan's Universal Studios even has a replica of Hogwarts School of Witchcraft and Wizardy for fans to visit.

WOMEN OF LETTERS

Throughout history, women have played a huge part in the creative pursuit of great literature and hard-hitting nonfiction across the globe. In fiction, from the greats of antiquity—the poet Sappho and first novelist Murasaki—to the modern pioneers—such as Virginia Woolf, Sylvia Plath, and Chimamanda Ngozi Adichie—women set in motion new ways of writing about the world. Female writers were instrumental in changing the face of nonfiction, too. Nelly Bly guided investigative journalism into its current form, and Mary Woolstonecroft and Harriet Beecher Stowe triggered great social change in the form of women's rights and civil rights. We can thank all of these women—and millions more—for shaping the world of books, magazines, essays, plays, and poetry available to us today, and for paving the way for many more of us to put pen to paper with the dream of being an author.

CLOCKWISE FROM TOP LEFT:
MARY WOOLSTONECROFT, VIRGINIA WOOLF,
NELLY BLY, AND HARRIET BEECHER STOWE

THE NIGHTINGALES
LONGEST-RUNNING "GIRL BAND" OF ALL TIME

FULL NAME: The Nightingales
FORMED: 1971, OMDURMAN, SUDAN

THE SUDANESE SUPREMES

Most likely you've heard of the iconic Motown girl band The Supremes from your grandparents or even your parents. But have you ever heard of The Nightingales? You should have! After 45 years, sisters Amal, Hadia, and Hayat Talsam are the longest-surviving girl band in the world. Their band began in 1971 and was nicknamed the "Sudanese Supremes." Motown's Supremes only stayed together for 18 years.

At the same time as the group was starting in the early 1970s, Sudan was going through a creative explosion. The Talsam teenagers experienced some criticism from traditional groups, but they were also widely celebrated. The group soon became one of the region's best-loved musical acts. The Nightingales have performed in the Sudan and in New York, and they are now planning a world tour—after 45 years of making music.

The Nightingales have been making music together for an incredible 45 years!

BEYONCÉ
ONE OF BEST-SELLING MUSIC ARTISTS OF ALL TIME

FULL NAME: Beyoncé Knowles-Carter
BORN: SEPTEMBER 4, 1981, HOUSTON, TEXAS, U.S.A.
NATIONALITY: AMERICAN

180 MILLION RECORDS SO FAR

Beyoncé is best known as a hugely talented singer and performer. But her talents don't end there: she is also a successful songwriter, performer, record producer, actress, businesswoman, philanthropist, and mother. One of the best-selling musical artists of all time, Beyoncé began as part of one of the best-selling all-female groups ever (Destiny's Child), is the most nominated woman in the history of the Grammy Awards (having won 17), is the highest-paid black musician in history, and has sold nearly 180 million records worldwide in her career to date. Truly astonishing.

Beyoncé Knowles was born and raised in Houston, Texas, where she performed in many competitions as a child. At the age of seven, she sang John Lennon's "Imagine" and won a talent competition against much older contenders. The performing spark was lit. Soon after, she became the lead singer of an all-female R&B group that would ultimately be called Destiny's Child. When

FABULOUS FIRSTS

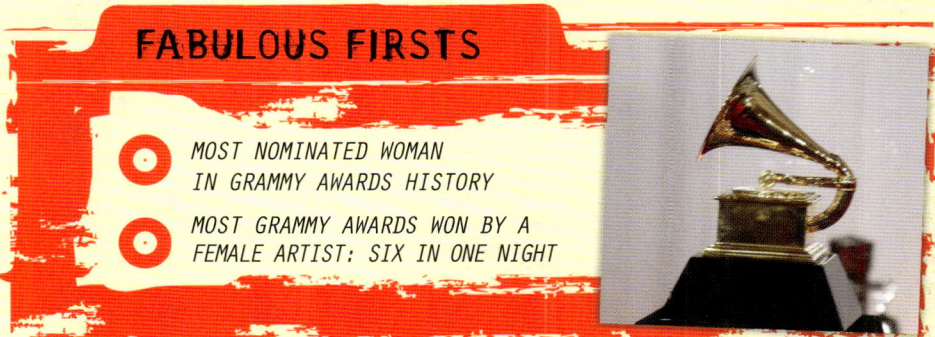

- MOST NOMINATED WOMAN IN GRAMMY AWARDS HISTORY
- MOST GRAMMY AWARDS WON BY A FEMALE ARTIST: SIX IN ONE NIGHT

A Grammy Award

Beyoncé was only 16, Destiny's Child released their first album. The group would go on to sell over 60 million records worldwide. At the age of 21, Beyoncé released her debut solo album, *Dangerously in Love*. Selling 11 million copies and earning five Grammy Awards, the album caused Beyoncé's popularity to skyrocket. In total, she has released five solo albums, each of which debuted at number one (the first woman in Billboard chart history to do so). She has starred in a number of movies, putting in critically acclaimed performances in *Dream Girls* and *Cadillac Records*. Beyoncé's sound is wide ranging, including R&B, funk, pop, and soul, and her talents include record producing and managing. Beyoncé is also well known for her impressive dancing and choreography, and she is considered to be one of the best entertainers in contemporary music. *Billboard* magazine named her "Artist of the Millennium."

A POWERFUL ROLE MODEL

Credited with helping to bring feminism back into popularity, Beyoncé is not afraid to speak her mind or share her talents. She helped sponsor the 2014 "Ban Bossy" campaign, led by Facebook's Sheryl Sandberg and the Girl Scouts Association (*see pages* 130–131). The campaign seeks to eliminate the word "bossy" in relation to women and girls and to promote leadership in its place. Powerful, talented, and beautiful, she is a role model for many girls and boys, as well as women and men, today. *Time* magazine includes Beyoncé in its "100 Most Influential People in the World" (of both 2013 and 2014).

Beyonce performing in Rio de Janeiro, Brazil, in 2011

MISTY COPELAND
FIRST AFRICAN-AMERICAN PRINCIPAL BALLERINA

FULL NAME: Misty Danielle Copeland
BORN: SEPTEMBER 10, 1982, KANSAS CITY, MISSOURI, U.S.A.
NATIONALITY: AMERICAN

Misty has performed in some of the most iconic roles in ballet, including as the swan Odette in Swan Lake.

BALLET ON A BASKETBALL COURT

Graceful, powerful, and talented, Misty Copeland has spun like a whirlwind through the world of contemporary ballet. Her personal popularity has increased interest in ballet across the U.S.A. and beyond.

Most professional ballerinas start dancing as toddlers and dedicate themselves to the art at a young age. By contrast, Misty took her first ballet class in a basketball court at her local youth club and began dancing at the late age of 13. Only two years later, she won first place in the Music Center Spotlight Awards. Misty's tremendous talent was soon obvious, and she earned full scholarships to study at both the San Francisco Ballet School and the American Ballet Theatre's summer program.

MAKING DREAMS AND HISTORY

In 2001, at the age of 19—and only six years after she started dancing—Misty joined the prestigious American Ballet Theatre (ABT) as a member of its troupe. By 2007, she became the company's second-ever African-American female soloist. Misty performed a number of iconic roles, including Clara in *The Nutcracker*, Odette in *Swan Lake*, and Juliet in *Romeo & Juliet*. These roles did not come without challenges, and Misty spoke out publicly about the fact that she was told her skin color was "wrong" for *Swan Lake*. However, her performances wowed audiences and critics alike. Misty was dedicated to her craft, but also outspoken in her ambition: to become the first black woman named a principal dancer, the top role in ballet. On June 30, 2015, Misty's dreams became reality—and she made history. The ABT chose her as the principal female dancer—making her the first African-American female principal in the company's 75-year history.

A star in or out of pointe shoes, Misty invests her time in charity work. She is seen here at an American Heart Association charity catwalk event, in 2011.

RISING STAR

In addition to her talents on stage, Misty is known as the advertising face of several companies and she has been featured in many magazines and TV shows. She is also an ace of social media and publicity and has published two best-selling books, the memoir *Life in Motion* and the children's picture book *Firebird*. Misty has brought legions of new fans to ballet, an art form often viewed as old-fashioned, and her work has helped to ensure ballet is now beloved by all ages and backgrounds.

Misty has been honored with a number of awards for her success and contributions. In 2013, she was named the National Youth of the Year Ambassador for the Boys & Girls Clubs of America (the club where she first learned ballet). That same year, she received the Young, Gifted & Black honor at the Black Girls Rock! Awards. *Time* magazine named Misty as one of its "100 Most Influential People" in 2015, and in 2016, *Variety* honored Misty in its "Power of Women" issue as one of five women using their celebrity to bring attention to worthy causes. In 2016, toy company Mattell—the makers of Barbie—launched their own Misty Copeland doll as part of their "Barbie's Sheroes" program, honoring women who break boundaries and help to expand possibilities for girls everywhere. In the eyes of many young people, this might even be the greatest honor to have been bestowed upon her!

Add your own great women here

Politics & world-building

 # CONTENTS

 # CONTENTS

HATSHEPSUT
ONE OF EGYPT'S MOST SUCCESSFUL PHARAOHS

FULL NAME: Hatshepsut
BORN: c. 1507 b.c., EGYPT
DIED: 1458 b.c., EGYPT
NATIONALITY: EGYPTIAN

A statue of Hatshepsut, from the Temple of Hatshepsut near Luxor, Egypt

FALSE BEARDS AND BAD PRESS

While her name is not as well known as the charismatic Cleopatra's, Hatshepsut may well have been one of ancient Egypt's most successful pharaohs (rulers). Her reign lasted over 20 years (from 1479 to 1458 b.c.), but the details of her life have been largely hidden from the history books. When her resting place was discovered, in 1903, the statues and tributes entombed with her were found to have been vandalized. This painted her in a harsh, unpopular light; however, today's academics believe that this was just a severe case of "bad publicity."

Hatshepsut was the sixth pharaoh of the 18th dynasty—and one of the few women to have ruled ancient Egypt. Before her, there had been two or three female rulers, but Hatshepsut was the first "official" female pharaoh. The throne usually passed from man to man, and the pharaohs enjoyed a godlike status. Following the death of her pharaoh husband, Thutmose II, Hatshepsut became regent (a temporary head of state) in order to rule in place of her infant stepson, Thutmose III. However, she soon proclaimed herself pharaoh. Most of the surviving imagery of Hatshepsut shows her with male characteristics, such as the "false beard" adorning her face—which the Egyptians saw as a symbol of power.

A STRONG RULER

Under Hatshepsut's rule, the empire was peaceful and wealthy, with a focus on art, trade, and construction projects. Among these was the Temple at Deir el-Bahri, a building now regarded as one of the wonders of the ancient world. When Hatshepsut died, her stepson took over. Egyptologists believe he had her monuments destroyed to erase her from history, most likely because her reign was "too" successful—a dangerous example of a powerful female ruler. In 2007, a royal mummy was discovered and identified as Hatshepsut. It is now on display in the Egyptian Museum in Cairo. It seems Hatshepsut couldn't be erased from history after all!

CLEOPATRA
MOST FAMOUS FEMALE RULER IN HISTORY

FULL NAME: Cleopatra
DATES FROM: C. 69 B.C., ALEXANDRIA, EGYPT
DIED: AUGUST 12, 30 B.C., ALEXANDRIA, EGYPT
NATIONALITY: POSSIBLY ANCIENT EGYPTIAN

Carved in 196 B.C., the Rosetta Stone features both Greek and Egyptian, including hieroglyphs, allowing officials to translate between the languages.

A WOMAN IN A MAN'S WORLD

Cleopatra was the last pharaoh (ruler) of the Ptolemy dynasty of ancient Egypt. In ancient Egypt, pharaohs were almost always men. An exception to the rule, Cleopatra brought peace and wealth to her struggling empire and was a strong and unifying ruler.

When Cleopatra came to power, her family had ruled Egypt for 100 years. Her background is disputed: she may have been Greek, black African, or Roman. At the death of her father, King Ptolemy XII, the throne was left to 18-year-old Cleopatra and her 10-year-old brother, Ptolemy XIII. The siblings ruled together, but Egypt struggled with famine, floods, and poverty. Cleopatra, clever, well educated, and fluent in several languages, decided to take matters into her own hands. She assembled an army against her brother so she could become sole pharaoh. Known for her grand gestures, Cleopatra reputedly had herself secretly delivered to the Roman ruler Julius Caesar, hidden inside a rug. He was captivated and offered Rome's support. With his help, Cleopatra defeated her brother and became ruler. Soon after, Caesar was assassinated, and Marc Antony came to power in Rome.

A POWERFUL LOVE STORY

Like Caesar before him, Antony was able to offer financial and military support to Cleopatra's empire, and she was able to do the same for him. Cleopatra saw herself as a reincarnation of the Egyptian goddess Isis and was known to have a powerful presence and personality that drew people in. Marc Antony was no exception. The love story between the two has been often re-told, including in a famous play by William Shakespeare. They had three children together, in addition to a son she had previously with Julius Caesar.

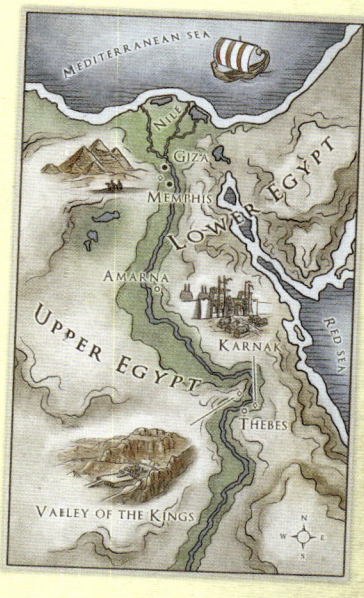

Cleopatra, Antony, and their children sat on elevated golden thrones at their palace at Alexandria, in Egypt, and became popular figures in both empires. For a time, they were strong rulers of the two great empires of Rome and Egypt, and their territories grew. Around 31 B.C., the couple combined Roman and Egyptian forces to defeat Roman rivals. But they were defeated themselves and fled to Egypt. The story goes that while on the battlefield, Antony was told that Cleopatra had died. It was a lie, but in grief and desperation, he killed himself. Then when Cleopatra was told of Antony's death, she, too, ended her life. As was their wish, the couple was buried together at an unknown location. The great empire of Egypt became a state within the Roman Empire.

An ancient coin featuring the great queen

THE LEGEND LIVES ON

Under Cleopatra's rule, Egypt grew its borders as well as its wealth and reputation. As a woman in a heavily male-dominated world, Cleopatra was a clever and ruthless politician. She united a country split by war and bankruptcy. Today memorialized in dozens of plays, operas, and films, *National Geographic* has called her the "world's first celebrity," and an asteroid (216 Kleopatra) has been named in her honor. Cleopatra remains an iconic and recognizable figure across the globe for her power, charm, and intelligence. Thousands of years after her death, her story continues to captivate and inspire.

ARAWELO
RULER OF ANCIENT SOMALIA AND FEMINIST ICON

FULL NAME: Arawelo
LIVED: c. A.D. 15 OR A.D. 7TH CENTURY A.D.
NATIONALITY: ANCIENT SOMALIAN

The current nation of Somalia is located on Africa's east coast.

Somalia

A DETERMINED FEMINIST

While there is little confirmed information about Arawelo, what is known adds up to a picture of a pretty phenomenal woman. Arawelo (also called Arawello, Araweelo, and Queen Ebla Awad) was a queen of ancient Somalia, in Africa. Most ancient African histories were passed down through storytelling rather than written accounts, so details vary widely. The dates are unconfirmed, but she lived and ruled some time between the first and seventh centuries.

Queen Arawelo is one of the earliest-known female rulers, alongside Cleopatra of ancient Egypt and the Queen of Sheba. At a time when rulers were almost always men, all three women remain important figures of female empowerment as the exception to the rule. (Rumor has it that the Queen of Sheba would send gifts to Arawelo in sisterly solidarity, but it is also believed that the Queen of Sheba did not rule until the 10th century!)

The Queen of Sheba, seen here in a 1911 illustration by Edmund Dulac, was rumored to have sent gifts to Arawelo.

REVERSING GENDER ROLES

Arawelo fought for female empowerment in a society traditionally ruled by men. She believed that society should be based on a matriarchy—a social system in which women are the leaders and decision-makers. Arawelo was anything but traditional in her idea of gender roles. Before Arawelo was queen, there was a major drought in the area. Arawelo and a group of women prevented mass starvation by collecting water and hunting. As queen, she thought that women should play an active role in society, not just be limited to the home, and that men should raise children. Arawelo believed that men traditionally started and participated in wars and that women were natural peacekeepers. Because of this, she believed that women, not men, should make decisions relating to conflict.

While some of Arawelo's tactics were potentially extreme (although some historians believe this could have been the result of false accusations that were recorded as history), she did manage to disrupt the norm and to improve women's role. She remains an enduring symbol of female empowerment—particularly to the people of Somalia, and Africa as a whole—more than 2,000 years after her death. Today, a nickname exists in the Somali language as a throwback to the great queen. The nickname "Caraweelo" means an assertive girl or woman.

Arawelo prevented mass starvation of her people, when she led a group of women to collect water and food to distribute.

BOUDICCA
FEARSOME WARRIOR

FULL NAME: Boudicca
BORN: UNKNOWN
DIED: C. A.D. 60
NATIONALITY: ANCIENT BRITISH

THE CELTIC QUEEN

Boudicca (also spelled Boadicea or Boudica) was an ancient British queen. Boudicca's husband, Prasutagus, was the king of the Celtic Iceni people of Eastern England (roughly in today's county of Norfolk), and Boudicca was their queen. Boudicca and Prasutagus had two daughters. When the king died, he left his empire to his daughters and to the Roman emperor Nero. As almost the whole of England was under the rule of the Roman Empire, the king hoped the inclusion of Nero in his will would help protect his family, especially as he had no male heirs. Sadly, the plan backfired. Instead, the Romans decided to rule the Iceni people themselves. They took over the Iceni kingdom, stealing property from the chief tribesman and violently harming Prasutagus' family. This made the Iceni people furious toward the Romans.

WARRIOR WOMAN

Responding with bravery and desperation, Boudicca raised a major rebellion against Roman rule. The uprising was believed to have included up to 100,000 fighters under Boudicca's leadership. In A.D. 60, they burned large Roman areas, including current-day Colchester, St. Albans, and London, and massacred 70,000 Romans. They were eventually defeated by the Romans after a courageous battle. Boudicca refused to be captured, and it is believed she poisoned herself so she could not be caught.

The story of Boudicca all but disappeared for hundreds of years, but then images of her began to make their way into paintings of the Italian Renaissance. She grew in popularity during Britain's Victorian era, when Queen Victoria was seen to embody her ideals (both "Boudicca" and "Victoria" mean "victory"). The poet laureate at the time, Alfred Lord Tennyson, wrote a poem about her, and she has since been memorialized in plays, fine art, music, and film. Today, she is a symbol of bravery and independence.

When the Romans ruled England, they built massive walls to defend their territories.

Boudicca is remembered as a legendary warrior for her bravery.

WU ZETIAN
ONLY FEMALE EMPEROR OF CHINA IN MORE THAN 4,000 YEARS

FULL NAME: Wu Zetian (Wu Ze Tian, Empress Wu)
BORN: FEBRUARY 17, 624, JINGZHOU, CHINA
DIED: December 16, 705, Luoyang, China
NATIONALITY: CHINESE

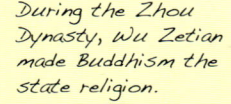

During the Zhou Dynasty, Wu Zetian made Buddhism the state religion.

DETERMINED RISE TO THE TOP

Wu Zetian, or Empress Wu, ruled China during the golden age of the Tang dynasty, a time of great culture, peace, and prosperity. Empress Wu was the only woman in Chinese history to rule as emperor.

The Tang dynasty was a time that brought new freedoms for women. Born into a noble family, Wu was taught to read, write, and play music. She became known for her beauty and intelligence and joined the royal court. After a number of years, she married the emperor, Kao Tsung, and they had several children. When he died, Wu manipulated the traditional order and put her youngest, weakest son in power. This allowed her to get a grip on power herself.

HER OWN DYNASTY

In spite of increased freedom for women at the time, traditional beliefs still said that women could not rule. To help her cause, Wu had biographies written of famous women and gave her mother's family important political jobs. Her belief was that the best ruler could govern over her subjects like a mother does over her children.

It appeared to work, and when her son gave up his post in 690, Wu Zetian was made the official emperor of China. She declared the period under her rule to be the Zhou Dynasty (690–705). Her rule was considered fair and just. She made life easier on the poor, lowering taxes and increasing farming. She also reduced the size of the army and filled government positions with educated scholars rather than military officials. In cultural and religious matters, she supported great art and architecture and made Buddhism the state religion. The famous 1000 Buddha Caves were built under her direction.

A statue of Wu Zetian at Huangze Temple, in Sichuan, China

In 705, at the extremely ripe old age of 80, Wu Zetian agreed to give up the throne to her third son. During Empress Wu's reign, she expanded the borders of the Chinese empire and made society stable and prosperous. She was the only female emperor of China in more than 4,000 years.

An ancient landmark in contemporary China, Empress Wu Zetian's tomb is located in Xian, China.

JOAN OF ARC
ONE OF HISTORY'S GREATEST SAINTS

FULL NAME: Jeanne d'Arc
BORN: JANUARY 6, 1412, DOMRÉMY, FRANCE
DIED: May 30, 1431, Rouen, France
NATIONALITY: FRENCH

MAID IN (WHITE) SHINING ARMOR

Nicknamed the "Maid of Orléans," Joan of Arc is one of history's greatest saints and a heroine of France. Believing God was on her side, Joan led France to victory in its long-running war against England. She became a symbol of French unity and a feminist icon.

Joan was born to a family of deeply religious peasant farmers in northeastern France. Because of the Hundred Years' War raging at the time, life was difficult in France. England occupied the area, and many in Joan's village had to flee. At age 13, Joan began hearing voices. She believed these voices were from God, and the message was to save France and return the crown prince Charles to the throne. At 16, Joan's father arranged a marriage for her, but she took him to court on the basis that it was against her divine mission. She won.

> 66 I am not afraid.
> I was born to
> do this. 99
>
> JOAN OF ARC

That same year, Joan made her way to see the crown prince. Along the way, she attracted a band of followers. They believed her claims that God had chosen her to save France, in spite of the fact that women did not hold military roles at the time, let alone command armies. Wearing men's clothes and short hair, she arrived at the crown prince's palace. Prince Charles' advisors tried to dissuade him, but Charles believed Joan's words that she had been sent by God to see him crowned. Joan had information he felt only a messenger from God could know. He granted her request for an army to lead to the town of Orléans, then under English occupation. Joan is believed to have set off for battle in white armor, riding a white horse.

JOAN THE HERO

Seventeen-year-old Joan of Arc defeated the English army at Orléans, despite having no military training—only determination and faith. News of her victory spread, and Joan became a hero. She was able to fulfil the second part of her destiny when she helped crown Charles as king of France in July of 1429.

Joan's downfall is disputed by history books. It could be that her lack of military training caught up with her in subsequent battles, or that her power was starting to threaten the new king and his court. Either way, during a siege at Rouen in 1430, Joan was thrown from her horse and taken captive by the Anglo-Burgundian enemy (the English and their French allies).

Joan was put on trial. Seventy charges were held against her, including heresy, witchcraft, and "dressing like a man." (Bear in mind for a moment how difficult it would have been to dress like a 15th-century woman in the heat of battle . . .) Accusations of heresy and witchcraft were very serious, and King Charles made no effort to come to her aid—despite the fact that he would not been crowned without her. The charges were made in the hope of getting rid of Joan and weakening the French king. Despite being uneducated and illiterate, Joan impressed the courts with her intelligence and legal wit. However, eyewitnesses said that court papers were later rewritten to show Joan in a negative light.

FROM TEENAGE WITCH
TO IMMORTAL SAINT

After a year in a military prison under death sentence and constant interrogations, Joan signed a confession saying that God had never spoken to her. It is likely the confession was forced. However, authorities still demanded her execution. On the morning of May 30, 19-year-old Joan was led to the center of Rouen, where she was burned at the stake for her crimes.

A monument of Joan of Arc riding into battle, in Orléans, France

In 1456, King Charles finally cleared her name, and in 1803 Napoleon Bonaparte declared her a symbol of French unity. In 1920, Pope Benedict XV recognized her as Saint Joan of Arc. Since her death, her fame and intrigue have continued to grow. Joan has been immortalized in countless paintings, plays, books, and films, and she is now a feminist icon and the patron saint of France.

QUEEN ELIZABETH I
ONE OF LONGEST-REIGNING MONARCHS AND RULER OF THE GOLDEN AGE OF PROGRESS

FULL NAME: Queen Elizabeth I
BORN: SEPTEMBER 7, 1533, GREENWICH, U.K.
DIED: MARCH 24, 1603, RICHMOND PALACE, RICHMOND, U.K.
NATIONALITY: ENGLISH

> *Though the sex to which I belong is considered weak, you will nevertheless find me a rock that bends to no wind.*

ELIZABETH I

A COMPLICATED FAMILY

Nicknamed the "Virgin Queen" for her choice not to marry or have children, Elizabeth I was often shown in paintings wearing white as a symbol of purity.

Born to King Henry VIII and his second wife, Anne Boleyn, Elizabeth was born into a complicated family and royal lines. King Henry had six wives and a number of children. The king was said to be disappointed with Elizabeth's gender at her birth, but he was certain a son and heir would follow. At this time, women could only be rulers if there were no other male heirs. When the young princess was just two and a half years old, her father had her mother executed for high treason against the state. This allowed the king to remarry. This new marriage did produce a male heir for the king, and this son became King Edward VI. However, he became terminally ill at a young age and died before he was old enough to rule on his own. Elizabeth took her rightful role as queen after a fight for the throne with her half-sister and cousin.

FABULOUS FIRSTS

 ONE OF LONGEST-REIGNING
MONARCHS

 RULER OF THE GOLDEN
AGE OF PROGRESS

*A portrait of young
Queen Elizabeth I
(date unknown)*

A POWERFUL RULER

Elizabeth was the queen of England and Ireland from 1558 to 1603. She was the fifth and last monarch of the Tudor dynasty (the royal house to which her family belonged). Queen Elizabeth recognized the importance of the popular consent of her people. As a result, she always worked with Parliament and consulted her close advisors. Elizabeth was considered a powerful ruler, defending her lands against invasion, including the Armada invasion from Spain. Her period of rule became known as the Elizabethan era. The period remains famous as a golden age of progress in arts and exploration. The playwright William Shakespeare and adventurer Sir Frances Drake were active in this period. As ruler, Elizabeth was also the head of the church, and she helped establish the English church her father had begun. The Church of England helped form a national identity at the time, and the church still exists today. Contrary to her father and half-siblings, Elizabeth was considered more tolerant of religious difference and more moderate in government.

STRENGTH AND STABILITY

Elizabeth's 44 years on the throne stabilized and strengthened the country during an era of major upheavals in Europe. Due to expectations of the time, Elizabeth was expected to marry and have a child (preferably male) as heir to the throne. She had several suitors, but Elizabeth never married. When she died, her nephew James VI (also known as James I) became king of Scotland, England, and Ireland, unifying the kingdoms.

CATHERINE THE GREAT
POWERFUL EMPEROR DURING RUSSIA'S "GOLDEN AGE"

FULL NAME: Sophie Friederike Auguste von Anhalt-Zerbst
BORN: MAY 2, 1729, STETTIN, PRUSSIA (NOW POLAND)
DIED: NOVEMBER 17, 1796, ST. PETERSBURG, RUSSIA
NATIONALITY: PRUSSIAN/RUSSIAN

Built in 1873, this monument to Catherine the Great is located in Ostrovsky Square, in St. Petersburg, Russia.

THE RISE OF EMPRESS CATHERINE

Catherine the Great was a powerful and successful ruler. She led the Russian empire for more than 30 years, during which it grew and flourished. She was the longest-serving female leader of the Russian empire (1762–1796).

Catherine the Great, Empress of Russia, was born Sophie Friederike Auguste von Anhalt-Zerbst to a family of German/Prussian heritage. Catherine was tutored in history, music, and religion, as well as French and German. In 1744, she moved to Russia to marry Grand Duke Peter, heir to the throne.

Catherine was intelligent, ambitious, and capable. Her relationship with her husband was not a happy one, and the two lived quite separate lives. When Peter's mother, Empress Elizabeth, died in 1762, Peter became Tsar Peter III. At the time, Russia was in the middle of the Seven Years' War with Prussia. Peter's first move as tsar was to pull Russia out of the war and side with Prussia (and secretly get rid of his wife). However, public opinion was against him, and Catherine had the support of both the army and the people. Six months after Peter was crowned tsar, he lost his crown to Catherine, who was proclaimed empress on July 9, 1762. Peter was assassinated eight days later.

The summer residence of the Russian royalty, Catherine Palace in Tsarskoye Selo, Russia, is full of grand rooms and opulent style.

An engraving of Catherine the Great (date unknown)

RUSSIA'S GOLDEN AGE

Catherine would go on to reign for an incredible 34 years. Early in her reign, Catherine was a liberal social reformer, but she grew more conservative with age. Following the values of the Enlightenment, Catherine had a group of delegates work out the wishes of the people in the hope of creating a liberal constitution. She expanded the borders of Russia's empire and improved diplomatic relations with neighboring countries. Catherine wanted Russia to be seen as the role model for civilization. Russia flourished under Catherine's rule. The empire went through a "Golden Age," a time of great arts, culture, and education, making it one of the great European powers. She hoped to modernize Russian life, making the day-to-day running more efficient and "westernized." The education of young women was a priority for Catherine, and she established the Smolny Institute, the first state university for women.

While Catherine courted scandal throughout her reign, she took her role of emperor very seriously. She was an intelligent, powerful, and capable leader who led Russia to become one of the great powers of Europe.

Catherine the Great created the first university for women, called the Smolny Institute and based in St. Petersburg, Russia.

CHING SHIH
ONE OF WORLD'S MOST SUCCESSFUL PIRATES

FULL NAME: Ching Shih (Zheng Shi or Madame Ching)
BORN: 1775, GUANGDONG, CHINA
DISAPPEARED: 1844, GUANGZHOU, CHINA
NATIONALITY: CHINESE

As leader of a massive pirate fleet, Ching Shih took the name of Madame Ching.

A CREW OF 70,000

Ching Shih, also known as Zheng Shi or Madame Ching, was one of the world's most famous and successful pirates, terrorizing the China Sea in the early 1800s. She is believed to have commanded up to 70,000 pirates in hundreds of ships.

As a young woman, Ching Shih was herself captured by pirates. In 1801, she married the notorious pirate Cheng I. He came from a family tradition of pirates, and through various alliances he was able to build a large coalition of pirate fleets known as the Red Flag Fleet. Ching Shih participated in her husband's piracy and when he died in 1807, she took over the leadership of the massive pirate fleet and became known as Madame Ching.

An 1864 French illustration of a Chinese junk (a particular type of ship used by pirates)

THE IMPORTANCE OF RULES—
EVEN FOR PIRATES

As pirate captain, Madame Ching proved a quiet and reasoned leader. She issued a strict code of laws, including no disobeying, no stealing from the group, and no deserting. Booty (stolen money or goods) was put into a shared pot to purchase supplies and then distributed evenly. Ching had a strict code for female captives, too. Captives deemed unattractive were released unharmed. A pirate could marry a beautiful captive, but he had to be faithful to her or he would be killed. If a pirate harmed a female captive, he would be injured or killed. These strict rules made Madame Ching's pirate army strong and obedient and helped ensure her incredible success.

Madame Ching terrorized the China Sea for booty, or stolen cash and treasure.

Madame Ching and her pirates could not be defeated, though countless navies and officials from around the world tried their best. In 1810, the Qing dynasty of China offered an amnesty to all pirates, whereby they could turn their back on piracy in return for safety. Madame Ching took advantage of the amnesty and gave up her life as a pirate—but only after long negotiations with the Chinese government to get the best deal she could. She got to keep her loot and is believed to have opened a gambling house. She lived for over 30 more years as a wealthy and well-respected woman. Madame Ching was one of the very few pirate captains to retire from piracy and die of old age.

Madame Ching continues to inspire people's imagination with her swashbuckling success. She has appeared in several novels and even made an appearance in the 2007 Pirates of the Caribbean movie, *At World's End.*

It was uncommon for any pirate to die either wealthy or of old age—Madame Ching was the exception. She got to keep all of her treasure and retire with dignity.

SOJOURNER TRUTH
ANTI-SLAVERY LEADER

FULL NAME: Isabella Baumfree (Sojourner Truth)
BORN: C. 1797, SWARTEKILL, NEW YORK, U.S.A.
DIED: NOVEMBER 26, 1883, BATTLE CREEK, MICHIGAN, U.S.A.
NATIONALITY: AMERICAN

Sojourner Truth,
in an 1864 portrait

$100 AND A FLOCK OF SHEEP

Sojourner Truth was an African-American woman who escaped from slavery and helped secure freedom for many others. She became one of the leading abolitionists (anti-slavery activists) and an early women's rights advocate. Her work had a massive impact on race and gender relations in the U.S.A. from the early 1900s onward.

Isabella Baumfree (her original name) was one of 12 children born to slave parents from Ghana and Guinea. The family was "owned" (in the language of the day) by a colonel and his family in New York. When the colonel died, the Baumfree family was separated and sold individually at auctions. At age nine, Isabella was sold for $100 with a flock of sheep and went to live as a slave with a new owner. She was sold several more times. Over the next few years, Isabella had several children. Children of slaves were automatically the property of the slave owner of the mother, so the children stayed with Isabella.

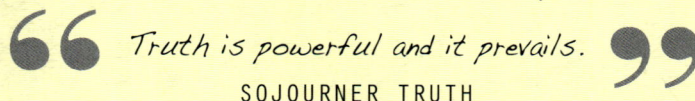

> *Truth is powerful and it prevails.*
>
> **SOJOURNER TRUTH**

The Northern U.S. states began to outlaw slavery earlier than the South, and New York started to do so in 1799. However, it wasn't until 1827 that all slaves were ordered to be freed. Isabella's owner promised to release her earlier and then changed his mind. So in 1826, Isabella escaped to freedom with her baby daughter Sophia. She had to leave her other children behind. She soon learned that her young son Peter had been illegally sold to a man in Alabama. Isabella took the case to court and got Peter released. Isabella became the first black woman to win a court case against a white man in a U.S. court. Though she was free at last, Isabella's life remained difficult, as she had a series of jobs as a domestic servant in various houses.

AIN'T I A WOMAN?

Isabella converted to Methodism (a branch of Christianity) and decided to devote her life to the abolition of slavery. In 1843, she changed her name to Sojourner Truth ("Sojourner" meaning traveling preacher). She joined a group supporting women's rights, pacifism, and abolitionism. Though unable to write, Sojourner dictated her life story, and 1850 saw the publication of her memoirs—*The Narrative of Sojourner Truth: A Northern Slave*. She began touring and speaking about her experience as an escaped slave and on women's rights. The speech she has become most famous for, known as the "Ain't I a Woman?" speech, was improvised and delivered in 1851 at the Ohio Women's Rights Convention declaring rights for all women and all African-Americans.

Her views were ahead of their time, outlining political equality for all, regardless of race or gender. This was a pretty radical view at the time, even among fellow abolitionists. She feared that women (both black and white) would be left without rights after the fight for the rights of black men were won. Sadly, she was right, as votes for women would not come until decades and much struggle later.

NEVER GIVE UP

During the U.S. Civil War, Sojourner was asked to contribute her views, and as part of this she met President Abraham Lincoln. In 1863, Lincoln delivered the Emancipation Proclamation, an order freeing slaves in the U.S. South. Sojourner welcomed the move, but she did not feel it went far enough, so she continued her own activism around transportation, property, and freedom. Sojourner lived to the age of 86, continuing her public speaking until the very end. Her views never weakened, and she continued to engage in subjects as diverse as voting rights for all, prison reform, capital punishment, and women's rights.

Sojourner Truth was an incredible woman who achieved a great deal in her long life. She is renowned as one of the leading pioneers of the anti-slavery movement and an early women's rights activist. According to Smithsonian magazine in 2014, Sojourner is one of the "100 most significant Americans of all time." In April 2016, the U.S. Treasury announced that Sojourner Truth would appear on the new $10 bill to honor her contributions to the United States.

NATIONAL AMERICAN WOMAN SUFFRAGE ASSOCIATION
FOUNDED IN 1869
SUPPORTS
MONDELL RESOLUTION
B. ANTHONY, 1874
D ALWAYS
1914

ELIZABETH CADY STANTON
WOMEN'S RIGHTS ACTIVIST AND LEADER OF THE SUFFRAGISTS

FULL NAME: Elizabeth Cady Stanton
BORN: NOVEMBER 12, 1815, JOHNSTOWN, NEW YORK, U.S.A.
DIED: OCTOBER 26, 1902, NEW YORK CITY, NEW YORK, U.S.A.
NATIONALITY: AMERICAN

Elizabeth Cady Stanton, in an 1890 portrait

A POLITICAL PIONEER

Elizabeth Cady Stanton was an early pioneer of the women's rights movement and a leader of the struggle for women's right to vote (suffrage). Elizabeth lived a very long life, which she dedicated to social activism in many forms: abolitionism (abolishing slavery), feminism, and women's rights.

Elizabeth was one of 11 children born to a family of lawyers. From a young age, Elizabeth revelled in reading and debating legal issues. This early learning led to her realization that women were second to men in matters of property, employment, and income. When Elizabeth married Henry Stanton in 1840, she left out the word "obey" from the marriage oath (over 170 years later, it is often still included in traditional Christian vows).

In 1848, Elizabeth was part of the landmark Seneca Falls Convention. There, she and others wrote up the "Declaration of Sentiments" and embarked on their campaign for women's voting rights. The declaration is credited with starting the first organized women's rights movement. During the U.S. Civil War of the 1860s, Elizabeth fought to abolish slavery. When the war ended, she turned her focus to women's rights again, campaigning on everything from voting to riding bicycles, divorce to property rights. She cofounded the National Woman Suffrage Association in 1869 with Susan B. Anthony (*see pages 120–121*) and remained its president until 1890. With her strong intellect and legal education, Elizabeth was an incredible asset to the women's rights movement in the U.S.A.

LUCY STONE
LEADING WOMEN'S RIGHTS ACTIVIST

FULL NAME: Lucy Stone
BORN: AUGUST 13, 1818, WEST BROOKFIELD, MASSACHUSETTS, U.S.A.
DIED: OCTOBER 18, 1893, BOSTON, MASSACHUSETTS, U.S.A.
NATIONALITY: AMERICAN

Lucy Stone was considered to be the heart and soul of the women's rights movement.

MY NAME AND MY IDENTITY MUST NOT BE LOST

Nicknamed the "heart and soul of the women's rights movement," Lucy Stone was hugely active in bringing about social change. Together, Lucy Stone, Elizabeth Cady Stanton (*see page* 118), and Susan B. Anthony (*see pages* 120–121) are known as the 19th-century "triumvirate" (trio) of women's voting rights and feminism. But while Lucy fought tirelessly for social change, her name is less recognizable than her counterparts.

Lucy was an activist through and through, and she wore her politics on her sleeve. When she married abolitionist Henry Blackwell in 1855, she stated: "A wife should no more take her husband's name than he hers. My name and my identity must not be lost."

SUPERB SPEAKER

Lucy was an excellent public speaker (even making it a paid career), and she used this skill as she lectured all over North America in favor of women's rights (and voting rights in particular) and against slavery. She helped establish the Woman's National Loyal League and helped pass the 13th Amendment abolishing slavery. She helped start the National Women's Rights Convention and the American Equal Rights Association. After the U.S. Civil War, the "triumvirate" parted ways, over Lucy's backing of the 15th Amendment. The amendment guaranteed all black men the right to vote. Lucy thought the law would be a step toward gaining the same rights for women, but the other two disagreed. Although they were in favor of these rights being given to African-American men, they didn't think this should happen while all women (black and white) still lacked these rights. All three continued to fight for women's right to vote, but sadly not one of them lived to see that vote made a reality. Lucy Stone died in 1893, almost 30 years before women were granted the vote.

SUSAN B. ANTHONY
LEADER OF THE SUFFRAGIST (WOMEN'S VOTE) MOVEMENT

FULL NAME: Susan Brownell Anthony
BORN: FEBRUARY 15, 1820, ADAMS, MASSACHUSETTS, U.S.A.
DIED: MARCH 13, 1906, ROCHESTER, NEW YORK, U.S.A.
NATIONALITY: AMERICAN

A U.S. 1979 silver dollar, featuring the suffragist leader

> " There will never be complete equality until women themselves help to make laws and elect lawmakers. "
>
> *Susan B. Anthony*

SUFFRAGETTE VS. SUFFRAGIST

You may have spotted a confusing mix of words in this chapter and thought it was simply a mistake. In fact, while both groups led the struggle for women's right to vote, "suffragettes" is the name given to the British group of (often more militant) activists, and "suffragists" for the American group. "Suffrage" is the term given to the right to vote.

Susan B. Anthony, in an 1860 portrait

A LONG LIFE FOUGHT FOR OTHERS

Susan B. Anthony remains one of the most recognizable figures of the American women's suffrage movement. Alongside Elizabeth Cady Stanton and Lucretia Mott, Susan fought tirelessly for women's rights. Photographs of Susan depict her as a conservative-looking older woman; however, she was anything but.

Susan was born into a politically active Quaker family. The family advocated against slavery (making them "abolitionists") and against the sale of alcohol (a movement called the "temperance" movement). While campaigning for temperance, Susan was denied a chance to speak publicly because she was a woman. This made her realize the importance of women's right to vote in their being taken seriously. She joined the women's rights movement officially in 1852 and decided to devote the rest of her long life to women's suffrage.

THE SUSAN B. ANTHONY AMENDMENT

In 1869, Susan and Elizabeth Cady Stanton cofounded the National Woman Suffrage Association, of which Susan became president in 1892. With Susan and Elizabeth at the helm, the group campaigned hard for women's voting rights, speaking and touring all over the country. In 1872, Susan even voted illegally in the U.S. presidential election. She was arrested and fined, but never paid the fee. She also continued to lecture against slavery and in favor of racial equality, as well as for the rights of women to own their own property, keep their own money, and be admitted to college. As far back as 1868, Susan was campaigning for equal pay for equal work—an issue still being fought today. Susan appeared before every session of Congress from 1869 to 1906, campaigning for the women's vote.

In 1920—14 years after Susan's death—all adult women in the U.S.A. were finally granted the right to vote, when the 19th Amendment was added to the U.S. Constitution. The amendment is also known as the "Susan B. Anthony Amendment."

Susan B. Anthony became the first woman to be honored on a U.S. coin, when in 1979 her portrait was added to one-dollar coins to recognize her contributions to civil rights. In April 2016, the U.S. Treasury announced an important revision to the new $10 bill, effective from 2020. The currency will now feature the 1913 march in support of women's rights, with portraits of five suffrage leaders: Susan B. Anthony, Sojourner Truth, Elizabeth Cady Stanton, Lucretia Mott, and Alice Paul.

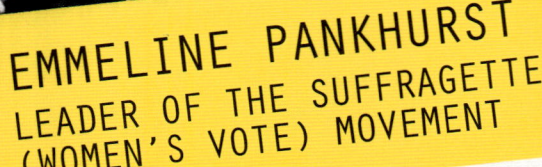

EMMELINE PANKHURST
LEADER OF THE SUFFRAGETTE (WOMEN'S VOTE) MOVEMENT

FULL NAME: Emmeline Goulden Pankhurst
BORN: JULY 15, 1858, MANCHESTER, U.K.
DIED: JUNE 14, 1928, LONDON, U.K..
NATIONALITY: BRITISH

> 66 *We shall fight against the condition of affairs so long as life is in us.* 99
> EMMELINE PANKHURST

YOUNG RADICAL

Emmeline Goulden was one of ten children born into a politically active family. Revolutionary for the mid-19th century, her parents supported an end to slavery and voting equality for women. Emmeline's early experience taught her the radical view that girls should have the same education as boys. By the time Emmeline left school, she was educated in everything from chemistry to bookkeeping. Emmeline married Dr. Richard Pankhurst, a radical liberal lawyer who also fought for women's right to vote. Sadly Richard passed away in 1898, leaving Emmeline a single parent to four children. Emmeline still found plenty of time for her activism, and their children, Sylvia, Christabel, Adela, and Harry, were also very involved in the movement.

DEEDS NOT WORDS

Emmeline Pankhurst quickly rose to become the leader of the British suffragette movement. In 1903, she founded the Women's Social and Political Union (WSPU), dedicated to practical activism to fight for equal voting. The WSPU's slogan was "Deeds Not Words." Emmeline was a controversial figure in British politics and was imprisoned many times for her tactics, which were sometimes violent. The activism she encouraged among her supporters was described as militant and included smashing windows, cutting telephone lines, and chaining themselves to railings in protest.

A statue of Emmeline stands in Victoria Tower Gardens, in London, England.

The protesters suffered extreme brutality at the hands of the police, and the WSPU offices were repeatedly raided and activists imprisoned. Some of the jailed women went on hunger strike to bring public attention to the cause, and while on hunger strike they were painfully force-fed. One member of the WSPU, Emily Wilding Davison, strongly supported Emmeline's controversial tactics. In 1913, she led a protest at the Epsom Derby, where she was fatally injured by stepping in front of King George V's horse. Tens of thousands of people attended her funeral service. While it was a tragic event, it garnered huge press and support for the suffragette movement.

When World War I broke out in August of 1914, Emmeline ordered that the suffragettes call a break from their protests, in order to focus energy on the war effort. In response, the government released suffragettes from prison and the media ran positive headlines.

SUFFRAGE AT LAST

After the war ended, the "Representation of People Act 1918" was issued: all men over 21 were granted the right to vote, as well as all women over 30 who were property owners or graduates. The law didn't yet apply to all women, but it was a start. Emmeline Pankhurst died on 14 June, 1928. Eighteen days later, Parliament issued the "Representation of People (equal franchise) Act 1928." After many years and a huge amount of struggle, British women were finally given equal voting rights to men.

Alongside Susan B. Anthony and Elizabeth Cady Stanton, Emmeline Pankhurst remains one of the most famous leaders in the global struggle for women's right to vote. In 1999, she was named by *Time* magazine as one of the "100 most important people of the 20th century." In 2016, the movie *Suffragette* was released, starring Meryl Streep (*see pages 76–77*) as Emmeline, and documenting the lives and struggles of women's fight for equality.

NELLIE BLY
GROUND-BREAKING INVESTIGATIVE JOURNALIST

FULL NAME: Elizabeth Cochrane
BORN: MAY 5, 1864, COCHRAN'S MILLS, PENNSYLVANIA, U.S.A.
DIED: JANUARY 27, 1922, NEW YORK CITY, NEW YORK, U.S.A.
NATIONALITY: AMERICAN

SPURRED INTO ACTION BY A NEWSPAPER COLUMN

The youngest of either 13 or 15 children (reports vary), Elizabeth Cochrane, or Nellie Bly as she became known, was determined and adventurous from the start. She became a famous American journalist who pioneered investigative and undercover reporting. This type of journalism was still cutting-edge for anyone, and Nellie became the master of her craft in an almost exclusively male world.

The story goes that Nellie's writing career began when she read an article in the *Pittsburgh Dispatch* called "What Girls Are Good For." The article put down working women, and it infuriated Nellie enough to write an angry letter to the editor. That letter led to an invitation to write for the paper! Beginning her journalism career at the small *Pittsburgh Dispatch*, Nellie wrote about stories that interested her: working women, poverty, and discrimination. Her editor tried to make Nellie write "women's interest" stories as well, but articles about fashion and society did not interest her.

UNDERCOVER REPORTING

Nellie moved to New York City, but she found it difficult to find work as a woman. Two years later, Nellie was in New York City writing for the big-time New York World. One of her first stories for the paper turned out to be a huge career boost for the 23-year-old reporter. Her assignment was to investigate "Blackwell's Island Madhouse," an infamous institution for patients with mental health troubles. Nellie believed that she could report most accurately if she went undercover and posed as a patient for ten days. She lived through the same horrors as the "real" patients and wrote down all of her experiences. The story was a huge success, exposing terrible conditions and bad patient care. As a result, the facility was investigated and healthcare and safety were improved. Nellie used this same method when she reported on inadequate jails and factories.

Nellie Bly, seen here in an 1890 portrait, was described as the best reporter in America by her contemporaries.

AROUND THE WORLD IN 72 DAYS

In 1889, Nellie undertook a massive adventure: traveling around the world and reporting on it for New York World. Her goal was to break the fictional record of Phileas Fogg, the character in Jules Verne's 1873 novel, *Around the World in Eighty Days*. She broke this record—as well as any real-life records—at only 72 days, 6 hours, 11 minutes, and 14 seconds. During the journey, Nellie traveled by ship, wooden boat, train, horse, donkey, rickshaw, and more. Readers loved the story, and Nellie was a big success. Both her exposé of Blackwell's Island and her travel adventure were turned into popular books. Nellie became the most famous female reporter of her era.

After her mega success and marriage, Nellie took a break from journalism between her early 30s and 50s and moved into business. She came back to journalism at the age of 55 and continued to write until her death two years later. In her obituary, fellow reporters called her the "best reporter in America." Nellie was a fearless and ground-breaking reporter, who never shied away from uncovering the truth. With her adventurous spirit and dedication to writing, she will be remembered as a legendary pioneer of investigative journalism.

HELEN KELLER
LEADING ACTIVIST FOR DISABILITIES AND SOCIAL CHANGE

FULL NAME: Helen Adams Keller
BORN: JUNE 27, 1880, TUSCUMBIA, ALABAMA, U.S.A.
DIED: JUNE 1, 1968, EASTON, CONNECTICUT, U.S.A.
NATIONALITY: AMERICAN

The first word that Helen learned was "water."

FRUSTRATED POTENTIAL

Many people know of Helen Keller as the woman born deaf and blind who overcame those obstacles to become a renowned activist for people with disabilities. But most aren't aware of her other outstanding roles, as an educator, journalist, humanitarian, and co-founder of the American Civil Liberties Union (ACLU). By any account, Helen Keller was a phenomenal individual.

As a baby, Helen was developmentally advanced. At just six months, she had started talking—and by the age of one, she was walking. But then, aged only 19 months, Helen was struck with an illness—called "brain fever" at the time, but likely to have been scarlet fever—that left her blind, deaf, and unable to speak. As Helen grew into a young child, her inability to communicate left her frustrated. She often became angry and violent. Her family didn't know what to do, and gaining support for such a serious condition was very difficult at the time. After examining Helen, a doctor recommended a visit to Alexander Graham Bell (the inventor of the telephone). He was conducting work with deaf children and directed the Kellers to the Perkins Institute, from which Anne Sullivan had just graduated. That recommendation was instrumental in bringing Helen out of her shell and allowing the world to benefit from her massive potential. Helen and Anne went on to have one of the most notorious and productive working relationships in history, lasting for almost 50 years. The award-winning play and movie, *The Miracle Worker*, tells the story of their relationship.

AN INCREDIBLE PARTNERSHIP

Anne taught the six-year-old Helen how to "finger spell" (a form of sign language in which each individual letter of a word is spelled out). Both Helen and Anne found it difficult, and Helen's tantrums grew worse, but Anne persevered. The first word that Helen mastered was "water," with Anne spelling out each letter then holding Helen's hand under running water. Following this realization that she could truly understand, Helen immediately dragged Anne around the family home and learned 30 new words in a single day.

Helen went to school, where she learned to speak and communicate, before going on to college. Anne sat right by Helen's side at Radcliffe College, interpreting the lectures for her. Helen became the first deaf-blind person to earn a Bachelor of Arts degree. Her communication skills improved. In addition to her knowledge of finger spelling and speaking, she learned Braille, typing, and touch-lip reading. Helen's story became known, and she met a number of famous people, such as Mark Twain—who became a good friend. Helen became a celebrity and began using her fame to campaign on behalf of people with disabilities. She was even asked to speak in front of Congress. From there, her activism broadened to include women's suffrage and peace, but she also continued to fight for the rights and welfare of blind people. In 1920, Helen co-founded the ACLU—a non-profit organization that defends the rights and liberties of every American. Because of her warm and engaging personality, she also became an excellent fundraiser. In her 60s, Helen had a prominent role within the American Foundation of Overseas Blind. On their behalf, she traveled to 35 countries—across five continents—between 1946 and 1957, giving talks and inspiring millions.

AN INSPIRATION TO THE WORLD

Helen continued her pursuit of a better world throughout her lifetime. In 1936, she was awarded the Theodore Roosevelt Distinguished Service Medal, and in 1964 the Presidential Medal of Freedom, for her incredible contributions. Helen was famously invited to the White House by every U.S. president from Grover Cleveland to Lyndon B. Johnson. Helen's autobiography, *The Story of My Life*, is still in print in more than 50 languages.

Helen's work was celebrated around the globe. Seen here is a Spanish stamp of the activist, circa 1980.

MOTHER TERESA
ONE OF THE WORLD'S GREATEST HUMANITARIANS

FULL NAME: Gonxha Agnes Bojaxhiu, Blessed Teresa of Calcutta
BORN: AUGUST 26, 1910, SKOPJE, MACEDONIA (OTTOMAN EMPIRE)
DIED: SEPTEMBER 5, 1997, CALCUTTA, INDIA
NATIONALITY: OTTOMAN-ALBANIAN/INDIAN

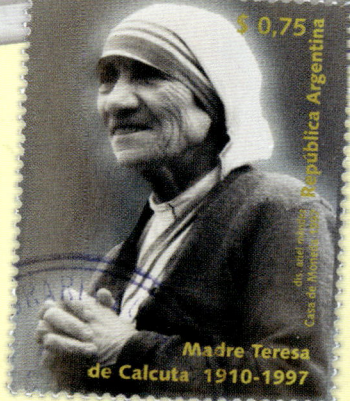

An Argentine postage stamp, circa 1997, honoring Mother Teresa

CHARITY BEGINS AT HOME

Gonxha Agnes Bojaxhiu was born into a devoutly Catholic, Albanian family. When she was just eight years old, her father died—very suddenly—amid the rumor that he was poisoned for his political beliefs. Young Agnes became very close to her mother, a caring and charitable woman, and this helped mold her into the woman she would become. With the strong belief that anything you have should always be shared, the family regularly distributed what little they owned among local people who were in need.

At the age of 12, while on a pilgrimage with her religious school, Agnes experienced her first calling to pursue a life of faith. Six years later, she decided to become a nun, moving to Ireland to join the Loreto convent in Dublin. It was at this time that she chose the name Sister Mary Teresa, after Saint Thérèse of Lisieux, France. Saint Thérèse, also known as the "Little Flower," is the patron saint of missions.

In 1931, at the age of 21, Sister Mary Teresa was sent to a Catholic school in Calcutta, India, to teach geography and history to Bengali girls from poor backgrounds. For this, she learned to speak both the Bengali and Hindi languages fluently. After taking her final vows, she officially became Mother Teresa. Between 1931 and 1946, Mother Teresa served as a teacher and then as a school principal. She dedicated herself to sharing her faith and using education as a means of helping others out of poverty.

Mother Teresa lived the simple life of a nun. This image shows her room at the Missionaries of Charity, in Calcutta, India.

A VOICE ON A TRAIN

While riding on a train through India on September 10, 1946, Mother Teresa experienced what she referred to as a "call within a call." At this time, she heard Jesus' voice telling her to focus her attention on the slums of Calcutta, to work with the city's sick and poor. In August of 1948, Mother Teresa put on the blue-and-white robes she would wear for the rest of her life and left for the city. Her goal was simple but broad—to aid the unwanted and unloved. She quickly set up a school and a hospital in Calcutta, creating a new congregation called the Missionaries of Charity. During the 1950s and 1960s, recognition for her work—as well as much-needed donations—poured in, and she was soon able to set up an orphanage, health clinics, and a nursing home. From there, her work would take her to New York City and Beirut to extend her support and charity. By the time of her death, in 1997, the Missionaries of Charity had 610 foundations in 123 countries around the globe.

"I BELONG TO THE WORLD"

Mother Teresa won several awards and honors for her life-long commitment to charity. She remained humble throughout, stating simply, "I belong to the world." In 1979, she won the Nobel Peace Prize in honor of her dedication to improving the suffering of so many. Six years after her death, she was beatified by the Catholic Church, meaning she was honored with the title of "Blessed." At the end of 2015, Pope Francis declared that Mother Teresa would be canonized—officially declared to be a saint—on September 4, 2016, in Rome, Italy. For the sheer number of lives she was able to touch, and for her undying commitment to the people most in need, she is considered to be one of the greatest humanitarians of the 20th century.

When Mother Teresa was beatified by Pope John Paul II on October 19, 2003 in St. Peter's Square in the Vatican, thousands of worshippers paid their respects.

THE GIRL SCOUTS AND GIRL GUIDES
THE LARGEST GLOBAL LEADERSHIP ORGANIZATION FOR GIRLS

FULL NAME: The Girl Scouts of America

WORLDWIDE ORGANIZATION: WORLD ASSOCIATION OF GIRL GUIDES AND GIRL SCOUTS

FOUNDED: MARCH 12, 1912 (FIRST OFFICIAL MEETING)

For everything from first aid skills to woodworking, business skills to cooperation, Girl Scouts can earn badges and pins.

100 YEARS OF CHANGING THE WORLD

Millions of Girl Scouts across the globe are united in the belief that girls can truly change the world. It is the largest leadership organization for girls on the planet, with a clear mission: "to build girls of courage, confidence, and character, who make the world a better place." This goal extends to every girl, regardless of where she's from, what she looks like, or how her body is built.

Juliette "Daisy" Gordon Low founded the Girl Scouts of the U.S.A. in 1912, after a meeting with the founder of the Boy Scouts movement, Robert Baden-Powell. The first Girl Scout meeting—held in Savannah, Georgia, on March 12, 1912—was unconventional for the time, made up of a group of girls of varied ethnicities, backgrounds, abilities, and disabilities. Daisy believed in the potential of all girls: the organization she set up, more than 100 years ago, now exists as a place for girls to grow and thrive all over the world. In 2012, this forward-thinking woman was honored with a Presidential Medal of Freedom, by President Barack Obama, for her "remarkable vision."

UNDERCOVER REPORTING

Since the organization began, more than 59 million American women and girls have belonged to the Girl Scouts. Famous members include Taylor Swift, Venus and Serena Williams, Carrie Fisher, Hillary Clinton—and nearly every female U.S. astronaut to have flown in space. Girl Scouts groups meet regularly to encourage friendship, leadership, and cooperation. This includes outdoor activities, cultural exchanges, and community service projects. For any number of activities and skills, girls can earn badges to celebrate their successes.

While they are famous for the tastiness of the cookies they sell, there's much more to the activity than that. The Cookie Program is the largest girl-led business in the world, selling around 200 million boxes of cookies ($800 million worth) each year. The program teaches girls confidence, people skills, and business sense. But just so you know—the Thin Mints are the most popular variety of cookie.

The group is actively involved in protecting the environment and in making the world a better place. Members attend camps and outdoor activities, promoting respect for the planet and for each other. Every year, more than 100 Girl Scout councils meet to discuss public policy and leadership opportunities. This includes everything from increasing girls' involvement in the STEM subjects (science, technology, engineering, and math) to reducing bullying. The agendas set out in these meetings are then shared with policy makers in Congress to ensure a better place for girls in our world.

A GLOBAL MOVEMENT OF LOVE AND COOPERATION

Highlighting its mission to include all girls, the Girl Scouts of Western Washington made headlines, in July of 2015, when they returned a donation of $100,000. A single benefactor gave money to the organization to support its summer camp. However, the donation came with a very specific piece of fine print: the money could not be used to support transgender girls—those born as "biologically" male, but who identify as being female. The rejection of the offer prevented 200 girls from going to camp, but the organization felt it was against the values of the group to accept the money. They started the "Girl Scouts is #ForEVERYGirl" campaign. Within 24 hours, they raised $100,000—and they eventually tripled that amount. The Girl Scouts received positive support and publicity for their bold message of inclusion.

Depending on where you live, you may have heard of this group by any number of names, such as the "Girl Scouts" and the "Girl Guides." The Girl Scouts is a member of the global association known as the World Association of Girl Guides and Girl Scouts (WAGGGS). The WAGGGS' family is made up of around ten million girls and adults, across 146 countries around the world, all centered on the same ideal—that of realizing the potential of all girls as responsible citizens of the world.

ROSA PARKS
CIVIL RIGHTS ACTIVIST

FULL NAME: Rosa Louise McCauley Parks
BORN: FEBRUARY 4, 1913, TUSKEGEE, ALABAMA, U.S.A.
DIED: OCTOBER 24, 2005, DETROIT, MICHIGAN, U.S.A.
NATIONALITY: AMERICAN

BORN INTO SEGREGATION

Rosa Parks was born in 1913 in Alabama, of mixed ancestry. Mostly of black African descent, Rosa's ancestors were also part Scottish-Irish and part Native American. However, because of the era in which Rosa was born, it was her black heritage that would define her day-to-day life.

Rosa with Martin Luther King Jr., in 1955

RESTRICTIONS REPLACED SLAVERY

The most major outcome of the U.S. Civil War was the end of slavery. This was a good thing for all Americans, but the resulting laws did little to create the level playing field hoped for by the more progressive abolitionists. In the U.S. South, a series of "Jim Crow Laws" restricted black citizens from using their new-found vote and segregated blacks and whites in public spaces.

HARD-WORKING ACTIVIST

The young Rosa worked hard to finish high school and got involved in both civil rights and voter activism at the same time as working many jobs. For a time, she was the secretary of the Montgomery, Alabama National Association for the Advancement of Colored People (NAACP).

ROSA'S REFUSAL

From 1900, the Montgomery buses permitted black commuters, but the seating was segregated and rules were set by the driver. White commuters almost always got seating priority. On December 1, 1955, after working a long day, Rosa paid her fare, boarded the bus, and sat in the "Colored" section. Shortly after, the bus began to fill up. A handful of white passengers stood in the aisle. The driver ordered Rosa and three other passengers to give up their seats for the white passengers. Rosa refused. The driver called the police. Rosa was arrested and charged with disorderly conduct. That little gesture by one individual spurred a 381-day boycott of the city's public buses, creating one of the largest and most successful movements ever against racial segregation.

A U.S. postage stamp, circa 2013, honoring the civil rights activist

The infamous Montgomery bus

CONSTITUTIONAL CHANGE

In June of 1956, segregation laws were declared unconstitutional. Rosa's action and refusal to stand down were a significant trigger in the end of U.S. segregation. She became known as the "first lady of civil rights" and the "mother of freedom." She continued to fight for civil rights throughout her life. She received many awards, including the Martin Luther King, Jr. Award and the Presidential Medal of Freedom.

EVA PERÓN (EVITA)
LABOR ACTIVIST AND "SPIRITUAL LEADER OF THE NATION"

FULL NAME: Maria Eva "Evita" Duarte de Perón
BORN: MAY 7, 1919, LOS TOLDOS, ARGENTINA
DIED: JULY 26, 1952, BUENOS AIRES, ARGENTINA
NATIONALITY: ARGENTINIAN

Casa Rosada (meaning "Pink House") is the Argentinian presidential residence. This balcony was made famous by Eva for her many speeches to the public.

FROM ACTRESS TO POLITICIAN

Commonly known as "Evita," Eva Perón's legacy lives on, more than 60 years after her death. Officially, Evita's role was always secondary to that of her husband and her political party. However, such was her determination and widespread popularity that she made a massive impact on Argentinian politics, despite a short life of only 32 years.

Evita was a youngster from a disadvantaged background, but she harbored dreams of becoming a star. As a teenager and young woman, she enjoyed moderate success as an actress and as a voice on the radio—and at the age of 20, she started her own radio production business. Then, in 1943, her life took a significant turn. Evita met the Argentine secretary of labor and social welfare, Juan Perón. With the support of the country's workers, Juan had a glittering dream of his own: to become the president of Argentina. The two were soon in a relationship, with Evita's charisma and beauty helping to increase Juan's popularity even further. The Argentine public loved her. Juan and Evita married in 1945, and Evita continued to campaign by her husband's side—an uncommon thing in South American politics at the time. Because of her own upbringing, Evita was able to appeal directly to disadvantaged groups and the working classes. The fact that people identified with her granted her a powerful political influence.

FIRST LADY OF ARGENTINA

When Juan ran for president, in 1946, he was elected. Evita continued her fight to improve the lives of the poor, championing wage and welfare reforms as well. Eva's public work spread further, including important work on health policy and disease prevention. She set up the Maria Eva Duarte de Perón Welfare Foundation to support those most in need. The foundation distributed food and medicines, making her very popular with Argentina's poorer classes. She was considered to be the unofficial secretary of labor and health for her work. But Evita's efforts didn't stop there. She maintained a very high public profile in her advocacy work, which also began to encompass women's suffrage (voting rights). She founded the Female Peronist Party, the first Argentine women's political party. Argentina eventually granted women the right to vote in 1947, thanks largely to Evita's campaigning.

"DON'T CRY FOR ME, ARGENTINA"

On the back of her tremendous, "unofficial" government work, Evita decided to stand for vice president in the 1951 election, as the running mate to her president husband. In the 1940s, it was simply astounding to see a woman on a presidential ticket—especially a South American woman who had not come from a background of wealth or status. Both the military and the elite classes opposed her nomination. That, paired with Evita's fast-declining health, caused her to step down from political life. The following year, Evita died of cancer at the tender age of 32. The public was devastated. In recognition of the people's grief, her grand funeral was of the type normally reserved for heads of state. The same year, the Argentinian Congress granted Evita the title of "Spiritual Leader of the Nation."

The exact nature of Evita's role in the politics of her country continues to be debated. However, her legacy remains a huge force in South America, and a fascination with the icon of Evita spans the globe. She was an actress, politician, feminist, labor activist, and so much more. Today, she can be remembered through Andrew Lloyd Webber's musical, *Evita*, which was later re-worked (in 1996) as a movie with Madonna (*see pages* 82–83) in the starring role. It is also very fitting that Evita's great-niece, Cristina Fernández de Kirchner, went on to become the first elected female president of Argentina, serving in office from 2007 to 2015.

MARGARET THATCHER
LFIRST WOMAN TO LEAD A MAJOR WESTERN DEMOCRACY

FULL NAME: Margaret Hilda Roberts Thatcher, Baroness Thatcher

BORN: OCTOBER 13, 1925, GRANTHAM, LINCOLNSHIRE, U.K.

DIED: APRIL 8, 2013, LONDON, U.K.

NATIONALITY: BRITISH

The Iron Lady is commemorated on a British stamp, circa 2014.

THE IRON LADY

Margaret Thatcher was the first woman to lead a major Western democracy, as well as the longest-serving British Prime Minister of the 20th century—and the only woman, to date, to have held that office. Nicknamed the "Iron Lady," she was known as one of the toughest and most divisive British politicians in history. Her time in office was one of great change, as well as major controversy.

Margaret, famously the daughter of grocers, was educated in a state (public) school, before going on to study chemistry at Oxford under Nobel-Prize-winning chemist Dorothy Hodgkin (*see page* 186). During this time, she became president of the student Conservative Party. Margaret trained as a lawyer, with a focus on taxes. In 1959, she was elected to Parliament—a post she would hold until 1992. She quickly rose through the ranks and, by 1970, Margaret was education secretary under Prime Minister Edward Heath. In 1974, Heath called a general election—and unexpectedly lost it. The Conservative Party needed a change of direction. In February of 1975, Thatcher won the party's leadership contest (surprising both herself and many other Conservatives). This made her the first woman ever to lead a Western political party. In May of 1979, the Conservative Party won the general election, got back into power, and Thatcher became Prime Minister of the United Kingdom—a post she would hold until 1990. She became the most senior elected woman of any Western country in history, and one of the most powerful women in the world.

Margaret made tough decisions that were not always popular, including sending troops to the Falkland Islands (flag seen here).

A DETERMINED LEADER

The late 1970s and early 1980s were a difficult time in Britain. Unemployment was up, the economy was down, and the manufacturing industries (such as coal mining and car manufacturing) were struggling. Margaret decided that harsh steps were necessary: she raised taxes, fought against the trade unions, privatized industries, and reduced welfare payments. When the Argentine government invaded the Falkland Islands (a British overseas territory close to Argentina), Margaret was militarily tough, too, sending in troops and winning back British control. On matters of foreign policy, Thatcher worked closely with her U.S. ally, Republican President Ronald Reagan. This included their negotiations to decrease hostilities during the Cold War, a time of raised tensions between Soviet countries and the West.

Margaret lost her position as Prime Minister in 1990, but she remained in Parliament until 1992. At that time, she was asked to join the House of Lords (becoming "Baroness Thatcher"). As her health declined, she appeared less and less in public and in politics. She died on April 8, 2013. She is not remembered fondly by all for her actions, but her tough stance, strong beliefs, and long role in power have ensured that she has a strong legacy in British politics. In 2011, a film of her life was released, titled *The Iron Lady* and starring Meryl Streep (*see pages 76–77*). Her influence on the politics of Britain and Europe continue and can be seen and heard today.

When Margaret died in 2013, her many supporters laid tributes in her honor.

ANNE FRANK
THE GIRL WHO GAVE US HER ACCOUNT OF THE HOLOCAUST

FULL NAME: Annelies Marie Frank
BORN: JUNE 12, 1929, FRANKFURT, WEIMAR REPUBLIC (MODERN-DAY GERMANY)
DIED: MARCH (EXACT DATE UNKNOWN), 1945, BERGEN-BELSEN CONCENTRATION CAMP, GERMANY
NATIONALITY: GERMAN

> *When I write, I shake off all my cares.*
>
> ANNE FRANK

The Nazis forced Jewish people to wear a yellow Star of David at all times.

HOLOCAUST NARRATIVE

The Diary of Anne Frank has become the most popular diary in the world, as well as one of the most read accounts of World War II's Holocaust. Anne's legacy, and her remarkable gift as a writer and storyteller, lives on as a testament to the horrors of war and the sheer determination of the human spirit.

HAPPY CHILDHOOD

Anne was born in Germany to parents named Otto and Edith. She had a sister three years older named Margot. The Franks were a typical, middle-class family who lived happily in Germany, until the rise to power of the National Socialist (or Nazi) Party. Anne and her relatives were of German–Jewish descent, and so—due to the increasing persecution of Jews and other minority groups by the Nazis—the family chose to relocate to the safety of Amsterdam, Holland, in 1933. At school, Anne loved to read and write and often played the class clown.

However, by 1940, the Nazis had invaded Holland. The Holocaust, a period of discrimination, persecution, and violence, was sweeping across Europe. Jewish people were subjected to strict rules. They could not own their own businesses or attend non-Jewish schools and were forced to wear a yellow star to mark them out as different. Despite these hardships, the Franks tried to lead normal lives. For her 13th birthday, Otto gave his daughter a red-checkered autograph book. This would become her diary, and she composed each entry as if she were writing to a special friend: "Dear Kitty." Sadly, in spite of it being a much-loved gift, even the earliest entries describe the discrimination that the Franks and fellow Jews suffered. In July of 1942, Margot got a letter ordering her to report to a Nazi work camp in Germany—a forced labor camp where the inhabitants often died as a result of their grueling manual tasks. The Franks had begun to discuss the possibility of escaping or hiding; that dreaded letter forced them to act even more quickly than planned.

A SECRET HIDING PLACE

On 6 July, 1942, the Franks moved into a hidden space above Otto's business, alongside four other families. The space would come to be known, throughout history, as the "Secret Annex." A handful of friends, including a woman named Miep Gies, knew their secret and brought them food and news from the outside world. Anne and her family would continue to live in this cramped hiding place for the next two years, which required long stints of silence and stillness to avoid discovery and capture. Anne went into hiding at the age of 13; her sister was 16. All the while, Anne kept her diary, honestly recording her life in the annex, with all its fear, boredom, anger, as well as the everyday teenage concerns about love and life. Anne often expressed an interest in becoming a writer when she grew up, and she hoped that her diary would be published.

Anne's diary entries end, abruptly, in 1944, when the annex was raided by the Nazis. The families had been discovered due to an anonymous tip-off. The Franks were sent to Auschwitz, the infamous concentration camp in Poland, before being moved on to Bergen-Belsen in Germany. Both girls died of typhoid, in 1945, when Anne was just 15. She and her sister were among the six million Jews who died during the Holocaust. One-and-a-half million of those were children. Remarkably, her diary survived. Miep Gies had kept it safe after the family's capture. Otto was the only member of the Frank family to survive the war. When he returned to Amsterdam, Miep returned the diary and, in 1947, Otto had it published.

PEACE WILL RETURN

Now 70 years old, Anne's diary has been read by millions and translated into 67 languages worldwide. In spite of the horrors Anne encountered, her diary remains a story of hope and courage. On July 15, 1944, not long before her capture, Anne wrote: "I see the world slowly being transformed into a wilderness . . . I feel the suffering of millions. And yet, when I look up at the sky, I somehow feel that everything will change for the better, that this cruelty too shall end, that peace and tranquillity will return once more."

SANDRA DAY O'CONNOR
FIRST FEMALE SUPREME COURT JUDGE

FULL NAME: Justice Sandra Day O'Connor
BORN: MARCH 26, 1930, EL PASO, TEXAS, U.S.A.
NATIONALITY: AMERICAN

Sandra is known as a moderate Republican, and her strong sense of justice has earned her a fearsome reputation.

While these next two women may sit on opposite sides of the political aisle in Washington, D.C., they both hold an important place in history for their role in guiding the course of American justice.

A HARD-FOUGHT PATH TO THE SUPREME COURT BENCH

Sandra Day O'Connor grew up on a ranch in Texas—a world away from the politics of Washington, D.C. After graduating with a degree in economics, she attended law school, coming third in her class. In spite of her high grades, there were very few law jobs available for women in 1952. Sandra had to work unpaid for a time, before finally getting a job as a deputy county attorney.

From 1952 to 1969, Sandra worked as a lawyer and as Arizona's Assistant Attorney General. In 1969, she became a Republican senator for Arizona. She served in that role for five years, before stepping up to be a Superior Court Judge. Sandra earned a reputation for being fair but firm. U.S. Republican President Ronald Reagan nominated her for the position of Associate Justice on the U.S. Supreme Court. With such a strong reputation, Sandra was unanimously approved by the U.S. Senate in a vote of 99 to 0. She went on to become the first female Supreme Court Justice in 1981. (Anyone following U.S. current affairs in 2016 will understand the significance of unanimous approval for such a role!)

A WELL-RESPECTED VOICE

Sandra believed strongly in the words of the U.S. Constitution, and she was trusted for her attention to detail and strong sense of justice. As a conservative Republican, Sandra usually voted in line with her party—but she thought deeply in all of her decisions and would occasionally go her own way. As a moderate, she became an important "swing vote" (final decision-maker) in many important cases, such as those concerning women's health, election policy, and healthcare. Sandra retired in 2006, after serving on the Supreme Court bench for 24 years. In 2009, U.S. President Barack Obama awarded her a Presidential Medal of Freedom. Since her retirement, she has taken on several new and challenging pursuits: she has worked on an online education program aimed at teaching people of all ages about politics, has authored several books, and continues to be a respected voice in American politics—among both Republicans and Democrats alike.

Retirement hasn't stopped Sandra from continuing to educate people about American justice. She is seen here presenting a civics curriculum, in Monterey, California, in 2013.

RUTH BADER GINSBURG
PIONEERING SUPREME COURT JUDGE

FULL NAME: Justice Ruth Joan Bader Ginsburg
BORN: MARCH 15, 1933, BROOKLYN, NEW YORK, U.S.A.
NATIONALITY: AMERICAN

Ruth, seen here in 1993, has been called an icon and one of the "100 Most Powerful Women" in the U.S.A.

THE NOTORIOUS R.B.G.

So beloved is the Democratic Supreme Court Justice Ruth Bader Ginsburg that she has become something of a pop culture icon. Often, she is simply known as "R.B.G." Bobblehead dolls exist in her likeness, and a Twitter feed called Notorious R.B.G. has been created in her honor, featuring T-shirts, mugs, and tote bags. There is even a coloring book dedicated to her!

Ruth was born and raised in a working-class neighborhood of Brooklyn, New York City—a far cry from Sandra Day O'Connor's Texas ranch childhood. However, she was also at the top of her school, finishing first in her class for her degree in government. Not long after, Ruth had a baby and balanced her role as a mother with enrolling at law school. She was reportedly one of only nine women in a class of 500. She did very well, and also became the first female member of the Harvard Law Review journal, before moving to Columbia. Once again, Ruth graduated at the top of her class—this time from Columbia Law School. In spite of her tremendous academic record, she could not find a job in law. But law's initial loss was academia's gain, as she worked as a professor and director of the American Civil Liberties Union's Women's Rights Project (*see also Helen Keller, pages* 126-127). During this time, she argued six important gender equality cases in the Supreme Court, becoming well known for her meticulous legal mind and strong activism.

With such a stellar record under her belt, U.S. President Jimmy Carter appointed Ruth to the U.S. Court of Appeals, where she served from 1980 to 1993. She stepped down when she finally made it to the pinnacle of her legal career. In 1993, President Bill Clinton nominated her for the U.S. Supreme Court. She was confirmed with a strong vote in her favor, of 96 to 3. This made her the second female to serve as Supreme Court judge, as well as one of the first Jewish judges to sit on the bench.

AN ICON OF LIBERALISM

Ruth has famously explained that people should not be judged by their gender, background, or appearance. As a liberal voice, she is in favor of gender equality, civil rights, healthcare for all, workers' rights, gay rights and equality in the institution of marriage, and the separation of church and state. Ruth has cast the deciding vote on a number of landmark cases. In 2010, at the age of 77, she became the oldest justice on the Supreme Court.

Ruth Bader Ginsburg continues to have a huge impact both on and off the bench. In 2009, she was named by *Forbes* magazine as one of their "100 Most Powerful Women," and in 2012, *Glamour* magazine listed her among their "Women of the Year." In 2015, *Time* magazine named her as an icon, as one of the legendary "Time 100." A slightly more unusual honor was bestowed upon Ruth in 2016, when the Cleveland Museum of Natural History named a species of praying mantis after her. This was due to the insect's resemblance to a type of neckwear she often wears, as well as in recognition of her impressive and ongoing fight for gender equality.

Justice Ginsburg has served on the U.S. Supreme Court, in Washington, D.C. (seen here), since 1993.

Insects are usually classified by the male of the species. However, the praying mantis named after Ruth was unusually classified according to the female.

ROSIE THE RIVETER
FICTITIOUS CULTURAL ICON

DATE FIRST CREATED: EARLY 1940s

WE CAN DO IT!

Sometimes you don't have to be a real person to be amazing! Just take Rosie the Riveter. Most of us will recognize her red bandana and muscular forearm, even if we don't know her catchphrase: "We can do it!"

Rosie was an advertising persona created during World War II to encourage women into the jobs left empty by men serving in the war. Songs, posters, and films were created showing capable but stylish women in overalls riveting, drilling, and welding. And they were everywhere. Housewives were suddenly being asked to do their part for the American war effort by swapping electric mixers for drills. It became the most successful recruitment tool in American history—as women took on these jobs, and factories could keep running. Suddenly women proved to themselves (and to the country) that they could do a man's job—and do it well. But when the war ended in 1944 and the men returned, government posters quickly changed. Women's place was once again in the home—or into lower paid jobs. Some women did so willingly, but some so loved this new freedom, they refused to look back: a huge factor in choices available to women today!

THE BIRTH OF ROSIE

Several versions of Rosie Riveter have survived the test of time. The most famous is the "Westinghouse poster" (not at the time called Rosie the Riveter at all!), with the speech bubble: "We Can Do It!" Created by J. Howard Miller, the image is believed to be of machine operator Geraldine Hoff Doyle. The second is the accurately named Rosie the Riveter done by Norman Rockwell for *The Saturday Evening Post* in 1943. It shows a muscular redhead with a rivet gun on her lap and a sandwich in her hand. Another Doyle, the model for this image was the phone operator Mary Doyle. Over the years, images of Rosie the Riveter have come to symbolize women's economic power. Today, Rosie is often used as an icon of feminism.

AUNG SAN SUU KYI
POLITICAL ACTIVIST AND WINNER OF THE NOBEL PEACE PRIZE

FULL NAME: Aung San Suu Kyi
BORN: JUNE 19, 1945, YANGON, MYANMAR (BURMA)
NATIONALITY: BURMESE

Aung San Suu Kyi (above) won a Nobel Prize for Peace (left) in 1991.

DEDICATED ACTIVIST FOR PEACE

Aung San Suu Kyi is an activist for peace and democracy in her home country of Myanmar (also known as Burma). She is respected across the globe for her steadfast commitment to her ideals and for bringing integrity to national politics.

Suu Kyi has led an international life. After graduating from colleges in India and Britain, she worked at the United Nations for three years. In 1988, she returned to Myanmar to care for her mother—and found the country in tatters under the harsh rule of U Ne Win. Opposition to his command was being silenced, and protesters were being brutally killed. Suu Kyi believed in the importance of democracy and began a peaceful movement against him, which grew in popularity. For this, the government placed her under house arrest, in 1989, for 15 of the next 21 years—in a move declared illegal by the United Nations. All communication between Suu Kyi and the outside world was cut off.

GLOBAL RESPECT

In spite of her imprisonment, Suu Kyi continued in her fight for human rights and democracy. In 1991, she was awarded the Nobel Prize for Peace in recognition of her work. However, it was not until 2012—two decades after the award—that she was finally able to make her acceptance speech. She was finally released in 2010 and immediately won a parliamentary seat in the National League for Democracy party. When the party won the national election, in 2015, they were in a position to select the next president. Suu Kyi became "state counselor," a position above the presidency. She remains highly respected by world leaders, by the general population of her home country, and by citizens all around the world.

HILLARY CLINTON
FIRST WOMAN IN U.S. HISTORY TO BE THE PRESIDENTIAL NOMINEE OF A MAJOR PARTY

FULL NAME: Hillary Diane Rodham Clinton

BORN: OCTOBER 26, 1947, CHICAGO, ILLINOIS, U.S.A.

NATIONALITY: AMERICAN

PRESIDENTIAL ELECTION 2016

During both the 2012 and 2016 campaigns, Hillary fought tough battles, in her pursuit of becoming the first female president of the U.S.A.

A POWERFUL LAWYER

Hillary was politically active from a young age. However, while she has been a Democrat for most of her life, Hillary's political interest started as a "young Republican," having been raised in a conservative household. After hearing a 1962 speech by civil rights activist Dr. Martin Luther King, Jr., Hillary knew she wanted to devote herself to public life. She became a Democrat in 1968. Hillary remained top of her class, first as college class president, then graduating with honors from Yale Law School. She married a fellow law student, named Bill Clinton, in 1975.

The young lawyer assisted on several political campaigns, while also working as a professor. Bill and Hillary were both successful in their own rights, and they had to make some important choices—as a married partnership—about their various career moves. From 1978 to 1992, Bill was governor of Arkansas. This gave Hillary her first taste of being a first lady (of the state), but her main job continued to be as a well-respected lawyer and children's advocate. The prestigious *National Law Journal* named Hillary as one of the "100 Most Powerful Lawyers in America"—in both 1988 and 1991.

As Secretary of State, Hillary speaks at the Clinton Global Initiative Annual Meeting in New York, in 2013.

A HISTORY OF FIRSTS

Bill was elected to two terms as U.S. President (in 1992, and again in 1996), making Hillary the First Lady of the U.S.A. She continued to practice law and wield a strong political influence during this time. In 2001, Hillary was elected as a senator for New York, making her the first U.S. First Lady ever to win a seat in public office, as well as the first female senator of New York. She served in this role from 2001 to 2009. In 2007, Hillary announced her plans for another first—to be the first female president of the U.S.A. She put her all into fighting a tough campaign, but Barack Obama won the Democratic nomination—and, ultimately, was elected as U.S. President in 2008, and again in 2012. President Obama hired Hillary as the 67th U.S. Secretary of State, in 2009. She became one of the most widely traveled Secretaries of State ever, and her focus on diplomacy, human rights, women's rights, and healthcare won her high praise.

Early in 2015, Hillary once again threw her hat into the ring for the position of U.S. President, in a close-fought battle with a more left-wing candidate, Senator Bernie Sanders. During her campaign trail and in televised debates, she outlined key issues of her potential presidency, such as those concerning healthcare, women's rights, education, changes to gun laws, climate change, and justice reform. On June 7, 2016, Hillary made history when she was declared the "presumptive presidential nominee" for the Democratic Party. This makes her the first woman in U.S. history to be the presidential nominee of a major party. This is by far the closest a woman has got to the White House—so far.

AND SETTING THE STAGE FOR HILLARY

It is hugely important to note that, 44 years before Hillary's landmark triumph, an incredible woman named Shirley Chisholm (1924–2005) set another first, when, in 1972, she became the first woman to run for the Democratic presidential nomination. Significantly, she was also the first black candidate of a major party ever to run for U.S. President, and she had to endure racism—and even assassination attempts—in her struggle to the top. But Shirley could not be deterred in her fight for change. In 1968, she became the first black Congresswoman and went on to serve seven terms. She fought for civil rights, women's rights, and demilitarization. In 2015, she was awarded the Presidential Medal of Freedom by Barack Obama in recognition of her incredible contributions to American politics.

If president, Hillary would be the first woman in charge of the White House, in Washington, D.C.

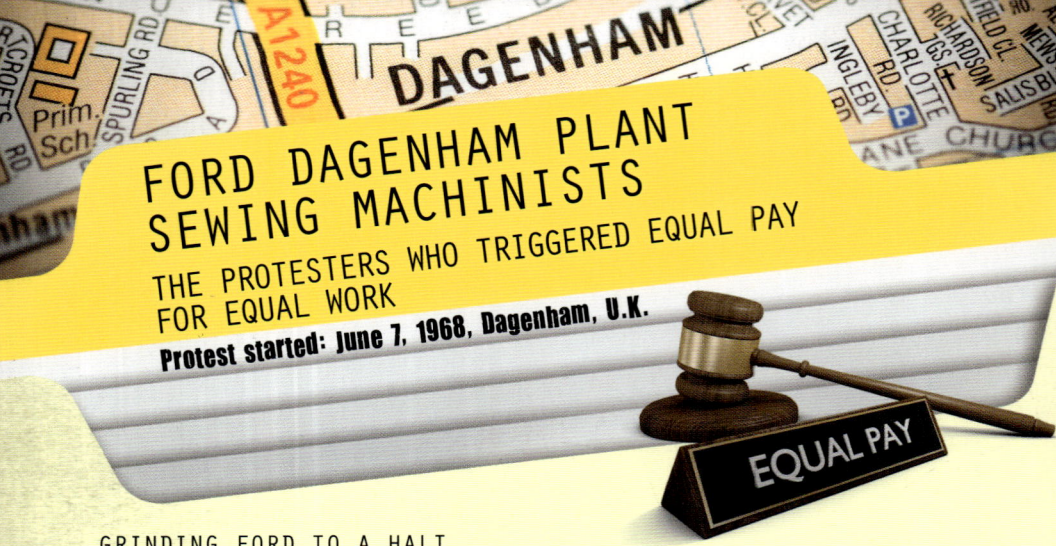

FORD DAGENHAM PLANT SEWING MACHINISTS
THE PROTESTERS WHO TRIGGERED EQUAL PAY FOR EQUAL WORK
Protest started: June 7, 1968, Dagenham, U.K.

EQUAL PAY

GRINDING FORD TO A HALT

On June 7, 1968, 187 female workers at Ford Motor Company's plant in Dagenham, U.K., put down their tools and walked out in protest. This strike created widespread attention that would ultimately lead to equal pay across the U.K.

Those striking workers were all sewing machinists, responsible for making the seat covers in Ford's British cars. The women were protesting the fact that they were paid less than the men for doing the same level of work and that they were not respected for the work they did, as their jobs were graded as "unskilled." Soon, 195 more women from another English Ford plant joined them, and some male workers also supported their campaign. The strike lasted for three weeks in total. Eventually, the strike caused car assembly at the entire plant to stop completely. Ford simply couldn't't sell any cars without the finished seats. It was suddenly apparent to Ford—and the world—just how important these jobs really were.

EQUAL PAY FOR EQUAL WORK

Not everyone supported the women and their strike for equal pay. Some trade unions and male workers saw it as a threat, believing men should be the breadwinners. But Ford was quickly realizing the severity of the strike. The Dagenham Strike, as it became known, gained the support of Barbara Castle, the British Secretary of State for Employment. The women were soon given a pay increase, but it took another six years—and another strike—to get the women's jobs reclassified as "skilled."

In 1970, the U.K. passed the Equal Pay Act. A direct result of the actions of the Dagenham workers, the law makes it illegal to have different pay scales for men and women. These brave women, many of whom had never been political before, stood up for what they believed in. And by doing so, they changed history.

KHARTOUM PLACE STAIRWAY, LOCATED IN AUCKLAND, NEW ZEALAND, IS A MEMORIAL AND FOUNTAIN DEDICATED TO NEW ZEALAND'S INCREDIBLE RECORD AS THE FIRST COUNTRY TO GRANT WOMEN THE RIGHT TO VOTE.

NICELY DONE NEW ZEALAND!

Not a person but a country, New Zealand deserves its own entry here for one incredible fact: on September 19, 1893, New Zealand became the first country in the world to grant all adult women the right to vote. Especially impressive for the 19th century, this meant all women over 21, including native Maori women.

The landmark law did not come easily, as suffrage (voting) campaigners fought hard for many years, led by activist Kate Sheppard. While a handful of global territories and individual U.S. states began to grant the vote, other democratic countries did not follow suit until decades later. Australia was next, in 1902, but countries such as Canada waited until 1917, the United Kingdom 1918, and the U.S.A. 1920. Even then, in in many cases, voting rights only extended to white women. The most recent countries to join the women-voters' party have been Qatar (2003), Kuwait (2005), the United Arab Emirates (2006), and most recently Saudi Arabia (2015).

A 1968 NEW ZEALAND STAMP CELEBRATING THE 75TH ANNIVERSARY OF UNIVERSAL SUFFRAGE (VOTING RIGHTS FOR ALL)

NEW ZEALAND FLAG

MALALA YOUSAFZAI
YOUNGEST-EVER WINNER OF THE NOBEL PEACE PRIZE

FULL NAME: Malala Yousafzai
BORN: JULY 12, 1997, MINGORA, PAKISTAN
NATIONALITY: PAKISTANI

> *All I want is an education, and I am afraid of no one.*
>
> MALALA

SPEAKING OUT

Malala was born in the Swat Valley of Pakistan, to a family of teachers. A militant group, called the Taliban, had been growing in power in the local area. As their power grew, they began to take over the region and force their beliefs on the local people. The Taliban have very strict rules on foreign involvement in the region and on appropriate behavior for its people. Education for girls and women is not allowed.

Named after an important female poet and warrior, Malala was intelligent and curious from the start. At the age of 11, she wrote a blog under a pen name about what it was like to live under Taliban rule as a girl trying to go to school. Her blog was followed up by a *New York Times* journalist, who made a documentary about her life. Malala started giving interviews on TV and in newspapers using her real name. At the age of only 14, she was nominated for the International Children's Peace Prize. However, not everyone was happy with this, and members of the Taliban issued a death threat against her.

"I AM MALALA"

The next year, 2009, Malala boarded her school bus as usual. A Taliban gunman got on the bus and asked for her by name. He shot her in the head. Malala was unconscious for days and was eventually sent to England for intensive treatment. The gunman had hoped to assassinate the outspoken girl and end her support for the education of women. Instead, Malala gained massive support around the world. The United Nations launched a petition called "I am Malala," demanding that children all around the world be in school by the end of 2015. *Time* magazine put Malala on its front cover as one of "The 100 Most Influential People in the World."

Malala continues to be a leading voice on the importance of education for all. She spoke on the subject at the United Nations building in New York City on her 16th birthday.

Malala was only 17 when she won the Nobel Peace Prize for her work on human rights. The Nobel Peace Center, seen here, is located in Oslo, Norway.

REMARKABLE ROLE MODEL

In 2013, she won the International Children's Peace Prize and the same year co-wrote a book about her life. On her 16th birthday, Malala spoke at the United Nations headquarters about the importance of education for everyone. In October 2014, Malala co-won the Nobel Peace Prize. Alongside Indian children's rights activist Kailash Satyarthi, Malala was honored for her work on human rights and education for all. At the age of only 17, this made her the youngest-ever winner. In spite of the threats that continue against her, Malala remains a strong activist for human rights and education for everyone.

Add your own great women here

Science & innovation

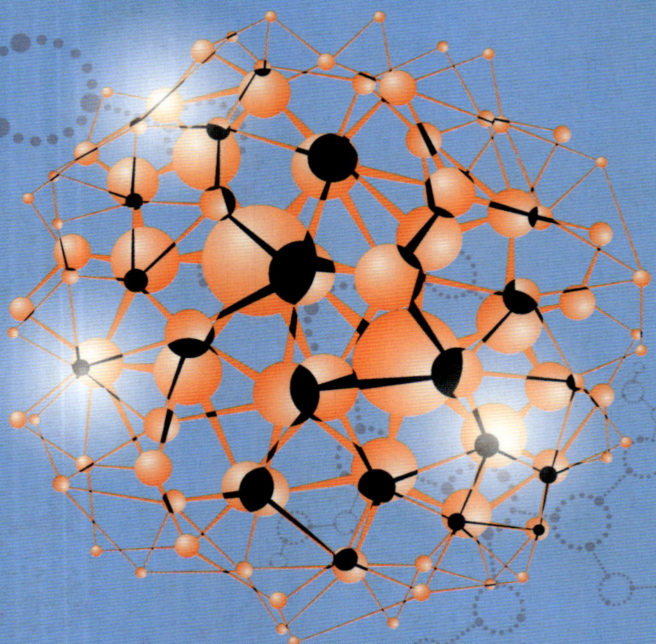

 # CONTENTS

CONTENTS

HYPATIA OF ALEXANDRIA
PROMINENT MATHEMATICIAN AND PHILOSOPHER OF THE ANCIENT WORLD

FULL NAME: Hypatia of Alexandria
BORN: A.D. C. 370, ALEXANDRIA, ANCIENT EGYPT
DIED: A.D. C. 415, ALEXANDRIA, ANCIENT EGYPT
NATIONALITY: ANCIENT GREEK

> 66 *Reserve your right to think, for even to think wrongly is better than not to think at all.* 99
>
> HYPATIA OF ALEXANDRIA

BRINGING IN THE CROWDS

This progressive woman was many things: mathematician, philosopher, astronomer, and head of the Platonist school in Alexandria, in ancient Egypt. This would be hugely impressive for anyone at any time—even more so when you consider that this was at a time when women did not have a voice or recieve an education. Hypatia was a popular teacher within the school, and she attracted large audiences to hear her lecture on philosophy and astronomy.

Hypatia is credited with writing detailed theories on the existence of knowledge. She is believed to have written several important works, but sadly none have survived. She strove to preserve the heritage of Greek mathematics and astronomy. Hypatia was a pagan and lived during a time of major religious trouble between Christians, Jews, and pagans. In fact, she was killed by a gang of Christian fanatics. Some historians believe her death was connected to the destruction of the Library of Alexandria—one of the largest and most important libraries of the ancient world. However, she remains a strong feminist symbol of perseverance and determination. Several books and plays have been written in tribute to her, and her brilliance lives on.

An illustrated example of Hypatia's work

MARIA AGNESI
PROMINENT MATHEMATICIAN: WROTE FIRST BOOK ON CALCULUS

FULL NAME: Maria Gaetana Agnesi
BORN: MAY 16, 1718, MILAN, NOW ITALY
DIED: JANUARY 9, 1799, MILAN, NOW ITALY
NATIONALITY: ITALIAN

CHILD PRODIGY

Maria's brain was in overdrive from childhood. Unusual for girls of the time, she had the best tutors available and mastered a number of languages (including Greek, Latin, Hebrew, French, and Spanish) from a very young age. Her father invited prominent thinkers to their home, and young Maria would debate with them fluently in many languages.

Maria was appointed professor of mathematics at the University of Bologna in 1750 (seen here in 2014)—the first woman appointed to such a position.

In 1738, Maria published a collection of 200 of these debates under the title *Philosophical Propositions*, covering everything from gravitational theory to philosophy. Ten years later, Maria wanted to communicate up-to-date mathematics to her younger brothers, whom she was responsible for educating. She wrote the math textbook that would become her best-known work: *Analytical Institutions for the Use of Italian Youth*. The 1,000-page text was an in-depth study of algebra, trigonometry, and geometry, including new developments in calculus. Her work was hugely respected at the time; her clear explanations of calculus, in particular, would pave the way for the future teaching of mathematics. Pope Benedict XIV was so impressed that he appointed Maria to be the professor of mathematics at the University of Bologna in 1750. Incredible stuff for a time when women could only very rarely get an education! This made her the first woman to be appointed as a university mathematics professor.

FABULOUS FIRSTS

> WROTE FIRST BOOK ABOUT CALCULUS

> FIRST WOMAN APPOINTED AS A
> UNIVERSITY MATH PROFESSOR

Maria Gaetana Agnesi

WOMEN AND MATHEMATICS

When Maria's father died, she was finally able to fulfill her ambition of caring for those less fortunate than herself. She carried out this work until she died, in 1799. Maria's brilliance and clear explanation of complex theories led her to be considered the first important female mathematician since Hypatia (*see page* 157).

Maria's clear explanations of mathematics paved the way for future teaching of the subject.

$16 \cdot x$

$I = \dfrac{i \times 10^3}{50T} = \dfrac{20i}{T}$

$\sum_N$

$\dfrac{a^2 C_1^3}{3T}$ $(y+A) =$

$\Pi = 3.1$

$m+n$ $E=mc^2$

$\text{grad}\,\phi(x,y)$ $M = \sqrt{\dfrac{3 \cdot 6 \cdot 10^3}{3 \cdot 18 \cdot 10}}$

$\nabla \phi(x,y,z) = \dfrac{\partial \phi}{\partial d} i + \dfrac{\partial \phi}{\partial d} j$

$\int \sqrt{a^2-x^2}\, dx = \dfrac{x}{2}\sqrt{a^2-x^2} + \dfrac{a^2}{2}\sin^{-1}\dfrac{x}{a} + C$

$C = \Pi r^2$

$\log ab$

$46 < x$

$ax + bx + c = 0$

$90°$

$\dfrac{x_1 + x_2}{2}$

MARIE-SOPHIE GERMAIN
IMPORTANT MATHEMATICIAN, PHYSICIST, AND PIONEER OF NUMBER THEORY

FULL NAME: Marie-Sophie Germain
BORN: APRIL 1, 1776, PARIS, FRANCE
DIED: JUNE 27, 1831, PARIS, FRANCE
NATIONALITY: FRENCH

Sophie Germain prime:
$$2p + 1$$

> ❝ *Without doubt, she must have the noblest courage, quite extraordinary talents, and superior genius.* ❞
>
> CARL FRIEDRICH GAUSS
> OF MARIE-SOPHIE GERMAIN

PUNISHED FOR LOVING MATH

The young Marie-Sophie was curious and intelligent. However, because of her gender, she was not allowed an education. But Marie found a way around it, instead learning from books in her father's library and corresponding with famous mathematicians using a male pen name. She even taught herself Greek and Latin in order to read books in those languages. Mathematics was seen as inappropriate for women, but Marie persevered. Her parents tried to punish her for her love of math, but nothing could deter the young Marie.

FABULOUS FIRSTS

> FIRST WOMAN TO WIN A PRIZE FROM THE ACADEMY OF SCIENCES, PARIS

A SOPHIE GERMAIN PRIME NUMBER

In 1809, the elite Paris Academy of Sciences opened a competition for work on the theory of elasticity. In January 1816, Marie became the first woman to win a prize from the Academy. Marie's best work was considered to be her research into number theory—in particular, proving the complicated "Fermat's Last Theorem." (Number theory is the study of integers, or whole numbers that do not have fractions or decimal points. Marie's work was the greatest breakthrough in this field until the 1960s.) Response to her work was mixed. Some ignored it completely, due to her gender and unorthodox methods, while others praised it highly and compared Sophie to the great Hypatia. The physicist Claude-Louis Navier said: "It is a work which few men are able to read and which only one woman was able to write."

Today, it is recognized that Sophie was a brilliant mathematician with imaginative approaches to the subject. Some feel that her informal education left her at a disadvantage, while others feel it added to her creativity. Her work is now seen as fundamental to the advancement of number theory and the theory of elasticity, which is used in the construction of tall buildings, as well as applied mathematics. A mathematical term was named after her. A "Sophie Germain prime" is a prime (p) such that 2p + 1 is also a prime number. For example, 11 is a Sophie Germain prime: 11 is a prime and (2 x 11) + 1 = 23, which is also a prime.

Prime numbers

MARY ANNING
IMPORTANT FOSSIL COLLECTOR WHOSE WORK INFLUENCED THE STUDY OF EVOLUTION

FULL NAME: Mary Anning
BORN: MAY 21, 1799, LYME REGIS, U.K.
DIED: MARCH 9, 1847, LYME REGIS, U.K.
NATIONALITY: BRITISH

The Jurassic Coast in Dorset, England (above), is famous for its fossils.

SHE SELLS SEASHELLS BY THE SEASHORE

Mary Anning had a very difficult childhood. She and her brother, Joseph, were the only two of their parents' nine children to survive to adulthood. As a baby, lightning struck at a fair that Mary went to with her family. The woman holding Mary was killed, but Mary survived. When she was only 11, Mary's father fell from a cliff and died while collecting rocks. Her family was poor and she did not get to have an education. But Mary did have the most amazing classroom right at her feet—the seaside town of Lyme Regis, in Dorset, England.

Mary and her family spent their days collecting shells on the beach and sold them to visitors at their stall on the seafront. Interestingly, the childhood tongue-twister, "She sells seashells by the seashore," is rumored to have been written about Mary and her shells.

FABULOUS FIRSTS

DISCOVERED THE FIRST COMPLETE
ICHTHYOSAUR, THE FIRST PLESIOSAUR,
AND THE FIRST PTEROSAUR FOSSILS

*Mary discovered the first complete
fossil of an Ichthyosaurus. The
prehistoric sea reptile (right) was
a very important find.*

SELF-TAUGHT SCIENTIST

Mary did not train as a scientist, but she did spend her life around ancient shells and stones. She schooled herself in geology and anatomy. In 1811, Mary and Joseph were fossil hunting, as usual, when they saw a skull sticking out from a rock. Mary carefully chipped away at it and uncovered a whole skeleton that looked like a crocodile. It would turn out to be the first complete fossil of the large, prehistoric sea reptile *Ichthyosaurus*. Later, Mary would also discover a fossil of another giant sea reptile, the first plesiosaur ever found, as well as a flying reptile called a pterosaur, and significant fish fossils.

The fossils that Mary found were later called "Jurassic," which is the term for a geological period in history from around 200 to 145 million years ago. Mary became well known as an important fossil collector in her lifetime, and respected scientists and collectors came to see her. However, because of her gender and background, she did not always receive proper credit for her work until after her death. As late as 2010, more than 150 years after her death, she was named by Great Britain's Royal Society as one of ten British women to have had the most influence on science.

Mary's fossil finds were incredibly important. They provided the scientific community with clues about life and evolution (explained by Charles Darwin not long after Mary's death). Her discoveries helped change the course of science, and she is considered one of the most influential people in the study of evolution.

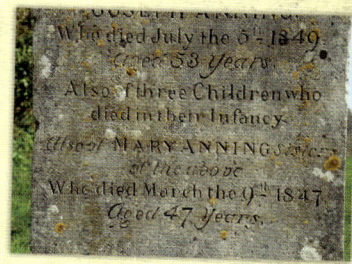

*Mary's gravestone in Lyme Regis
churchyard, Dorset, England, U.K.*

ADA LOVELACE
WORLD'S FIRST COMPUTER PROGRAMMER

FULL NAME: Augusta Ada King, Countess of Lovelace
BORN: DECEMBER 10, 1815, LONDON, U.K.
DIED: NOVEMBER 27, 1852, LONDON , U.K.
NATIONALITY: BRITISH

> 66 *The more I study, the more insatiable*
> *do I feel my genius for it to be.* 99
>
> ADA LOVELACE

ENCHANTRESS OF NUMBERS

Augusta Ada King, Countess of Lovelace (commonly known as Ada Lovelace) was the daughter of Anne Isabella Byron and the famous Romantic poet Lord Byron. Her father left when she was a baby, and her mother encouraged young Ada's interest in science and mathematics—to keep her from following her poet father's footsteps. In spite of this, Ada blurred the line between science and art, in an approach she called "poetical science". At a time when most women were not educated, Ada was taught by some of the best scientists of the day. Ada was often sick as a child, but this was no obstacle to her love of science. Fascinated by flying, Ada set about creating wings. She investigated different materials and methods of propulsion, such as steam, and researched the anatomy of birds. She wrote a book on her findings, called *Flyology*.

From the age of 17, Ada was known as a brilliant mathematician, capable of greatness. She made friends with several leading scientists, including Charles Darwin (a pioneer of the theory of evolution), Michael Faraday (an early pioneer of electricity), and Charles Babbage (a computer pioneer). Babbage was very impressed with Ada, nicknaming her the "Enchantress of Numbers."

FABULOUS FIRSTS

> *FIRST COMPUTER PROGRAMMER*

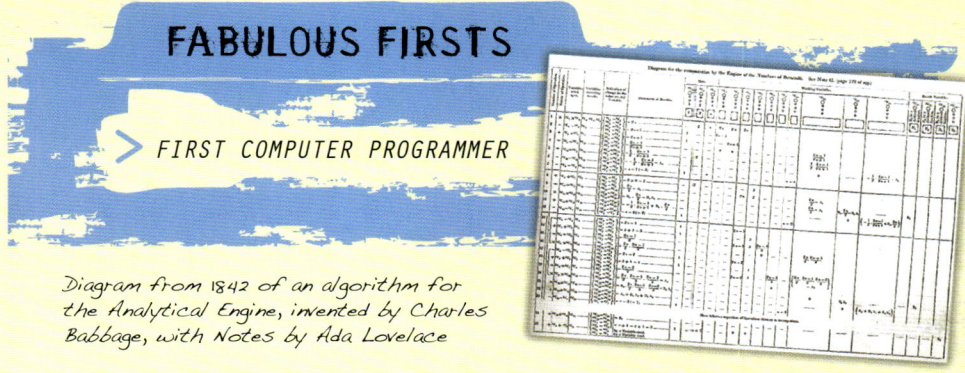

Diagram from 1842 of an algorithm for
the Analytical Engine, invented by Charles
Babbage, with Notes by Ada Lovelace

A "POETICAL" SCIENTIFIC APPROACH TO COMPUTERS

It was Ada's work with Charles Babbage that proved to be the most significant. Babbage had created the Difference Engine, the first mechanical computer, now seen as the prototype for today's programmable computers. Improving on the original, he then created the Analytical Engine, featuring input (equivalent to today's programs and data), a type of central processing unit, and a "store" (today's computer memory) able to hold 1,000 numbers of 40 decimal points each and capable of performing arithmetical operations. It was operated using early computer programming language.

From 1842 to 1843, Ada had the task of using the engine to translate an article, and she kept a detailed set of notes as she worked. These notes contain what is now considered to be the first computer program. It is an "algorithm": a sequence of numbers, or a set of instructions, that can be followed by a machine. Babbage saw computers as able to solve math problems. Ada's "poetical science" approach allowed her to see even further. Ada was the first person to understand what a computer could really do, and she believed that, one day, society might be able to use technology as an important tool—exactly as we do today. Unfortunately, the engine was never completed, but it has now been recognized as an early computer. Furthermore, Ada's notes and methods are seen to represent the world's first computer program and explanation of "software."

As a Victorian woman and mother, Ada's achievements as a pioneer in computing were not widely known. It wasn't until 100 years later, when World War II codebreaker Alan Turing said that Ada's work had been an inspiration to him, that she received recognition. Today, the modern computer language *Ada* is named after her, and Ada has gained a new fan club. Every October since 2009, Ada Lovelace Day celebrates the achievements of women in science, technology, engineering, and math around the world.

MARIA MITCHELL
PIONEER OF ASTRONOMY AND FIRST AMERICAN WOMAN TO WORK AS A PROFESSIONAL ASTRONOMER

FULL NAME: Maria Mitchell
BORN: AUGUST 1, 1818, NANTUCKET, MASSACHUSETTS, U.S.A.
DIED: JUNE 28, 1889, LYNN, MASSACHUSETTS, U.S.A.
NATIONALITY: AMERICAN

> 66 *We especially need imagination in science. It is not all mathematics, nor all logic, but it is somewhat beauty and poetry.* 99
>
> MARIA MITCHELL

1851 portrait of Maria Mitchell, by H. Dassell

NANTUCKET SKIES

Maria Mitchell was a very busy woman. In addition to her main passions of astronomy and teaching, she also found time to be a librarian, linguist, and supporter of women's rights. Not bad for a woman living 200 years ago! Maria is best known for her role as the first professional female astronomer in the U.S.A.

Maria was one of ten children. Her family was Quaker, so the boys and girls were provided with an equal education, which was pretty advanced for the 1800s. She grew up on the island of Nantucket, a harbor town that relied on shipping and was the whaling capital of the world. The study of the skies was important for safe navigation of the ships—so Nantucketers took this very seriously. Maria's father, William, was responsible for calculating exact locations for these ships and relied on sky-watching to do so. Maria was in awe of her father's work—and from the age of 12, she helped him. By the time she was 14, she was working on her own to assist the ships. Maria's mother, Lydia, was a librarian and further encouraged Maria's study.

FABULOUS FIRSTS

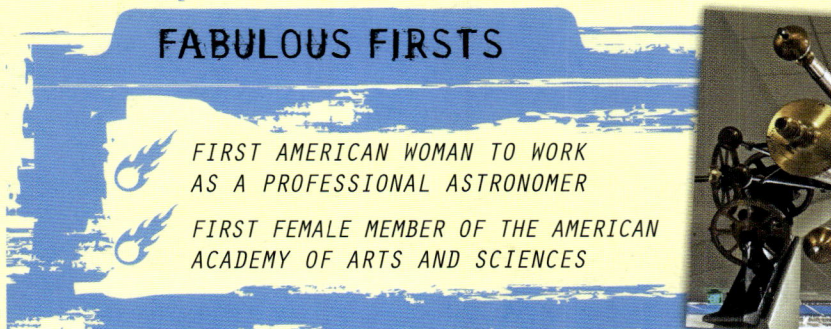

🔥 FIRST AMERICAN WOMAN TO WORK AS A PROFESSIONAL ASTRONOMER

🔥 FIRST FEMALE MEMBER OF THE AMERICAN ACADEMY OF ARTS AND SCIENCES

Miss Mitchell's telescope, on display at the Smithsonian National Museum of American History, in Washington, D.C.

MISS MITCHELL'S COMET

Maria started work as a teacher and then a librarian. But her love of the night sky never wavered. Each night, she would climb to the rooftop of the bank where her father worked to look through the family's telescope. On October 1, 1847, Maria saw a strange object and believed it to be a comet. She was reluctant to make her observation public for fear that no one would believe a woman. But her father encouraged her. The President of Harvard's Observatory also urged Maria to announce her discovery, for the chance of a medal from the King of Denmark. And, one year later, she did! The comet Maria discovered is called Comet 1847-VI (nicknamed "Miss Mitchell's Comet"), and the discovery made her famous—she went on to travel the world, studying astronomy, visiting observatories, and meeting other famous scientists of the day. She also became the first female member of the prestigious American Academy of Arts and Sciences.

Maria believed strongly in women's rights to an education, especially as she'd had one herself. She was a co-founder of the Association for the Advancement of Women.

Maria remained involved in astronomy throughout her entire life. After her death, the Maria Mitchell Observatory, based in Nantucket, was created in her honor. She was also inducted into the U.S. National Women's Hall of Fame. Her original telescope can today be seen at the Smithsonian National Museum of American History, in Washington, D.C.

Maria discovered Comet 1847-VI ("Miss Mitchell's Comet") in 1847— much like the comet seen above.

FLORENCE NIGHTINGALE
VICTORIAN PIONEER OF NURSING AND SANITATION

FULL NAME: Florence Nightingale
BORN: MAY 12, 1820, FLORENCE, ITALY
DIED: AUGUST 13, 1910, LONDON, U.K.
NATIONALITY: BRITISH

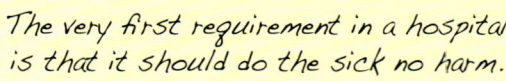

> *The very first requirement in a hospital is that it should do the sick no harm.*
>
> FLORENCE NIGHTINGALE

STATISTICS OVER SOCIALIZING

Born in 1818, Florence Nightingale was a bright child. Home-schooled by her father, she excelled in science and math and became fascinated by statistics and research. In Great Britain, during the reign of Queen Victoria, poorer girls worked as servants or in factories, while rich girls like Florence were expected to get married, look after the household, and attend parties.

Young Florence was very religious and did not want a party lifestyle. She believed that God intended her to carry out important work, and she turned down a marriage proposal to pursue her calling. As a teenager, she felt she was destined to be a nurse. Her parents were shocked; at the time, nurses were not considered respectable, and their working conditions were extremely harsh. However, in 1851, Florence was allowed to go to nursing school. She loved it. Soon she began work at a women's hospital in London, where she made several useful changes and was quickly promoted to superintendent.

AMAZING ACHIEVEMENTS

*SINGLEHANDEDLY REVOLUTIONIZED
SANITATION AND NURSING*

*Florence Nightingale
in an 1868 engraving*

THE LADY WITH THE LAMP

In 1853, the Crimean War started, with Russia on one side and Turkey, France, and Great Britain on the other. The battles were brutal, but a lack of medical care actually caused more death than the fighting itself. Florence was asked by the British government to lead a group of 38 nurses (later known as the "Nightingale Nurses") in the Crimea. Conditions were unbelievably terrible in the Army hospitals: not enough beds, dirty equipment, moldy food, filthy water, and rats. Florence knew that these conditions meant the patients could not recover. She worked very hard to clean the hospitals and made sure the food and water were fresh. This reduced the number of deaths by two-thirds. Florence also had a personal touch, talking to patients with dignity and respect. She earned the nickname "The Lady with the Lamp" for her nightly habit of visiting the wards by lamplight. Back home in Britain, she was hailed a heroine and received personal praise from the Queen.

THE FOUNDER OF MODERN NURSING

Florence wanted to use her fame for good. When she returned to England, in 1856, she met with Queen Victoria and other important figures to discuss her ideas for improvements. Hospitals got cleaner and doctors and nurses received better training, which meant less death and disease. In 1860, the Nightingale Training School opened in London to teach these new and better skills to nurses.

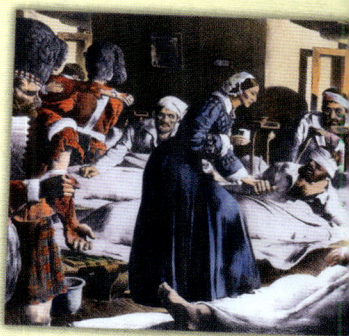

For the last 40 years of her life, Florence, though in poor health, remained dedicated to improving the lives of others. In 1907, she became the first woman to receive the Order of Merit. Florence Nightingale is considered the founder of modern nursing. During her lifetime, she saved countless lives, and she left an incredible legacy that still influences healthcare to this day.

*Florence nursing soldiers
during the Crimean War
(c. 1930 lithograph by
Robert Riggs)*

BERTHA BENZ
FIRST LONG-DISTANCE DRIVER AND FIRST CAR MECHANIC

FULL NAME: Bertha Ringer Benz
BORN: MAY 3, 1849, PFORZHEIM, GERMANY
DIED: MAY 5, 1944, LADENBURG, GERMANY
NATIONALITY: GERMAN

1886 Benz Motorwagen, in the Dresden Transport Museum, Germany

Bertha Benz's role in the Benz Motorwagen automobile company was a quiet one at first, due to strict gender laws. However, in addition to raising five children, Bertha was a strong business partner and financier of the company she co-owned with her husband Karl Benz.

THE WORLD'S FIRST-EVER ROAD TRIP

One day in August of 1888, Bertha's role in the business picked up speed—literally. Without telling her husband, Bertha took two of her young sons—in the newly built Benz Patent-Motorwagen No. 3—on the first-ever road trip. She drove the three-wheeled automobile a huge distance, crossing 66 miles in 12 hours, at a time when other automobiles had only traveled a dozen feet. This made her the first person to drive a car over a long distance—as well as the world's first car "thief!" Bertha claimed that the trip was to visit her mother, but the real purpose of her stunt was pure business. Karl was a great engineer, but he did not understand the importance of marketing. Bertha wanted to prove to her husband that publicity was important, and that the success of the automobile would come from its usefulness to ordinary people. She had faith in her husband and his invention, so she took to the road.

170

FABULOUS FIRSTS

- *FIRST ROAD-TRIP DRIVER*
- *FIRST GAS ATTENDANT*
- *FIRST CAR MECHANIC*
- *CO-INVENTOR OF THE FIRST BRAKE PADS*

INVENTOR WITH A HANDY HAT PIN

During her journey, Bertha racked up several more firsts. As the automobile had no real gas tank, she had to stop along the way to buy the necessary solvent fuel at an apothecary, playing the part of a gas attendant. When the ignition stopped, she used her garter to repair it, and when a fuel pipe became blocked, she used a hatpin to fix that, too, so she was the first car mechanic. The invention's wooden brakes failed, so Bertha stopped by a shoemaker to install leather, co-inventing the world's first brake pads. When she finally arrived at her destination, she sent her husband a telegram to let him know of her success. Bertha's trip attracted a lot of publicity, which is what she had hoped for—but also frightened several onlookers with this new-fangled invention, made worse with a woman behind the wheel. Bertha reported all of the technical problems and offered suggestions. As a result, the Benzes introduced improvements, including the invention of the first gear system and brake linings. Immediately, orders came flying in, and the the Benz company quickly became the world's largest automobile manufacturer.

Bertha's role in the advancement of the automobile industry remained one of innovation and partnership. Her contributions are seen as essential to today's car industry. In 2008, the Bertha Benz Memorial Route was introduced, following Bertha's landmark drive from Mannheim to Pforzheim (in the Black Forest), Germany.

The first-ever road trip (by Bertha Benz) was from Mannheim to Pforzheim, an incredible distance of 66 miles.

Autobahn
Mannheim

CLARA BARTON
CIVIL WAR NURSE AND FOUNDER OF THE AMERICAN RED CROSS

FULL NAME: Clarissa "Clara" Harlowe Barton
BORN: DECEMBER 25, 1821, NORTH OXFORD, MASSACHUSETTS, U.S.A.
DIED: APRIL 12, 1821, GLEN ECHO, MARYLAND, U.S.A.
NATIONALITY: AMERICAN

> " *It irritates me to be told how things have always been done. I go for anything new that might improve the past.* "
>
> CLARA BARTON

ANGEL OF THE BATTLEFIELD

Clarissa Harlowe Barton (or "Clara," as she was called) chose to spend her long life in the service of others. She was a teacher, a government official, and (in her most dangerous role) a U.S. Civil War nurse and carer. Her most famous act was to set up a volunteer-based charity called the American Red Cross.

When Clara was working as a government official in Washington, D.C., in 1861, civil war broke out. Large numbers of troops—many wounded and hungry—flooded into the city. Clara started bringing supplies such as bandages, food, and clothing to the troops herself, as well as offering personal and emotional support and serving as a nurse. However, Clara quickly realized that more help was needed to bring such supplies to the battlefield. She quickly took on this task and became known as the "Angel of the Battlefield." She discovered another important role she could assist in: helping to find soldiers who had disappeared in the war. President Abraham Lincoln helped her to set up just such an organization.

1948 U.S. postage stamp showing Clara Barton, founder of the American Red Cross

On May 31, 1889, the Johnstown Flood caused catastrophic damage. The American Red Cross, led by Clara Barton, undertook a major disaster relief effort. This was the first peacetime effort to be led by the organization.

A LIFE LIVED FOR OTHERS

In 1869, Clara visited Europe for a break, but her kind heart could not be put on hold for a vacation. She came across the Red Cross, in Switzerland, and was moved by its work (on a neutral basis) to protect the sick and wounded during wartime. After Europe had signed the Geneva Convention, embodying the work of the Red Cross, Clara fought hard for the U.S.A. to follow suit. And she won. When she returned to the U.S.A., she worked with the Red Cross to establish an American branch of the organization. In 1882, the American Red Cross was founded, with Clara as its president.

Clara devoted her life to helping others. In addition to her work with the Red Cross, she campaigned for women's rights, including their rights to an education and to vote in elections. Clara was a tireless humanitarian and activist, and her work lives on, over 100 years after her death.

Clara Barton in 1865, at the end of the U.S. Civil War

The American Red Cross provides disaster relief, emergency support, and education in the U.S.A.

American Red Cross

PRINCESS THERESA OF BAVARIA
BAVARIAN PRINCESS AND JILL-OF-ALL TRADES

FULL NAME: Theresa von Bayern, Princess of Bavaria
BORN: NOVEMBER 12, 1850, MUNICH, NOW GERMANY
DIED: DECEMBER 19, 1925, LINDAU, NOW GERMANY
NATIONALITY: GERMAN (BAVARIAN)

Theresa von Bayern was many things: a Bavarian princess, ethnologist, zoologist, botanist, and travel writer—as well as a fluent speaker and writer of 12 languages. At the time, girls did not attend school and women were not deemed fit to go to university. Instead, the ever-curious Theresa was taught at home by tutors.

UNORTHODOX INTERESTS FOR A PRINCESS

Princess Theresa was uncommon for any woman of her time, let alone a princess. She was interested in geology, anthropology, zoology, and botany, rather than in marriage or home-keeping. At the age of 21, Princess Theresa began a tour of Europe and North America, preferring to travel in disguise. During these trips, she collected specimens of flora and fauna (plants and animals) and wrote a number of books on natural history under a pen name. Her work became part of the collection of the State Museum of Ethnology, in Munich, and furthered the work of plant and animal classification experts in Europe. The Princess was the first woman to earn both an honorary membership into the Bavarian Academy of Sciences and Humanities and an honorary doctorate from the Ludwig Maximilian University of Munich.

SOFIA KOVALEVSKAYA
FIRST MAJOR RUSSIAN FEMALE MATHEMATICIAN AND FIRST FEMALE PROFESSOR IN EUROPE

FULL NAME: Sofia Kovalevskaya
BORN: JANUARY 15, 1850, MOSCOW, RUSSIA
DIED: FEBRUARY 10, 1891, STOCKHOLM, SWEDEN
NATIONALITY: RUSSIAN

Statue of Sofia Kovalevskaya in Polibino, Russia

SUPER STUDENT

Sofia Kovalevskaya (also known as Sonya Kovalevsky) came from a long line of mathematicians. As a young girl, she was home-schooled, but when she reached college age, she was stuck; women in Russia were not allowed to attend university, and her father would not let her study abroad. But Sofia was determined to continue her pursuit of math. Purely to allow her the freedom to travel, she found a young man who would agree to marry her (although they would stay together for over 20 years and have a daughter together). From there, she went on to study in Germany. However, she still wasn't allowed to attend formal classes, so she studied privately. In spite of this disadvantage, her doctoral dissertation so impressed the faculty that she was given her degree without an exam or classes!

A WOMAN OF MANY TALENTS

In addition to her contributions to mathematics, science, and mechanics, Sofia wrote fiction, and her work was translated into several languages. In 1888, she won a prize from the French Academy of Sciences for research into the rotation of Saturn's rings. The next year, she was appointed as chair of the Swedish Academy of Sciences, becoming the first woman nominated for such a role at a modern European university.

Sadly, Sofia's life was cut short by influenza, and she was only able to publish ten papers in her lifetime. But even in her short life, she made a strong mark on science and math. Just imagine what she might have been capable of if she'd lived past 41. A number of tributes exist in Sofia's honor. These include the Sonya Kovalevsky High School Mathematics Day—a program of workshops across the U.S.A. to encourage girls in math—and the Sofia Kovalevskaya Award, presented every two years to promising young researchers. The lunar crater Kovalevskaya was also named in her honor.

ANNIE JUMP CANNON
PIONEER OF ASTRONOMY AND MODERN STAR CLASSIFICATION

FULL NAME: Annie Jump Cannon
BORN: DECEMBER 11, 1863, DOVER, DELAWARE, U.S.A.
DIED: APRIL 13, 1941, CAMBRIDGE, MASSACHUSETTS, U.S.A.
NATIONALITY: AMERICAN

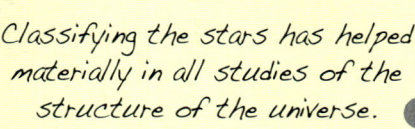

> Classifying the stars has helped materially in all studies of the structure of the universe.
>
> ANNIE JUMP CANNON

FOR THE LOVE OF STARS

Annie's parents were supportive from the start. Her father was a state senator, while her mother sparked Annie's interest in the stars at a young age and encouraged her love of science and math. Annie suffered an unknown illness during childhood, which left her with severe hearing loss for the rest of her life.

As a young girl, Annie knew the constellations, and that love of the stars eventually took her to Wellesley College, where she studied astronomy and physics. From there, she worked at the Harvard Observatory on a team nicknamed "Pickering's Women," first as an assistant and eventually as a professor. It was a large project, and Annie's role was to study the stars in the Southern Hemisphere and to classify them.

The American Astronomical Society (or A.A.S.) awards the annual Annie J. Cannon Award to young female astronomers.

Annie Jump Cannon became one of the top American astronomers, known for her work on star classification and variable stars. Annie is shown here at work at the Harvard College Observatory.

SPEEDY STAR COUNTER

Annie soon realized that the existing star classification system was inefficient. So she created her own. This system, known as the Harvard Classification Scheme, was based on stellar (star) temperature. It was soon adopted as a standard universal system that is still being used today. Annie manually classified more stars in her lifetime than any other human being. In total, she is believed to have classified as many as 350,000 stars, as well as hundreds more variable stars. She was incredibly efficient. At one point, she may have classified as many as three stars per minute!

A STELLAR TRAILBLAZER

Annie's patience and determination helped her excel in what was still very much a male world. Her work helped pave the way for the acceptance of female astronomers that followed. Annie received a number of honorary degrees—for example, she was the first woman to receive an honorary doctorate from the University of Oxford, U.K., in 1925. The American Astronomical Society still awards the Annie J. Cannon Award to distinguished young astronomers, and a lunar crater (Cannon) is named after her. Annie is considered a trailblazer for women in science, and her work was essential to the development of modern astronomy.

Annie classified as many as 350,000 stars in her lifetime—more than any other individual.

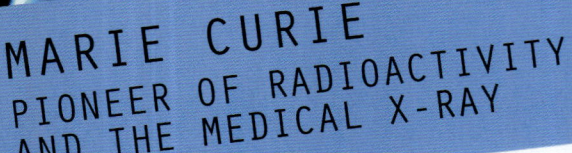

MARIE CURIE
PIONEER OF RADIOACTIVITY AND THE MEDICAL X-RAY

FULL NAME: Marie Skłodowska-Curie
BORN: NOVEMBER 7, 1867, WARSAW, POLAND
DIED: JULY 4, 1934, PASSY, FRANCE
NATIONALITY: POLISH/FRENCH

> 66 *I was taught that the way of progress was neither swift nor easy.* 99
>
> MARIE CURIE

EARLY EDUCATION

Marie Skłodowska-Curie would become one of the best-known scientists of all time, but she did not have an easy start to life. Her Polish family was politically active, and early in Marie's life they lost their fortunes as a result. Marie lost her mother and one of her sisters when she was only a child, but their father made sure that Marie and her siblings were well educated and supported. In the 1800s, it was uncommon for girls to go to college, but Marie studied in Warsaw and Paris, gaining a PhD in physics.

FABULOUS FIRSTS

 FIRST WOMAN TO WIN A NOBEL PRIZE

 FIRST PERSON TO WIN TWO NOBEL PRIZES, AND THE ONLY PERSON TO THEM WIN IN TWO DIFFERENT SCIENCES

 ESTABLISHED THE FIRST MILITARY X-RAY CENTERS

 FIRST WOMAN TO TEACH AT THE SORBONNE UNIVERSITY, IN PARIS

TWO NOBEL PRIZES

In 1903, Marie won international recognition with a Nobel Prize in Physics, with her husband Pierre Curie, and Henri Becquerel, for their work on radiation. This research was the basis for the development of X-rays in surgery. Initially, only the two men were to be honored. However, a progressive committee member fought to have Marie's name added, making her the first woman to be awarded a Nobel Prize. In 1911, Marie won the Nobel Prize in Chemistry for her discovery of the elements radium and polonium and for the isolation of radium. She was the first person to win two Nobel Prizes, is one of only two people to have earned a Prize in two different fields, and is the only person ever to win in multiple sciences.

Unusually, Marie never patented her work, in the hope that the results of her research would be used to treat everyone, and she and her husband selflessly gave their Nobel Prize winnings to family and students to encourage further research. Curie developed the important theory of radioactivity (a term she coined) that outlined the ways in which radiation changes an element's atoms. This opened up the gates to further uses for radioactivity, and also paved the way for the future study of atoms. She founded the Curie Institutes in Paris and Warsaw, still major medical research centers today. During World War I, she also established the first military radiological centers, including mobile X-ray units. Curie drove these mobile units to the front lines herself, and she was made the head of radiological services by the International Red Cross.

French flag   Polish flag

THE MOST INSPIRATIONAL WOMAN IN SCIENCE

Curie's work was hugely important for any scientist of her day, but the obstacles she overcame as a female scientist in the early 1900s make her achievements even more impressive. In 1934, Marie Curie died from the radiation poisoning she sustained living her years of research. In 2009, *New Scientist* magazine named her as the most inspirational woman in science, and 2011 was declared the Year of Marie Curie and the International Year of Chemistry by the United Nations. Her work lives on in the numerous museums and charities around the world that bear her name, and an asteroid has even been named in her honor.

For Marie Curie, her work was everything. At her wedding she wore a dark blue dress so she could go right back working at the lab!

$$b^2 \quad a^2 + b^2 = c^2$$

EMMY NOETHER
INFLUENTIAL MATHEMATICIAN IN ABSTRACT ALGEBRA AND PHYSICS

FULL NAME: Amalie Emmy Noether
BORN: MARCH 23, 1882, ERLANGEN, GERMANY
DIED: APRIL 14, 1935, BRYN MAWR, PENNSYLVANIA, U.S.A.
NATIONALITY: GERMAN

Portrait of Emmy Noether (date unknown)

CALLED A GENIUS BY *THE* GENIUS

Everyone has heard of Albert Einstein, with his wild, genius hair. But how many of us know of Emmy Noether? So brilliant a mathematician was she, even Einstein called her a genius! A number of leading scientists and mathematicians of her time described her as one of the greatest mathematicians of the 20th century.

Amalie Emmy Noether was a hugely inspirational mathematician known for her groundbreaking work on abstract algebra and theoretical physics. She was an instructor at the University in Göttingen in Germany (where she worked without pay for years because of her gender), until the Nazi regime fired all Jewish professors. Emmy moved to the U.S.A. to teach at Bryn Mawr College in Pennsylvania.

Emmy's work was vital to the development of abstract algebra and ring theory. At the heart of her work were "Noether's Theorem," "Noetherian Rings," and "Noetherian Induction." The very development of abstract algebra is attributed to Emmy. So whether you love it or loathe it, the next time you open your algebra textbook, remember Emmy Noether!

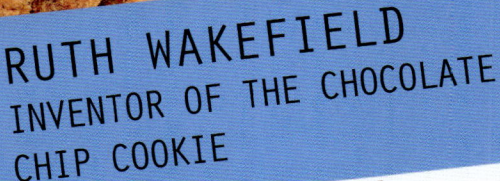

RUTH WAKEFIELD
INVENTOR OF THE CHOCOLATE CHIP COOKIE

FULL NAME: Ruth Graves Wakefield
BORN: JUNE 17, 1903, EAST WALPOLE, MASSACHUSETTS, U.S.A.
DIED: JANUARY 10, 1977, PLYMOUTH, MASSACHUSETTS, U.S.A.
NATIONALITY: AMERICAN

Chocolate chip cookies

A "FAILED" EXPERIMENT?

It's strange to think of a time when chocolate chip cookies didn't exist. But spare a thought for those who had to choose chocolate cookies OR sugar cookies. Hard times. Fortunately, Ruth Wakefield came to the rescue in a kitchen mishap with miraculous results!

Ruth was a dietician and food lecturer in the 1930s. She and her husband Kenneth bought a Massachusetts tourist lodge and named it the Toll House Inn. Ruth was responsible for creating and preparing the guests' meals, which included her specialty: chocolate cookies. The story goes that, one day in the mid-1930s, Ruth was preparing cookie dough when she found she was out of baker's chocolate. Thinking on her feet, she added broken pieces of Nestlé's semi-sweet chocolate, in the hope that it would melt in the same way as her usual baker's variety. Fortunately for us, her experiment "failed." Instead, the dough was pocked with bits of chocolatey goodness. Or so the story goes . . . However, this amusing story has been disputed as pure marketing. With her experience, surely Ruth would have known what she was doing in creating this groundbreaking recipe.

Accidentally or not, Ruth had come up with the now-world-famous chocolate chip cookie. Originally, she called them "Toll House Crunch" cookies, and Ruth's fame—and that of her cookies—grew, both locally and nationally. Her recipe was published, and sales of Nestlé's semi-sweet chocolate bars rocketed to meet the demand. Ruth and the head of Nestlé came to a mutually beneficial agreement. Nestlé would print the Toll House Cookie recipe on its packaging. Ruth would be given a lifetime supply of chocolate. And the chocolate chip cookie would come to be loved by millions around the world. Thank you, Ruth Wakefield!

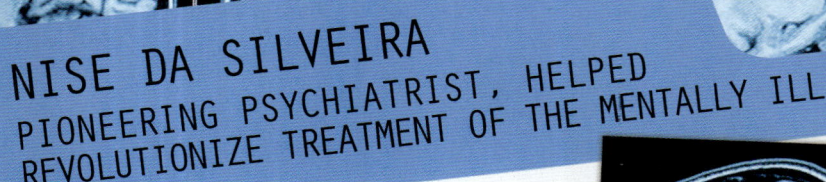

NISE DA SILVEIRA
PIONEERING PSYCHIATRIST, HELPED REVOLUTIONIZE TREATMENT OF THE MENTALLY ILL

FULL NAME: Nise da Silveira
BORN: FEBRUARY 15, 1905, MACEIÓ, BRAZIL
DIED: OCTOBER 30, 1999, RIO DE JANEIRO, BRAZIL
NATIONALITY: BRAZILIAN

CAT scan of a human brain

THE POWER OF LISTENING

Nise was revolutionary in the early 1900s. Not only was she a rarity as a woman earning a medical degree, she was also a pioneer of gentler and more effective psychiatric treatments. At that time, patients with mental illness were treated with harsh "cures", such as injections of high doses of harsh drugs, electroshock treatment (shocking the brain with electricity), and lobotomies (surgery to remove parts of the brain). Nise believed these treatments to be harmful to the patients, who could instead be treated with listening in the form of analysis and therapy. In Europe, the prominent psychiatrist Carl Jung was pioneering an approach that focused on a person's unconscious mind. Nise was a strong collaborator with Jung and introduced his "Jungian" methods of analysis to Brazil.

Nise was a pioneer of animal-assisted ("pet therapy") therapy in hospitals and clinics.

ART AND ANIMALS

Nise was a pioneer of several treatment methods still in use today, including the following: occupational therapy (working with the patient to increase their skills in ordinary, daily activities); art therapy (treatment and expression through art); and animal-assisted therapy (using pets as a calming, therapeutic aid). These treatments are much more nurturing of the patient and teach strategies for coping with everyday life. Nise's work helped to ensure that the future field of psychiatry, especially in South America, was much gentler and more effective for the sufferers of mental illness.

RACHEL CARSON
PIONEER OF THE ENVIRONMENTAL MOVEMENT

FULL NAME: Rachel Carson
BORN: MAY 27, 1907, SPRINGDALE, PENNSYLVANIA, U.S.A.
DIED: APRIL 14, 1964, SILVER SPRING, MARYLAND, U.S.A.
NATIONALITY: AMERICAN

Top: Rachel Carson Wildlife Sanctuary, Maine, U.S.A.

U.S. stamp circa 1981, showing Rachel Carson

STUDYING THE SEA

Rachel Carson was many things: marine biologist, conservationist, writer, and a pioneer of the global environmental movement. Her research and writings led directly to the creation of the now-essential U.S. Environmental Protection Agency. Growing up on a farm in Pennsylvania, Rachel was fascinated by nature from a young age. She began her career working for the U.S. Bureau of Fisheries as an aquatic biologist. She wrote a number of books on the environment, including her 1951 bestseller, *The Sea Around Us*.

SILENT SPRING

Moving from water to land, Rachel became interested in conservation and pollution. She was one of the first researchers to write about the harm that pesticides do to the environment (especially a pesticide called DDT, which was later banned) and the problems they cause for nature. In 1962, she wrote the landmark book *Silent Spring*. The title referred to the idea that, one day, pesticides could kill so many creatures that there might be a spring without any birdsong. The impact was phenomenal. Big-money chemical companies were outraged. However, the U.S. government investigated the claims and backed up Rachel's findings.

Her book led to major changes in U.S. policies around pesticide use. It also sparked an environmental movement that would later become the U.S. Environmental Protection Agency, begun six years after Rachel's death. Rachel Carson is an example of an individual who made huge waves. Undeterred by opposition from big industry, she carefully and thoroughly conducted her research, with groundbreaking results. Many people today credit Rachel with kick-starting the now-global environmental movement. As an early pioneer of environmentalism, Rachel worked tirelessly to preserve the world for future generations.

GRACE HOPPER
PIONEER OF COMPUTER PROGRAMMING LANGUAGES AND SOFTWARE DEVELOPMENT

FULL NAME: Rear Admiral Grace Hopper
BORN: DECEMBER 9, 1906, NEW YORK CITY, NEW YORK, U.S.A.
DIED: JANUARY 1, 1992, ARLINGTON, VIRGINIA, U.S.A.
NATIONALITY: AMERICAN

DISMANTLED ALARM CLOCKS

Grace was a curious child who liked to take things apart—alarm clocks were a particular favorite. In 1928, she graduated with a degree in mathematics and physics (rare subjects for women at the time) and soon after, earned both a masters and a PhD. During World War II, Grace joined the U.S. Naval Reserve and was assigned to Harvard's Bureau of Ordnance Computation Project. There, she worked on the Mark series of computers, which reminded her of the dismantled alarm clocks from her childhood.

Admiral Hopper devoted her life to making computers easier to use and available to everyone. Her most famous saying is, "If you've got a good idea, then go ahead and do it. It's always easier to ask forgiveness than it is to get permission." In 1949, she risked her career by providing businesses with computers. Next, she helped pioneer the first large-scale, electronic, digital computer. She encouraged programmers to share portions of programs, which were written out and copied by hand—an important step in the evolution of computer programming. She was a pioneer of COBOL, one of the most successful programming languages ever. She also coined the term "debugging" for fixing computers, after an actual moth got trapped in the Mark II.

Grace coined the now-common term "debugging" when an actual bug got stuck in her computer.

AMAZING ACHIEVEMENTS

PIONEER OF COMPUTER PROGRAMMING LANGUAGES
AND SOFTWARE DEVELOPMENT

FIRST-EVER RECIPIENT OF COMPUTER
SCIENCES MAN OF THE YEAR AWARD

Commodore Grace M. Hopper,
U.S. Navy, AKA "Grandma
COBOL"

AMAZING GRACE

This trailblazing woman believed that for computers to be used by the wider world, programming languages needed to be understood by regular people. Her abilities as a public speaker and teacher helped make her dream a reality, and she continued working until her death at the age of 86. (In fact, at the time of her military retirement, she was the oldest active-duty commissioned officer—at 79 years, 8 months). She earned 40 honorary degrees and won numerous awards, including the first-ever Computer Sciences Man of the Year Award, in 1969.

Admiral Hopper's achievements crossed the boundaries of the military, academia, and industry. Nicknamed "Amazing Grace" and "Grandma COBOL," she pioneered programming languages, data processing, and software development. Both the Cray XE6 "Hopper" supercomputer and a Navy ship are named after her. Without Hopper, there's a good chance your baby brother and your great aunt wouldn't know how to send an email, surf the Web, or post photos on Facebook. Thank you, ma'am!

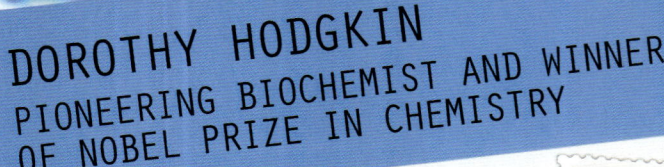

DOROTHY HODGKIN
PIONEERING BIOCHEMIST AND WINNER OF NOBEL PRIZE IN CHEMISTRY

FULL NAME: Dorothy Crowfoot Hodgkin
BORN: MAY 12, 1910, CAIRO, EGYPT
DIED: JULY 29, 1994, ILMINGTON, U.K.
NATIONALITY: BRITISH

1996 British postage stamp showing Dorothy with her work

"OXFORD HOUSEWIFE WINS NOBEL"

Dorothy Crowfoot Hodgkin was a British biochemist whose pioneering work confirmed the structure of penicillin, vitamin B12, and insulin. She also developed protein (or X-ray) crystallography—an innovation that won her the Nobel Prize in Chemistry in 1964, making Dorothy the only British female Nobel Prize winner in science. ("Oxford housewife wins Nobel" was how the British Daily Mail chose to honor the great scientist's hard-earned success.) Protein crystallography makes it possible to determine molecular structures, which is essential in gaining a better understanding of chemicals (such as penicillin, vitamin D, vitamin B12, insulin, and cholesterol) and therefore vital to medical advancement.

Dorothy developed rheumatoid arthritis in her 20s, which made her hands and feet swollen and painful. Despite this, she carried out the amazingly precise and detailed work using the tiny crystals—smaller than a grain of salt—needed for her research. For her work on insulin and vitamin B12, Dorothy was only the second woman ever to receive Britain's Order of Merit, in 1965 (the first was Florence Nightingale, *see pages* 168–169). She was also the first woman to win the important Copley Medal from the Royal Society.

While Dorothy devoted her life to chemistry, she also found time to dedicate to peace work and education, doing volunteer work for many peace organizations. In addition to her work as a researcher, Dorothy was also a professor, and one of her chemistry students, Margaret Thatcher, would go on to become the British Prime Minister (*see pages* 136–137). Rumor has it that Thatcher had a portrait of Dorothy Hodgkin put up at 10 Downing Street in the 1980s.

CHIEN-SHIUNG WU
"THE FIRST LADY OF PHYSICS"

FULL: Chien-Shiung Wu
BORN: MAY 31, 1912, LIUHE, CHINA
DIED: FEBRUARY 16, 1997, NEW YORK CITY, NEW YORK, U.S.A.
NATIONALITY: CHINESE/AMERICAN

Chien-Shiung Wu, the "First Lady of Physics," seen here in 1958

QUEEN OF NUCLEAR RESEARCH

Chien-Shiung Wu was an experimental physicist in atomic energy, radiation, and molecular chemistry. Her pioneering work in this field led to massive advancements in nuclear physics. Wu's work prompted comparisons with Marie Curie and led to her being nicknamed the "First Lady of Physics" and the "Queen of Nuclear Research."

Wu was born in China, where she studied mathematics and physics. In 1936, she moved to San Francisco, California, to continue her studies at Berkeley. Wu is best known for her work on the Manhattan Project—a research and development program for harnessing nuclear energy that led to the creation of the first atomic bomb—as well as beta decay. Beta decay is radioactive decay in which protons transform into neutrons, and vice versa. It was complicated stuff, for which Wu won a number of awards, including the Bonner Prize, Comstock Prize, and the National Medal of Science. She was also the first person to receive the Wolf Prize in Physics. To this day, Wu is considered to be one of the top experimental physicists in history.

FABULOUS FIRSTS

FIRST PERSON TO WIN THE WOLF PRIZE IN PHYSICS

MARY LEAKEY
ONE OF THE WORLD'S GREATEST PALEOANTHROPOLOGISTS

FULL NAME: Mary Leakey
BORN: FEBRUARY 6, 1913, LONDON, U.K.
DIED: DECEMBER 9, 1996, NAIROBI, KENYA
NATIONALITY: BRITISH

Mary Leakey

WE ARE FAMILY

Mary, along with the Leakey family of paleoanthropologists, is famous for some of the most significant archaeological discoveries of the 20th century. She was hugely important in tracing the "missing links" between ancient and modern humans. Mary was nicknamed the "Grand Dame of Archaeology," and the skull fossils found by Mary—and her husband Louis—greatly advanced our understanding of human evolution.

The ascent of man

Mary started work on archaeological digs, such as this, at the age of only 17.

COMPELLED BY CURIOSITY

As a youngster, Mary was a talented artist with a curious mind, and that combination served her well. At the age of just 17, she worked as an illustrator on an English archaeological dig—her first big break. In the years that followed, Mary and Louis became one of science's best-known husband-and-wife teams. Together, they discovered several fossils of skulls and other remains that advanced the study of the origin of life. The Leakeys spent much of their lives in Africa, where, in 1948, Mary made her first fossil find: a 16-million-year-old partial skull of *Proconsul africanus*. This was soon discovered to be a common ancestor of apes and humans that later evolved into the two separate groups. Individually, and with Louis, Mary would go on to discover several other important fossils—including *Australopithecus boisei*, *Homo habilis*, and 3.6-million-year-old footprints at Laetoli in Tanzania—that helped tell us about human evolution and migration, as well as early human skills in using tools.

Mary Leakey's work continues to live on after her death, with the Leakey Foundation and her children and grandchildren continuing the family tradition.

Mary's work contributed to the theory of evolution that humans evolved from a common ancestor of the great apes.

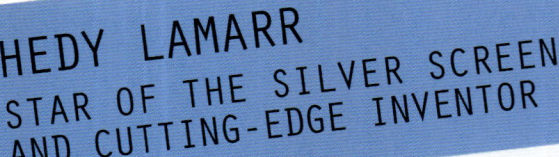

FULL NAME: Hedwig Eva Maria Kiesler
BORN: NOVEMBER 9, 1914, VIENNA, AUSTRIA-HUNGARY
DIED: JANUARY 19, 2000, CASSELBERRY, FLORIDA, U.S.A.
NATIONALITY: AUSTRIAN/AMERICAN

STAR OF THE SILVER SCREEN

Born Hedwig Kiesler, Hedy Lamarr would go on to become a star of the silver screen, as well as an inventor ahead of her times.

After a brief acting career in Germany, Hedwig moved to Hollywood and signed a contract with the Metro-Goldwyn-Mayer film studio, under the name Hedy Lamarr (she would become an American citizen in 1953). She was promoted as the "world's most beautiful woman." Her first American film, *Algiers*, propelled her to immediate box-office success. From the 1930s until the 1950s, Hedy remained a leading lady of Hollywood's "golden age," starring alongside Clark Gable, Jimmy Stewart, and Spencer Tracy. In 1960, she was given a star on the Hollywood Walk of Fame. Despite being called one of the most gorgeous and glamorous women in Hollywood, Hedy was skeptical of such labels. She is famously quoted as saying, "Any girl can be glamorous; all you have to do is stand still and look stupid."

When Hedy moved to Hollywood, she was promoted as the "world's most beautiful woman."

THE "OSCARS" OF INVENTING

That said, Hedy Lamarr was incredibly far from stupid. In 1942, at the peak of her movie career, she gained recognition for her scientific brilliance as well as her star quality on screen. That year, in the midst of World War II, Hedy co-invented and patented (alongside experimental composer George Antheil) a radio-signalling system known as "frequency hopping," or the "Secret Communication System." The system worked by changing radio frequencies, in order to block an enemy from decoding messages It was designed to help in the war against the Nazis. However, the invention would soon have a far greater reach. The "spread spectrum" technology, as it came to be known, was a landmark step in developing the technology involved in the security of everything from military communication to today's cell phones. It also paved the way for both Bluetooth and Wi-Fi technology. While the decoding element was recognized as important in its day, it wasn't until 1997 that the greater impact was understood, so that Hedy and George could be recognized for their amazing invention. That year, they received the Electronic Frontier Foundation (EFF) Pioneer Award and Hedy became the first female recipient of the BULBIE Gnass Spirit of Achievement Award—the "Oscars" of inventing.

INVENTIVE ACTRESS

The idea of a movie star who invents as a hobby may seem surprising to most people, but Hedy Lamarr was far from average. Her first husband was a weapons maker, so Hedy spent many evenings dining with generals and manufacturers—so she knew more about ammunitions and submarines than most. In addition, she had always been interested in inventions and new ideas, including an unsucessful experiment with cola-flavored bouillon cubes. Another rumor is that Hedy was bored by her acting roles and turned to invention as a challenge. Hedy and George were inducted into the National Inventors Hall of Fame in 2014.

WiFi, Bluetooth, and cell phones? Thanks, Hedy Lamarr!

SYLVIA SCHUR
INVENTOR OF THE CORN-DOG-ON-A-STICK

FULL NAME: Sylvia Zipser Schur
BORN: JUNE 27, 1917, NEW YORK CITY, NEW YORK, U.S.A.
DIED: SEPTEMBER 8, 2009, CHICAGO, ILLINOIS, U.S.A.
NATIONALITY: AMERICAN

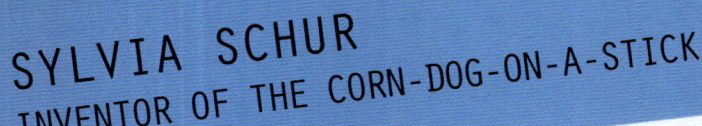

Tomato juice and clam broth in a drink: the one and only Clamato!

AN AMERICAN DELICACY

Since the start of the 20th century, several food vendors have laid claim to the invention of the corn dog. However, it is food expert Sylvia Schur who is credited with serving up the delectable State Fair favorite: a corn-dog-on-a-stick. Sylvia was a food editor and writer best known for her recipes for Betty Crocker and menus for leading restaurants of the time. However, she was also a food innovator and came up with such classics as Cran-Apple Juice and the less appealing-sounding Clamato (a blend of tomato juice and clam broth). But back to the fairground treat. If you're unlucky enough to have avoided this all-American delicacy, you're really missing out. It's exactly how it sounds: a standard hot dog sausage skewered with a stick, dipped in batter, and then deep fried. *Hot diggity dog!*

The iconic corn-dog-on-a-stick can be found at State Fairs across the U.S.A.

WOMEN IN MATHEMATICS

From Hypatia of Alexandria born in fourth-century ancient Egypt to Maryam Mirzakhani born in Iran in 1977, women's contributions to the vast field of mathematics have withstood the test of time. Calculus, number theory, abstract algebra, and geometry—these subjects have all been invented by or furthered by women of incredible vision, often with little or no recognition. So the next time you open your math book, spare a thought for these brilliant mathematical minds.

CLOCKWISE FROM TOP LEFT: HYPATIA OF ALEXANDRIA, MARIA GAETANA AGNESI, SOFIA KOVALEVSKAYA, AND EMMY NOETHER

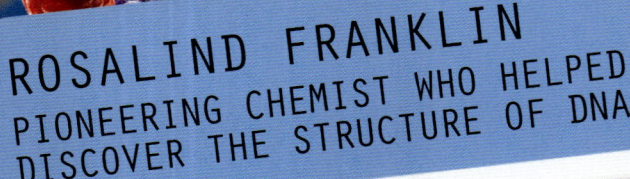

ROSALIND FRANKLIN
PIONEERING CHEMIST WHO HELPED DISCOVER THE STRUCTURE OF DNA

FULL NAME: Rosalind Franklin
BORN: JULY 25, 1920, LONDON, U.K.
DIED: APRIL 16, 1958, LONDON, U.K.
NATIONALITY: BRITISH

THE BUILDING BLOCK OF LIFE

Rosalind Franklin was one-quarter of the group to make the landmark discovery of the structure of DNA, the "building block of life." However, her important role was not fully acknowledged until after her death.

Rosalind came from a politically active family. Relatives were government officials, suffragettes, and trade union organizers. Rosalind, on the other hand, knew by the age of 15 that she wanted to be a chemist. With hard work and precision, she managed to do so spectacularly—earning a PhD in chemistry from Cambridge University.

THE MOST BEAUTIFUL X-RAY PHOTOGRAPHS EVER TAKEN

Rosalind was at the cutting edge of several discoveries, including the structure of coal and the development of X-ray crystallography (used to study the structure of atoms). Later, her research also encompassed RNA, viruses, and graphite. But it was her work on the structure of DNA that led to the most significant breakthrough. DNA (deoxyribonucleic acid) was first discovered in 1898, with the understanding that it was linked to genetics. However, it was not until scientific methods caught up that research could be carried out on its structure. This is where Rosalind came in. Using the X-ray crystallography method she had been perfecting, Rosalind took pictures of the DNA molecule. These were described as the most beautiful X-ray photographs ever taken. A co-worker named Maurice Wilkins

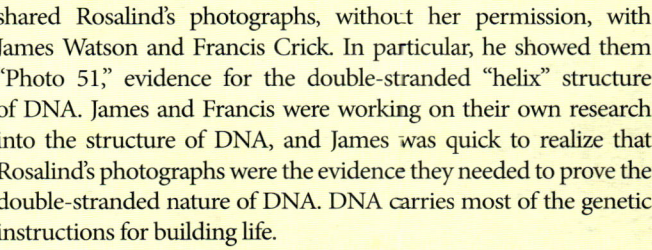

shared Rosalind's photographs, without her permission, with James Watson and Francis Crick. In particular, he showed them "Photo 51," evidence for the double-stranded "helix" structure of DNA. James and Francis were working on their own research into the structure of DNA, and James was quick to realize that Rosalind's photographs were the evidence they needed to prove the double-stranded nature of DNA. DNA carries most of the genetic instructions for building life.

THE FORGOTTEN WINNER

Nine years later, in 1962, Maurice, James, and Francis won the Nobel Prize in physiology and medicine for their work on DNA. Rosalind was never mentioned, even though the trio's work relied heavily on her photographs. Rosalind continued her research for a few years after her breakthrough, but then she died of cancer, in 1958, before the Nobel Prize was granted. The Prize rules explain that up to only three people are eligible for an award and that the list can only include living persons. In more modern times, Roslind's key role would have been acknowledged, but the sexism experienced by female scientists 50 years ago—coupled with her untimely death—made this an impossibility.

It is believed Rosalind was just a year or two away from independently reaching the same conclusions as the trio, and that the trio would not have come to their conclusion without Rosalind's photograph. In all, the work of all four—Rosalind, Francis, James, and Maurice—together made a huge breakthrough for science and humankind: the revelation of the structure of DNA.

An illustration of the DNA double-helix strand, as captured in Rosalind's "Photo 51"

Although Rosalind's name was left out of the 1962 Nobel Prize win, she was undoubtedly the fourth member of the group instrumental in the discovery of the structure of DNA.

JANE GOODALL
WORLD'S LEADING PRIMATOLOGIST AND CONSERVATIONIST

FULL NAME: Jane Goodall
BORN: APRIL 3, 1934, LONDON, U.K.
NATIONALITY: BRITISH

Tanzanian flag

JUBILEE, THE TOY CHIMPANZEE

When she was tiny, Jane Goodall was given a lifelike chimpanzee toy by her father. Jubilee, the toy chimp, inspired her lifelong love of animals—and of humanlike chimpanzees in particular.

At 23, Jane traveled from London to a friend's farm in Kenya. She contacted the famous paleoanthropologists Mary and Louis Leakey (*see pages* 188–189) with the idea of discussing animals. However, the Leakeys had bigger ideas. They were looking for a chimpanzee researcher to do some work alongside their research into early humans, and Jane was perfect. In 1960, she traveled to Gombe National Park in Tanzania, East Africa, to study chimpanzee culture. Jane worked as part of what became known as the "Trimates" (three researchers studying primates). The other two were Birute Galdikas, who studied orangutans, and Dian Fossey, who studied gorillas. The three women are now known as the founding mothers of primatology.

FABULOUS FIRSTS

FIRST (AND ONLY)
PERSON ACCEPTED INTO
CHIMPANZEE SOCIETY

Jane Goodall during a 2009 lecture about chimpanzees

A HUMAN IN CHIMP SOCIETY

With no college scientific training, Jane was open and adaptable in her research. She named the chimpanzees as she worked (the most famous was "David Greybeard"). She observed their unique personalities and emotions, including joy, sorrow, anger, and jealousy. Her findings were controversial as they showed similarities between humans and chimps in behavior, emotion, and community. Her work included the breakthrough discoveries that chimps could construct and use tools—previously, only humans were thought able to do this. Jane's patient, calm, and unorthodox approach of bonding with the chimps led to one truly unexpected outcome: she is the only human ever to be accepted into chimpanzee society.

In 1977, Jane established the Jane Goodall Institute to continue chimpanzee research in Gombe National Park, but she soon realized that she could not care for the chimps without also looking after the humans. Over the next 40 years, the institute has grown to support community-based conservation and sustainability programs in Africa for both animals and humans. In 1991, Jane and a group of students from Tanzania started Roots & Shoots, a global environmental and humanitarian youth program in over 130 countries. The program has wide-ranging goals for animals and humans. These include protecting the great apes and ensuring healthy animal habitats; using cutting-edge technology for lasting conservation; promoting sustainable livelihoods for local communities; and improving gender and health programs.

WORLDWIDE ANIMAL ACTIVIST

At 82, after over 50 years of working and living with chimps, Jane remains passionate about animals and the environment. Ever the activist, she travels around the world to lecture and campaign on everything from chimpanzees and conservation to education and health, sustainability, and action against animal testing. She is also a peace activist, and in 2002, she was named a UN Messenger of Peace. Jane has won a huge number of awards and honors, including an Order of the British Empire (making her Dame Jane Goodall). Jane's work has been essential to the study of evolution, chimp and human behavior, intelligence, and even parenting. She is considered to be the world's expert on chimpanzees.

SYLVIA EARLE
TIME MAGAZINE'S FIRST HERO FOR THE PLANET

FULL NAME: Sylvia Earle
BORN: AUGUST 30, 1935, GIBBSTOWN, NEW JERSEY, U.S.A.
NATIONALITY: AMERICAN

A LIVING LEGEND

Sylvia Earle has been called a "Living Legend" by the Library of Congress. She is an oceanographer, explorer, marine biologist, and author, and has been *National Geographic*'s explorer-in-residence since 1998. She was also the first female chief scientist of the U.S. National Oceanic Atmospheric Association (NOAA). Remarkably, Sylvia has led more than 100 research expeditions and totalled over 7,000 hours underwater. She has also set a record for solo diving at depths of around 1,000 meters. She has clearly been very busy, devoting her time to what she loves: safeguarding life in the ocean.

Sylvia has earned more than 100 national and international honors. She was named as *Time* magazine's first Hero for the Planet, in 1998, and received the UN Champions of the Earth Award in 2014. In addition to her work on protecting and exploring the world's oceans, Sylvia is also an expert on the impact of oil spills and has helped to protect ocean life after a number of oil disasters. Sylvia has been the expert at the forefront of ocean exploration and protection for over 40 years. Her views on marine conservation are some of the most respected in the world.

FABULOUS FIRSTS

FIRST FEMALE CHIEF SCIENTIST OF THE U.S. NATIONAL OCEANIC ATMOSPHERIC ASSOCIATION

FIRST TIME *MAGAZINE* HERO FOR THE PLANET

Sylvia has spent a total of over 7,000 hours underwater!

WOMEN IN TECHNOLOGY

Technology is a massive field, with countless contributors from all over the world. Many contributions from the women in this book are still in use today. From very different backgrounds and places in history, the work of Ada Lovelace and Rear Admiral Grace Hopper has played a massive part in how we use computers today. Both women had the vision to see that technology could be a useful tool for everyday people—Ada in her computer programming that was way ahead of its time, and Grace for her ability to make programming languages accessible to all. Meanwhile, actress Hedy Lamarr's co-invention now known as "spread spectrum" would go on to become the technology we use in today's Wi-Fi and Bluetooth. And Maria Telkes had the foresight to use technology for solar power, all the way back in 1947. Her ideas sparked the solar technologies in modern use.

CLOCKWISE FROM TOP LEFT:
REAR ADMIRAL GRACE HOPPER,
ADA LOVELACE, MARIA TELKES,
AND HEDY LAMARR

TEMPLE GRANDIN
PIONEER OF ANIMAL WELFARE AND AUTISM ADVOCACY

FULL: Temple Grandin
BORN: AUGUST 29, 1947, BOSTON, MASSACHUSETTS, U.S.A.
NATIONALITY: AMERICAN

Puzzle ribbon for autism awareness

FINDING HER VOICE

Temple Grandin is now a renowned author, animal expert, and advocate for autistic communities, respected across the globe. However, it took a lot of support and understanding for her to find her voice—but find it, she certainly has.

At age two, Temple was diagnosed with a condition that would later be labeled as autism. Today, autism is understood as a brain condition that can affect a person's ability to communicate and engage with other people. However, at the time, Temple was considered to have a form of brain damage. Her parents were blamed for causing the condition and even told to send her to an institution. But her parents refused to give up on her. Instead, they found the best care, including intensive speech therapy, and by the age of four, she was able to speak. She continued to find it difficult to interact with people, but she focused on her studies and was a good student.

Temple has incredible empathy with animals, and her contributions to their welfare have been huge.

"ANTHROPOLOGIST ON MARS"

Temple studied psychology, followed by a PhD in animal science. She is now a respected expert on animal welfare, based on her insight into the minds of animals. She has written several important books on the subject, including *Animals Make Us Human* and *Animals in Translation*. Temple places great importance on reducing animals' stress. She works with companies that run animal slaughterhouses to improve the quality of life for their animals.

Temple has been part of the Autism Society of America, and she first found fame for her own experience when she began to speak publicly in the 1980s. She has described how she feels like an "anthropologist on Mars" in social settings. Temple is considered a "high-functioning" autistic person, which means that she is able to live an independent life and wants to interact with people, even if she finds it difficult. She has incredible insight into what it means to be an autistic person in a non-autistic world. She is able to describe to others what it feels like to be extremely sensitive to noise and change. Temple works to encourage research and education into autism, and her view is that each person and their condition are unique. Without her autism, Temple does not believe she would have been able to make the outstanding contributions she has to animal welfare.

Temple's contributions to the field of animal welfare and insight into autism have been huge. As a result, she has earned several honorary degrees and was made a fellow of the American Society of Agricultural and Biological Engineers. In 2010, HBO made a T.V. movie starring the actress Claire Danes, called *Temple Grandin*. The film won five Emmy Awards and helped the public learn more about the real world of autism.

HBO won five Emmy Awards for the T.V. movie Temple Grandin. When the real Temple took to the stage at the Awards show, she stole the spotlight.

KATHRYN SULLIVAN
OCEANOGRAPHER, ASTRONAUT, AND FIRST AMERICAN WOMAN TO WALK IN SPACE

FULL: Kathryn Dwyer Sullivan
BORN: OCTOBER 3, 1951, PATERSON, NEW JERSEY, U.S.A.
NATIONALITY: AMERICAN

LONG-DISTANCE TRAVELER

Kathryn has a rare claim: she has been both to the depths of the ocean floor and the heights of Earth's orbit. She has been on three space missions totalling more than 22 days in space. After studying geology in college, Kathryn participated in several expeditions to

As part of NASA, Kathryn has logged more than 22 days in space.

study the seabeds of the Atlantic and Pacific oceans. In 1978, she was selected as an astronaut for NASA. Her first flight, in 1984, was on board the space shuttle *Challenger*, during which she operated a system to show how satellites could be refuelled in orbit. She and her co-astronaut, David Leestma, performed a 3.5-hour spacewalk, which meant Kathryn was the first American woman to walk in space. Her next voyage was in 1990, on board the space shuttle *Discovery*, which deployed the Hubble Space Telescope. This was followed by the 1992 voyage on space shuttle *Atlantis*, during which she conducted experiments into Earth's atmosphere.

FROM PLANETS TO POLITICS

In 1993, Kathryn left the sky and returned to the sea—swapping NASA for the NOAA (the National Oceanic and Atmospheric Administration), where she became its chief scientist. In 2011, President Barack Obama appointed her to the position of Undersecretary of Commerce for Oceans and Atmosphere, and as the administrator of the NOAA.

In 2004, Kathryn was inducted into the Astronaut Hall of Fame. She has also won the Haley Space Flight Award, for distinguished performance on the Hubble Space Telescope mission, as well as the Adler Planetarium Women in Space Science Award, and the National Audubon Society's Rachel Carson Award (*see page* 183), for environmental leadership.

MARYAM MIRZAKHANI
MULTIPLE GOLD-MEDAL-WINNER OF INTERNATIONAL MATHEMATICAL OLYMPIADS

FULL NAME: Maryam Mirzakhani
BORN: MAY 3, 1977, TEHRAN, IRAN
NATIONALITY: IRANIAN

THE BEAUTY OF MATHEMATICS

Maryam has always enjoyed a challenge. Despite a childhood ambition to become a writer, and poor grades in math in middle school, in high school she discovered a passion for complex mathematics. Maryam is an Iranian mathematician now working in the U.S.A. In 1994, at the age of 17, Maryam won her first gold medal at the International Mathematical Olympiad (IMO) and became the first female Iranian student to make such an achievement. In 1995, she won again, with a perfect score. The IMO is a very prestigious annual competition for math and one of the oldest of the International Science Olympiads. The first was held in 1959 and roughly 100 countries take part each year.

In 2014, Maryam won the most prestigious prize in mathematics—the Fields Medal—for her work on the dynamics of geometry. This made her the first woman (as well as the first Iranian) to win this award. In addition to her own research, Maryam is a mathematics professor at Stanford University, in California, U.S.A.

FABULOUS FIRSTS

1. FIRST FEMALE IRANIAN STUDENT TO WIN GOLD AT THE INTERNATIONAL MATHEMATICAL OLYMPIAD

1. FIRST WOMAN, AND FIRST IRANIAN, TO WIN THE FIELDS MEDAL

Science & innovation

& innovation

Inventors

Tabitha Babbitt (1779–1853, U.S.A.)—circular saw
As a member of the Shaker religious community, Tabitha decided not to patent any of her inventions, so that everyone could use them. The circular saw is still widely used today, over 200 years later.

Adeline D.T. Whitney (1824–1906, U.S.A.)—wooden alphabet blocks
Adeline was a writer of books for both children and adults. She held traditional views and felt that the home was the source of all good things. In 1881, she created a set of wooden alphabet blocks for young kids. These brightly colored blocks are still played with today and have become a lasting symbol of childhood.

Martha Jane Coston (1826–1904, U.S.A.)—signal flares
Martha was only 21 when her inventor husband Benjamin died, leaving her broke and caring for four children. One day, while searching through her late husband's papers, she found notes on a signalling system he was creating for the Navy. For the next ten years, Martha worked hard to develop this system of colored flares. Her final inspiration came from a fireworks display in New York City. In 1859, she was granted a patent (in Benjamin's name) for the Coston Flare. Her system allowed marines in distress at sea to send emergency signals. It saved countless lives. Martha's flares revolutionized communication and safety. A variation of her invention is still used today.

Ellen Fitz (1836–?, U.S.A./Canada)—modern mounted globes (patented in 1875)
Ellen was an American governess working in Canada, who had a sideline in inventing. In 1875, she patented her invention for the modern, mounted globe that we know from classrooms across the world today.

Margaret E. Knight (1838–1914, U.S.A.)—paper bag and several other inventions, including a rotary engine and internal combustion engine

Margaret was one of the first women to hold a patent (in 1870). With no engineering training, she spent her evenings drawing blueprints of a machine to make flat-bottomed paper bags. Unfortunately, before she finished, a man named Charles Annan saw her machine being cast, copied it, and filed a patent of his own. But Margaret fought her case. She took her models and drawings to the patent office in Washington. Annan's defence was simply that a woman could not have invented such a complicated machine. Margaret was able to show her work, prove she was the inventor, and earn the patent.

Josephine Garis Cochrane (1839–1913, U.S.A.)—first mechanical dishwasher

Josephine was a wealthy "socialite" who hosted lots of dinner parties. She got tired of cleaning up—and tired of waiting for someone else to invent a dishwasher, proclaiming, "If no one else is going to invent a dishwashing machine, I'll do it myself!" She had the early design patented in 1886 and installed one in her own kitchen. Soon, she opened a factory and began mass-producing the machines for restaurants and hotels.

Maria Beasley (mid to late 1800s, U.S.A.)—life raft

Maria was one of the rare women from history who actually made a fortune from her patents. Between 1878 and 1898, received at least 15 patents, including those for a barrel-making machine, a foot-warmer, and an anti-derailment device for trains. But it is the amazing life raft (left) for which she remains most famous.

Letitia Geer (mid to late 1800s, U.S.A.)—medical syringe

In 1899, Letitia invented a type of medical syringe that would be cheap to produce and easy for people to use with only one hand. That was over 100 years ago, and a version of her original is still widely used in hospitals and research labs all over the world.

Anna Connelly (mid to late 1800s, U.S.A.)—fire escape
Very little is known about Anna Connelly, except that her name is listed alongside the first registered patent for a fire escape, in 1887. This was still early days for women filing for patents in their own name. A particular design of external fire escape for apartment buildings is named after her. Anna and her invention are believed to be responsible for saving the lives of thousands.

Mary Walton (mid to late 1800s, U.S.A.)—elevated railway and anti-pollution devices
While details are sparse, Mary is widely recognized as playing a major part in the creation of the elevated railway found in many large cities. Mary patented devices for reducing both air and noise pollution (in 1879 and 1881) from the overhead trains. Without this, widespread elevated trains would not be in use today—and city-dwellers would not be able to breathe because of the severe traffic fumes.

Margaret A. Wilcox (mid to late 1800s)—first car heater (1893)
All we know of Margaret Wilcox is that she was a very early mechanical engineer who created the first car heater. It worked by directing air from around the engine over the driver and passenger's feet. This system paved the way for today's in-car temperature control systems.

El Dorado Jones (1860–1932, U.S.A.)—airplane engine muffler and electric iron
Nicknamed the "Iron Woman," El Dorado is credited with several inventions and patents. She had a factory producing her inventions that employed no men, and only women over the age of 40.

Mary Anderson (1866–1953, U.S.A.)—windshield wiper
Mary did everything: real estate, ranching, wine-making, inventing . . . In 1903, she created the invention for which she'd become known—windshield wipers. Mary came up with the idea after watching bus drivers reach out of their vehicles to clear snow and rain from their windshields. By 1916, windshield wipers had become standard equipment on all american cars. And today, no vehicle could cope without them.

Elizabeth Magie Phillips (1866–1948, U.S.A.)—Monopoly board game

Originally titled *The Landlord's Game*, *Monopoly* has gone on to sell billions of games and spin-offs worldwide. Elizabeth Magie invented the game for friends as a light-hearted way of demonstrating the negative effects of capitalism and greedy landlords, as well as the benefits of tax. She had it patented in 1904. In 1935, Elizabeth sold the rights to Parker Brothers, who paid her $500 and no royalties. The company quickly created a fake story about a male inventor and changed its political history. The real story has only just become known.

Sarah Boone (c. 1870–1900, U.S.A.)—ironing board

Sarah Boone was a female African-American inventor—a rarity in the late 1800s. In her 1892 patent for the ironing board, she wrote that she wanted to "produce a cheap, simple, convenient and highly effective device, particularly adapted to be used in ironing the sleeves and bodies of ladies' garments." Millions of poeple still use her invention today.

Florence Parpart (late 1800s to early 1900s, U.S.A.)—modern electric refrigerator (1914)

Little is known about Margaret, other than from her patent applications. Not only did Margaret invent the hugely important modern electric fridge we still use today, she also did her own advertising, production, and sales of her invention.

Melitta Bentz (1873–1950, Germany)—drip coffee and coffee filters

As coffee-drinking grew in popularity in the early 1900s, so too did inventions for its improvement. Melitta made lots of coffee for her household and was tired of bad flavors and coffee grounds getting stuck in her teeth. So one day, she tried using paper from her son's schoolbook as a filter and made a hole in the brass coffee pot. It worked! Soon, Melitta patented the invention (in 1908) and set up her own successful business. Modern coffee-drinkers and coffee shops have Melitta to thank for their cup of joe every morning!

Katharine Burr Blodgett (1898–1979, U.S.A.)
—inventor of invisible glass (1938) and smoke screens

Katharine was an American inventor and physicist, the first woman to be awarded a PhD in physics from the University of Cambridge, U.K., as well as the first woman to work as a scientist for General Electric (GE). Katharine's clear glass was used in projectors and cameras at Hollywood's heyday (it was first used in *Gone with the Wind*), as well as in everything from scientific products to submarine periscopes. During World War II, she invented the smoke screen, saving many lives by hiding troops from enemy view.

Mária Telkes (1900–1995, Hungary)—solar house and solar technologies

A physicist and solar-power engineer, Dr. Mária Telkes built the first 100 percent solar-power system for her own house, in 1947. This innovation has sparked solar technologies that are still in use today.

Marion O'Brien Donovan (1917–1998, U.S.A.)—disposable diaper

Marion patented the first disposable diaper, in 1946, as the "boater." Her invention was initially not well received by the all-male heads of the paper companies she pitched it to. Marion eventually sold her invention for $1,000,000. She went on to earn a degree from Yale and gained many more patents for her creations.

Stephanie Kwolek (1923–2014, U.S.A.)—Kevlar

Stephanie was an American chemist and inventor. She won numerous awards for her work and was inducted into the National Inventors Hall of Fame. But it is for the invention of Kevlar that she is most famous. Kevlar is used in over 200 products today, including everything from skis to race cars, tennis shoes to bullet-proof vests.

Shirley Jackson (born 1946, U.S.A.)—Telecommunication inventions

Theoretical physicist Shirley's experiments, and her belief in sharing her learning, have led to just about every imaginable invention connected to telecommunication. This includes the invention of the portable fax machine, touch-tone phones, solar cells, fiber-optic cables, and the technology behind caller ID and call waiting. Shirley was also the first African-American woman to earn a PhD at MIT.

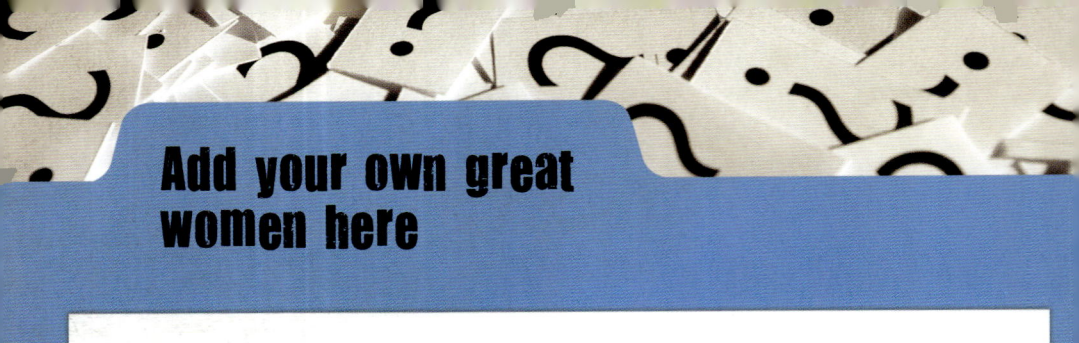

Add your own great women here

Sports & endurance

CONTENTS

CONTENTS

NIKE
GODDESS OF VICTORY

FULL NAME: Nike
DATES FROM: C. 550 B.C., GREECE
NATIONALITY: GREEK

THE ORIGINAL AND ULTIMATE WINNER

With her outstretched wings and laurel wreath, the ancient Greek goddess Nike was an impressive figure. In ancient times, mythical figures personified great ideals, and the strong and beautiful Nike stood for victory, strength, and speed. Nike was a popular goddess, depicted on pottery, coins, and statues. The oldest-surviving statue of her dates as far back as 550 B.C. Today, the popular sportswear brand, Nike, is named after her, and she can still be seen representing victory on every Olympic medal.

Nike athletic shoe showing the famous "swoosh" trademark

Statue of the Greek goddess Nike

CYNISCA OF SPARTA
FIRST WOMAN TO WIN AN OLYMPIC VICTORY

FULL NAME: Princess Cynisca of Sparta

DATE: C. 440 B.C., GREECE

NATIONALITY: GREEK

ANCIENT OLYMPICS—FOR MEN ONLY

The ancient Olympic Games are thought to have started almost 3,000 years ago, all the way back in 776 B.C. People from all over the ancient Greek world came to watch and compete. But in order to do either, you had to be male; women were not even allowed to set foot in the main stadium. Women were only permitted to enter equestrian (horse) events—and even then they could only participate by owning and training the horses and chariot teams, not by riding or driving the chariots.

EXPERT EQUESTRIAN

Most women in ancient Greece were not trained in sports or hunting, but in Sparta it was different. Women were raised to excel at these things so that they could raise strong children. The Spartan princess Cynisca was an expert equestrian and horse trainer. Cynisca entered her (all-male) team at the Olympics, where it won the four-horse chariot race event twice, in 396 B.C. and 392 B.C. Sadly, Cynisca probably wasn't allowed into the stadium to see her victories, but she became the first woman to win an Olympic title!

FABULOUS FIRSTS

⊕ FIRST WOMAN TO WIN VICTORY AT THE OLYMPIC GAMES

⊕ FIRST WOMAN TO GAIN RECOGNITION AS AN ATHLETE

Olympic laurel wreath of victory

THE WREATH OF VICTORY

Cynisca is now known as the most distinguished female athlete of the ancient world. She was honored with a statue at the Temple of Zeus in Olympia, with a plaque declaring her the only woman to win the wreath of victory. A hero shrine to her was also placed in Sparta at Plane-tree Grove, an honor usually reserved only for Spartan kings. The plaque there read:

Replica of an ancient Greek wall plaque showing a four-horse chariot, like the kind used by Cynisca in her Olympic win

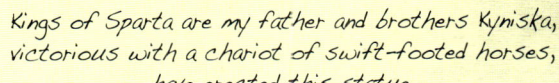

Kings of Sparta are my father and brothers Kyniska,
victorious with a chariot of swift-footed horses,
have erected this statue.
I declare myself the only woman
in all Hellas to have won this crown.
Apelleas son of Kallikles made it.

RIDING OUT IN FRONT

Cynisca's win had a great impact on other female chariot racers in the ancient Greek world, and, later, all the female athletes who followed. Her success also influenced society's respect for female athletes. Today, this Spartan princess symbolizes the social rise of women and their greater equal rights.

MARY "QUEEN OF SCOTS"
THE MOTHER OF GOLF

FULL NAME: Mary "Queen of Scots" Stuart
BORN: DECEMBER 8, 1542, LINLITHGOW PALACE, SCOTLAND
DIED: FEBRUARY 8, 1587, FOTHERINGAY CASTLE, ENGLAND
NATIONALITY: SCOTTISH

QUEEN OF SPORTS

At first glance, Mary, Queen of Scots, may seem like an unlikely contender for this sports and endurance chapter. Troubled by political and familial woes throughout her life (including three marriages, cousinly treachery, and her eventual execution), Mary is often portrayed as a figure of pity. But in reality, the six-foot-tall royal was graceful, quick-witted, and sporty—which is exactly what brings her here!

FROM SCOTLAND TO FRANCE

At a very young age, Mary was sent to France to be educated at the royal court in preparation for her marriage to the French king. This union would make her Queen of France and Scotland. During that time, she became an avid golfer and is thought to have introduced the game to France. She is believed to have coined the term "caddie" (the person who carries a golfer's clubs), based on the name for her French military aides, known as cadets. As an adult, Queen Mary caused a scandal by playing golf on the now-famous Links at St. Andrews, Scotland, days after her second husband's murder. This "unusual" behavior was even used as partial evidence of her guilt of being involved in the crime, eventually leading to her lengthy imprisonment.

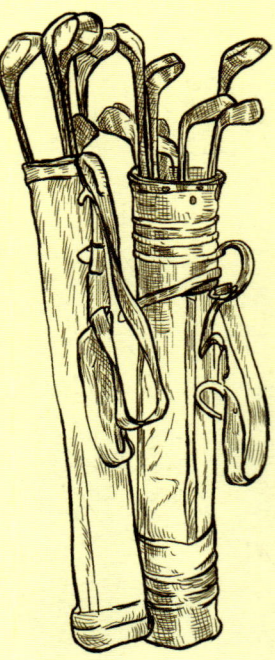

In addition to popularizing the sport of golf, Mary Stuart coined the term "caddie"

66 *In my end is my beginning.* 99

MARY
"QUEEN OF SCOTS"
STUART

GOLFING PIONEER
It was incredibly unusual for any woman to be involved in sports at the time, especially a queen, but that didn't deter her. Mary is considered the first woman to have ever played golf, and her legacy remains as the "Mother of Golf."

Mary Stuart in a French engraving by A. Celliez Lehuby, 1851

ELIZA POLLOCK
OLDEST FEMALE OLYMPIC MEDALLIST

FULL NAME: Lida Peyton "Eliza" Pollock
BORN: OCTOBER 24, 1840, HAMILTON, OHIO, U.S.A.
DIED: MAY 25, 1919, WYOMING, OHIO, U.S.A.
NATIONALITY: AMERICAN

GOLDEN ARCHER

Born in Hamilton, Ohio, Eliza Pollock was an American archer from the early 1900s. She competed for the U.S. team in the 1904 Olympic Games, wearing a long dress with a high collar, which was the style at the time. Eliza won two bronze medals, in the Women's Double and National Rounds, as well as a gold medal in the Team Round. Eliza is the oldest female Olympic medallist and the oldest female Olympic gold medallist—at 63 years and 33 days—in history. Her gold was in the team event; the oldest woman to win a solo Olympic gold medal was also in archery, in 1908. This accolade belongs to British woman Sybil "Queenie" Newall, who made history aged 53 years and 275 days.

Archer Eliza Pollock in 1907, ready to compete in her distinctive dress

The oldest woman ever to take part in the Olympic Games was Hilda Lorne Johnstone. Hilda competed in Equestrian Dressage at the 1972 Olympics, at the age of 70 years and 5 days. Overall, Hilda represented Great Britain in three separate Summer Olympic Games.

HILDA HEWLETT
AVIATION PIONEER AND ENTREPRENEUR

FULL NAME: Hilda Hewlett
BORN: FEBRUARY 17, 1864, LONDON, U.K.
DIED: AUGUST 21, 1943, TAURANGA, NEW ZEALAND
NATIONALITY: BRITISH

Hilda Hewlett, 1911

A WOMAN OF MANY SKILLS

Hilda Hewlett was one of nine siblings, but she certainly stood out among the crowd. From a young age, Hilda had a wide range of skills and interests, which helped create the well-rounded woman she would become. She studied at the National Art Training School, specializing in woodwork, metalwork, and needlework. Soon after, she spent a year training as a nurse. She was also an early motor car and bicycle enthusiast and took part in motor rallies as a driver and mechanic. All of this would serve Hilda well in her career to come—as a pilot and aviation entrepreneur.

PIONEER PILOT

In 1911, Hilda became the first woman in the U.K. to earn a pilot's license, after completing the test (in her own biplane) and gaining the nickname "Grace Bird." (She also taught her son Francis to fly, and he went on to have a distinguished military career—as well as being the first military pilot to have been taught to fly by his mother!) Hilda participated in a number of air shows and competitions, many of which she won. She co-founded and managed both one of Britain's first flying schools and an aircraft manufacturing business, producing ten different types of aircraft, including a number that the British used during World War I.

FLYING PRESIDENT

Hilda eventually moved to New Zealand with her family, where she became the first president of the Tauranga Aero and Gliding Club. Hilda was a real pioneer, both as the first British female pilot and thanks to her incredible contributions to aviation and airplane production.

"CHATTY" COOPER STERRY
FIRST FEMALE CHAMPION OF THE MODERN OLYMPIC GAMES

FULL NAME: Charlotte "Chatty" Cooper Sterry
BORN: SEPTEMBER 22, 1870, EALING, U.K.
DIED: October 10, 1966, HELENSBURGH, U.K.
NATIONALITY: BRITISH

In 1884, Wimbledon hosted its first ladies' competition. Chatty would go on to win this five times.

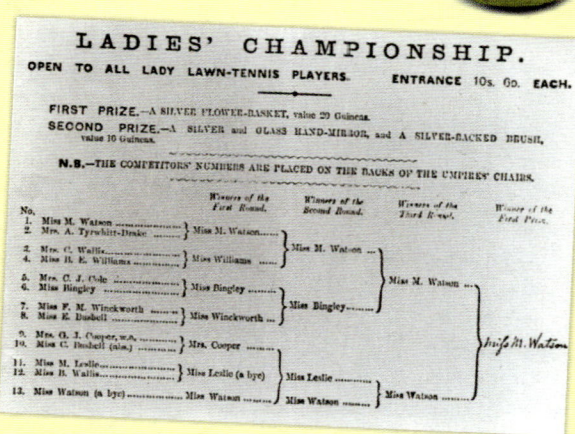

POWERFUL PLAYER IN A LONG DRESS

A five-time winner of the famous Wimbledon tennis tournament in England, Charlotte "Chatty" Cooper Sterry was an amazing tennis player. Chatty played in an ankle-length dress, which was standard attire for female players at the time. She was also deaf from the age of 26, but Chatty took this in her considerable stride. She had an offensive (attacking) style of play and excellent volleying skills, both of which were very rare for women of the day. Chatty was also one of the very first female players to serve overhand—now standard in both women's and men's tennis. She was known as an elegant but deceptively powerful athlete. At that time, tennis players did not play during the winter, so Chatty took up hockey in order to keep fit, and played for her local county of Surrey.

FABULOUS FIRSTS

FIRST FEMALE CHAMPION OF THE MODERN OLYMPIC GAMES

OLYMPIC GLORY

At the 1900 Summer Olympic Games in Paris, Chatty won the trophy (the equivalent of today's gold medal) in both the singles and doubles competitions. This made her the first female champion of the modern Olympic Games, following in the footsteps of Cynisca, over 2,000 years earlier. Chatty was inducted into the International Tennis Hall of Fame in 2013. At 37 years and 296 days old, Chatty is still Wimbledon's oldest-ever ladies' singles champion.

Around 1900, tennis players around the world dressed in long dresses for women and hats and ties for men. This photo shows one of the first tennis clubs in Canada, c. 1900.

JEANNE CALMENT
THE OLDEST PERSON IN HISTORY

FULL NAME: Jeanne Louise Calment

BORN: FEBRUARY 21, 1875, ARLES, FRANCE

DIED: AUGUST 4, 1997, ARLES, FRANCE

NATIONALITY: FRENCH

> " Always keep your smile.
> That's how I explain
> my long life. "
>
> JEANNE LOUISE CALMENT

FILM STAR AT 115

Imagine being born before there were cars. Or telephones. Or televisions. Or even moving-picture films. Now imagine you lived long enough to find yourself starring in such a film—at the age of 115! That is exactly what happened to Jeanne Calment. She was born in 1875 and survived to become the oldest woman in history, as well as the oldest verified living person ever, according to the *Guinness Book of World Records*. The incredible Jeanne lived to the unbelievable age of 122 years and 164 days.

44,694 DAYS YOUNG

Jeanne was born in Arles, France, where she lived for her entire life. She remembered meeting the world-renowned painter Vincent van Gogh, when he came into her uncle's art shop to buy canvasses for his paintings. She also recalled seeing the Eiffel Tower being built in 1889. At the age of 21, Jeanne married a wealthy store owner named Fernand. Jeanne did not work, and instead pursued a wide range of hobbies that kept her active, including tennis, hunting, cycling, swimming, piano, opera, and rollerskating.

Jeanne outlived her husband and daughter, and even her grandson. At the age of 85, Jeanne took up fencing and continued to ride her bike until her 100th birthday. She even smoked from the age of 21 to 117! In 1990, aged 115, Jeanne starred as herself in the movie *Vincent and Me*, becoming the oldest actress ever to appear in a film. In 1995, a movie was made of her life, called *Beyond 120 Years with Jeanne Calment*. She even featured on a 1996 album called *Time's Mistress*, in which Jeanne was recorded speaking over a backing of rap music.

Jeanne Calment is the oldest actress ever to appear in a movie, at the age of 115!

The Eiffel Tower in Paris, France, was built in 1889.

CHOCOLATE: THE KEY TO A LONG LIFE?

Jeanne Calment said her long life and "youthful" appearance were the result of a diet of olive oil, port wine, and two pounds of chocolate every week, as well as her calm nature. "That's why they call me Calment," she would say. Jeanne's birth date and long life have been well documented. Since she died, there have been several claims of people being even older, but not a single one has been proven. Jeanne Calment remains the oldest living person in history, male or female, and she lived her life full of humor and joy until the very end.

AMELIA EARHART
PIONEER OF AVIATION

FULL NAME: Amelia Earhart
BORN: July 24, 1897, ATCHISON, KANSAS, U.S.A.
DISAPPEARED: 1937
NATIONALITY: AMERICAN

> *Women must try to do things as men have tried. When they fail, their failure must be but a challenge to others.*

AMELIA EARHART

PIONEER OF AVIATION

Amelia Earhart accomplished many great aviation achievements in her short life. Born in Kansas, Amelia had an unconventional upbringing, as her mother did not want to mold "boring but nice" little girls. She and her sister had a good deal of freedom, and Amelia was described at the time as a "tomboy." At the age of seven, she had her first experience of "flying." Amelia modeled a ramp after a rollercoaster she had seen and ran a sled down it at great speed, exclaiming that it was "just like flying!" Beginning in childhood, Amelia kept a scrapbook of possible career options, mostly focusing on women in "men's jobs."

FROM LESSONS TO LICENSE

Amelia trained in nursing and enroled in medical studies at Columbia University. At the age of 23, she caught the pilot bug when she paid $10 to be flown a few hundred feet up in the air at an airbase. She dropped out of Columbia and worked odd jobs to save up for flying lessons. Six months later, she bought her first plane, which she named "The Canary." In 1923, aged 26, Amelia became the 16th woman in the entire world to earn a pilot's license. She was the first female pilot to fly solo and nonstop across the Atlantic Ocean, in 1932, and

FABULOUS FIRSTS

⭑ FIRST WOMAN TO FLY SOLO, NONSTOP, ACROSS THE ATLANTIC

⭑ FIRST PERSON TO FLY OVER BOTH THE ATLANTIC AND PACIFIC OCEANS

Atlantic Ocean

Amelia with her Lockheed Electra, in which she made her final flight

she was also the first person to fly over both the Atlantic and Pacific oceans. She hoped to inspire other women in their passion for flying, and she became a faculty member at Purdue University aviation department, teaching other women about careers in aviation. Amelia was also an early supporter of the Equal Rights Amendment.

UNEXPLAINED DISAPPEARANCE

In 1937, Amelia was attempting to make the first-ever, around-the-equator, circumnavigational flight of the globe. She disappeared on July 2, 1937, over the Pacific Ocean, near Howland Island. Many searches have been conducted over the years, but her body and that of her co-pilot, Fred Noonan, have never been found. There are several theories about her disappearance, from the technical—faulty navigation and communication systems—to the downright bizarre—claims she faked her own death to start a new life as a banker. Uncommonly, Amelia was famous in her own lifetime, and she remains a feminist icon of independence to this day. She inspired a generation of aviators, both male and female, and taught the important lesson that a person can achieve anything with enough determination.

Pilot Amelia Earhart, pictured in 1936

HAMMOND

AMY JOHNSON
PIONEER OF AVIATION AND LONG-DISTANCE RECORDS

FULL NAME: Amy Johnson
BORN: JULY 1, 1903, HULL, U.K.
DISAPPEARED: JANUARY 4, 1941
NATIONALITY: BRITISH

> 66 *I believe I can do anything. If I decide I want to be a doctor tomorrow, I'm going to be a doctor.* 99
>
> AMY JOHNSON

BREAKING RECORD AFTER RECORD

While Amelia Earhart may be the most famous American aviatrix (or female pilot), Amy Johnson remains the most famous British pilot and aviation pioneer of all time.

From a young age, Amy had amazing support from her parents. She graduated from college with a Bachelor of Arts degree in economics—a rare achievement for women of the time. Amy worked in a lawyer's office before taking up flying as a hobby, and then changed course to focus her energy on aviation. At the age of 26, she earned her pilot's license and, later the same year, became the first woman in the world to obtain a ground engineer's license (the airplane equivalent of a car mechanic). This meant Amy was able to both fly and fix her own planes, giving her a lot of freedom to pursue the endurance records that lay in her future. Amy's parents helped her buy her first aircraft, which she named "Jason." Jason and Amy received worldwide recognition in 1930, when she became the first female pilot to fly solo from England to Australia—an incredible feat even today. She returned home to a hero's welcome. The next year, Amy and co-pilot Jack Humphreys became the first pilots to fly from London to Moscow in one day, followed by records set for a flight from Britain to Japan.

In 1932, Amy set yet another solo record, when she flew from London to South Africa, breaking the record previously set by her new husband, Jim Mollison. Jim and Amy co-piloted a number of record-breaking flights during their brief marriage, including one from Britain to India. In May of 1936, Amy made her final record-breaking flight, regaining her Britain-to-South Africa record.

WARTIME SERVICE AND DISAPPEARANCE

During World War II, Amy joined the newly formed Air Transport Artillery (ATA). Her job was to transport Royal Air Force aircraft around the country. Amy rose through the military ranks to First Officer. In 1941, she went on an assignment for the Air Force. Flying in terrible weather conditions, Amy's plane went off-course and ran out of fuel. She parachuted into the sea, but due to poor conditions and a strong sea current, Amy could not be rescued. Her body has never been recovered. Mystery continues to surround Amy's death, and the reasons behind her final flight remain a well-kept secret of the British government. Rumors abound: was she mistaken for a German bomber and shot down by "friendly" fire, or was she on an ill-fated, top-secret government mission?

I BELIEVE I CAN DO ANYTHING

Amy Johnson remains Britain's most famous female aviator of all time. In addition to her impressive determination and skill in flying, she had incredible courage and stamina, setting numerous long-distance records and rising to brave challenges throughout her short life. Amy continues to inspire pilots and record-breakers to this day.

Record-breaking pilot Amy Johnson

London

Darwin

INCREDIBLE ACHIEVEMENTS

 FIRST FEMALE AVIATOR TO GAIN A GROUND ENGINEER'S LICENSE

 FIRST FEMALE PILOT TO FLY SOLO FROM ENGLAND TO AUSTRALIA

 SET SOLO RECORDS FOR SOLO FLIGHTS FROM LONDON TO SOUTH AFRICA

WITH CO-PILOT JACK HUMPHREYS, FIRST TO FLY FROM LONDON TO MOSCOW IN ONE DAY

Amy was the first female pilot to fly solo from England to Australia, in 1930.

MILDRED "BABE" ZAHARIAS
ALL-ROUND GREATEST ATHLETE

FULL NAME: Mildred Ella "Babe" Didrikson Zaharias
BORN: JUNE 26, 1911, PORT ARTHUR, TEXAS, U.S.A.
Died: September 27, 1956, GALVESTON, TEXAS, U.S.A.
NATIONALITY: AMERICAN

ALL-AROUND ATHLETIC ACE

In a single childhood baseball game, Mildred hit five homeruns—and earned herself the lifetime nickname of "Babe" (after the baseball legend Babe Ruth). It was a sure sign of things to come. At 15, Babe was the high-scoring forward on her school's basketball team. She was talent-scouted for the Golden Cyclones, and then she quickly became their star player. For two years, she was the All-American basketball forward.

From there, her interest—and talent—soon turned to track and field. At the 1931 National Event, she won first place in eight events. Naturally, Babe was quickly spotted for a place at the 1932 Olympics. Babe broke four world records and won two golds and a silver. She won the javelin throw and the 80-meter hurdles, twice breaking the world record, and made a world record high jump (later disqualified on technique). Babe pitched a game for the St. Louis' Cardinals baseball team, with one of her impressive pitches spanning an incredible 300 feet.

One of Babe's baseball pitches measured over 300 feet!

FROM OLYMPIAN TO STAR GOLFER

Around the time of the 1932 Olympics, Babe took up golf—the sport for which she'd ultimately become famous. In 1947, she became the first American woman to win the British Ladies' Amateur Championship. One spectator is rumored to have whispered of Babe, "She must be Superman's sister." Babe is considered the greatest female golfer of all time: her amateur and professional victories come to a total of 82. Babe was the first woman to compete in a men's Professional Golf Association (PGA) tournament, in 1938. There would not be another to do so for 60 years. She was also a founding member of the Ladies' Professional Golf Association. By 1950, Babe had won every golf title available.

U.S. stamp, circa 1981, celebrating Babe Zaharias

AMAZING ATHLETE

Voted the second greatest female athlete of the 20th century by *Sports Illustrated,* and the tenth greatest by ESPN, Babe was also named "Woman Athlete of the Half Century" by the *Associated Press* in 1950. In 1951, she was inducted into the World Golf Hall of Fame. While Babe was very skilled at sports—and just about everything she tried—she also worked hard and practiced tirelessly. And for that, fans adored her.

In addition to her achievements in golf, basketball, and track and field, Babe was also a professional harmonica player and competitive seamstress, making many of her professional golfing outfits. At the time of her death, she was still the top-ranked female golfer.

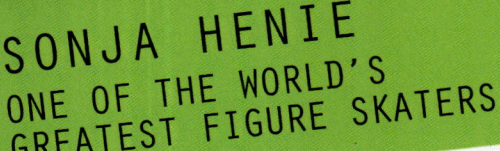

SONJA HENIE
ONE OF THE WORLD'S GREATEST FIGURE SKATERS

FULL NAME: Sonja Henie
BORN: APRIL 8, 1912, OSLO, NORWAY
DIED: OCTOBER 12, 1969, ON THE WAY HOME TO OSLO, NORWAY
NATIONALITY: NORWEGIAN, LATER AMERICAN

LITTLE ICE PRINCESS

As a very little girl, Sonja was studying to be a ballerina. But at the age of only six, she discovered her life calling: ice skating. Her brother helped her learn, and at the age of just ten, Sonja won the Norwegian Championship. Only a year later, she made her Olympic debut at the first Winter Games, in Chamonix, France, in 1924. At 14 years old, she won her first World Figure Skating Championship (which she would go on to win ten years in a row). The following year, Sonja entered the Winter Olympics again—winning her first gold medal at the age of 15.

Nicknamed the "Ice Queen of Norway" and the "White Swan," Sonja the child star quickly became adored worldwide. She would win two more gold medals, in 1932 and 1936, as

FIRST INTERNATIONAL ATHLETE-ACTRESS-SUPERSTAR OF MODERN TIMES

SINGLEHANDEDLY PUT FIGURE SKATING ON THE MAP

well as six European Championships. Sonja became known for her talent, looks, tricks, dancer's grace—and her pure-white skates, the color of Norwegian snow. Sonja won more Olympic and World titles than any other ladies' figure skater before she retired from competition in 1936. She was voted the fourth greatest female athlete of the 20th century by *Sport Illustrated*.

FROM WHITE SWAN TO SILVER SCREEN STAR

The same year, Sonja moved to America, to bring skating to Hollywood. Her film debut was a musical, *One in a Million* (1936), followed by *Thin Ice, Happy Landing,* and *Sun Valley Serenade*. Alongside her film career, Sonja also had a world-touring show called the *Hollywood Ice Revue*. At the height of her acting career, she is believed to have been one of the highest-paid stars in Hollywood.

Sonja Henie is remembered today as one of the greatest figure-skaters in history and an early superstar of both ice and screen. According to *Vanity Fair*, she was the first international "athlete-actress-superstar" of modern times. Through her talent and charisma, Sonja Henie truly put figure skating on the map.

Sonja brought figure skating to the silver screen of Hollywood.

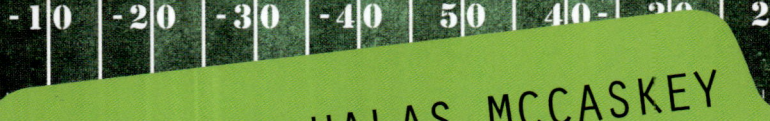

VIRGINIA HALAS MCCASKEY
"FIRST LADY" OF AMERICAN FOOTBALL

FULL NAME: Virginia Halas McCaskey
BORN: JANUARY 5, 1923, CHICAGO, ILLINOIS, U.S.A.
NATIONALITY: AMERICAN

Logo of the National Football League, the NFL

WOMEN IN AVIATION

The Chicago Bears remain one of the most internationally recognized teams in the National Football League (NFL). Created by George Halas, the Bears' team was a founding member of the NFL in 1920.

The NFL now makes more money than any other professional sports league in the world. When George Halas died, in 1983, he left his beloved Bears to his oldest child, Virginia Halas McCaskey. Virginia is the principal owner of the team (owning 80 percent), and she is believed to be worth $1.3 billion. Her nickname is the "Matriarch of the Bears." She is the oldest team owner in the NFL, at the age of 93. For most of her 30-year ownership, Virginia has held a strong but silent role. In 2009, Virginia was named by *Forbes* magazine as one of the most powerful women in sports.

Chicago Soldiers' Field in 2012: the oldest NFL stadium and home of the Chicago Bears since 1971

WOMEN IN AVIATION

History has seen some remarkable women take to the skies. Amelia Earhart and Amy Johnson set incredible transcontinental distance records on solo and duo flights in the 1930s and 1940s. Hilda Hewlett was a pioneer of aviation and plane-building in the early 20th century. The Night Witches flew death-defying missions during World War II against unimaginable odds. And in 1963, Russian Valentina Tereshkova became the first-ever civilian to fly in space. These amazing aviatrixes have inspired generations of women and men to take to Earth's skies—and beyond!

CLOCKWISE FROM TOP LEFT: HILDA HEWLETT, VALENTINA TERESHKOVA, AMY JOHNSON, *NACHTHEXEN* "NIGHT WITCHES," AND AMELIA EARHART

VALENTINA TERESHKOVA
FIRST WOMAN AND FIRST CIVILIAN EVER TO FLY IN SPACE

FULL NAME: Valentina Vladimirovna Tereshkova
BORN: MARCH 6, 1937, MASLENNIKOVO, RUSSIA
NATIONALITY: RUSSIAN

Collectable coin to celebrate 20 years of Russian space travel

Front page of "Moscovskaya Pravda" Soviet newspaper on June 17, 1963

CORRESPONDENCE COSMONAUT

Valentina Tereshkova was born in 1937 in a small rural town in Russia. She only attended classes for a small part of her schooling, and most of her education was done through correspondence courses. At a young age, she became fascinated by the idea of parachuting. She eventually trained as an amateur skydiver, and at 22, made her first jump. Two years later, Valentina discovered her other passion and became the secretary of the *Komsomol* (Young Communist League) and later joined the Communist Party.

CIVILIAN PIONEER

At the age of 25, Valentina's skydiving expertise led to her selection for the female cosmonaut corps. To be chosen, candidates had to be expert parachutists, under the age of 30, less than 5 feet, 7 inches tall, and weigh less than 154 pounds. She was selected from more than 400 applicants and five finalists to pilot the spacecraft *Vostok 6*. On June 16, 1963, Valentina took off on her solo mission. With this achievement, she became the first woman to fly in space. As an honorary member of the Soviet Air Force, she was also the first civilian to do so.

INSIDE *VOSTOK 6*

Valentina orbited Earth 48 times and spent three days in space. All on her own in the spacecraft, she made notes of her observations and photographed the horizon. With this single flight, she managed to log more time in space than the combined total of all (male)

FABULOUS FIRSTS

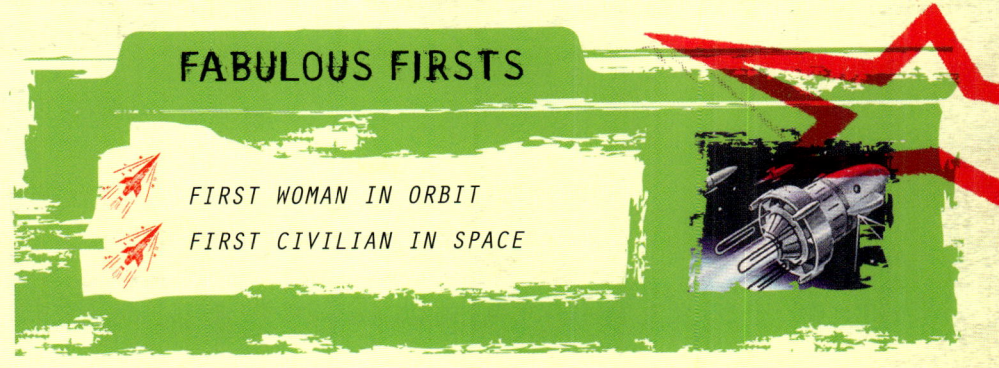

FIRST WOMAN IN ORBIT

FIRST CIVILIAN IN SPACE

American astronauts before her. After Valentina's flight, it would be another 19 years before a woman would take to orbit. In the Soviet Union itself, the female cosmonaut group was closed down in 1969.

POST-SOVIET AMBASSADOR

Soon, Valentina swapped her space suit for a business suit and became both an engineer and a well-respected politician. She studied at the Zhukovsky Air Force Academy and became a cosmonaut engineer with a PhD in engineering. She remains a hero in post-Soviet Russia and was honored as a flag-carrier at the 2014 Winter Olympics. She has been respected as an ambassador to the Soviet Union abroad and was a member of the World Peace Council. Valentina has been awarded an incredible number of medals and honors in her lifetime, including the Hero of the Soviet Union medal (Russia's highest medal of honor), the United Nations Medal of Peace, and the Simba International Women's Movement Award.

A LIVING LEGEND

Valentina is considered one of the Soviet Union's three top cosmonauts of all time, alongside Yuri Gagarin and Alexey Leonov. The Moon's *Tereshkova Crater* was named after her. Despite now being in her 70s, Valentina has offered to fly on a one-way trip to Mars, should the opportunity ever arise.

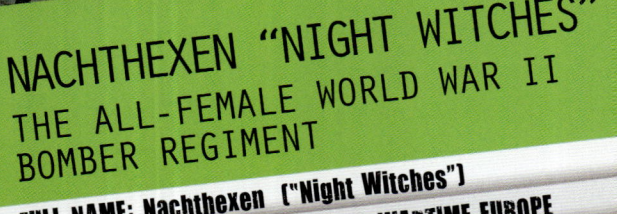

NACHTHEXEN "NIGHT WITCHES"
THE ALL-FEMALE WORLD WAR II BOMBER REGIMENT

FULL NAME: Nachthexen ("Night Witches")

ACTIVE: 1942–1944, THROUGHOUT WARTIME EUROPE

NATIONALITY: SOVIET

A FORMIDABLE FEMALE FORCE

"Night Witches," or *Nachthexen*, was the German nickname for the aviators from the all-female, 588th Soviet Night Bomber Regiment. The pilots saw the name as a badge of honor. The regiment flew bombing missions for the Soviet Air Force against the German military during World War II. These women trained not only as pilots and navigators, but also as engineers. At its largest, the group had 40 two-person crews, flying over 30,000 missions and dropping 23,000 tons of bombs. Each pilot flew more than 800 missions, often carrying out eight per night. The Night Witches were unique among the female combatants of World War II. Other countries permitted a small number of women to fly planes, but their roles were limited to support and transportation. The Soviet Union was the first country to allow women to fly combat missions. The 588th Regiment was the most highly decorated female unit in the Soviet Air Force.

INCREDIBLE SKILL

The Night Witches flew biplanes made of wood and canvas that were originally built for training and crop-dusting. This made them very light, so they were easy to maneuver. But they were also very slow and could only carry six bombs at a time. Because of the weight of the bombs and the low altitude at which they flew, the planes did not carry parachutes. Their courageous female pilots had limited technology and planes that could easily catch fire. They flew in the dark and had no radar, only maps and compasses. The planes also had open cockpits, so the pilots would get extremely cold and often suffered numbness and frostbite. They might return from a mission with their plane, map—and even their helmet —studded with bullet holes.

FABULOUS FIRSTS

 FIRST FEMALE PILOTS TO FLY COMBAT MISSIONS

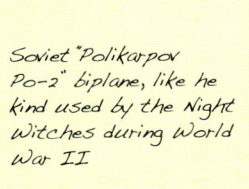

Soviet "Polikarpov Po-2" biplane, like the kind used by the Night Witches during World War II

Close-up of a Russian stamp showing Marina Raskova, a pilot and commander of the Night Witches regiment

The maximum speed of the biplanes was slower than the "stall" speed of German aircraft, so the Night Witches used an attack method of idling the engines and gliding before dropping a bomb. This "stealth" mode left only the whooshing sound of the wind to give away their location. German fighters came up with the nickname of "Night Witches" because the sound of the wind against the biplanes sounded like flying broomsticks. German fighters in their highly advanced aircraft feared the Night Witches because of their bravery and stealth. The legacy of these women was mostly kept secret outside of the Soviet Union until recently, when their incredible accomplishments have finally come to light.

BILLIE JEAN KING
SOCIAL ACTIVIST AND ONE OF THE GREATEST TENNIS PLAYERS OF ALL TIME

FULL NAME: Billie Jean King
BORN: NOVEMBER 22, 1943, LONG BEACH, CALIFORNIA, U.S.A.
NATIONALITY: AMERICAN

ON-COURT CHAMPION

Billie Jean King became interested in tennis at a young age. Growing up in California, she learned to play on the public courts around her neighborhood. At the age of 15, Billie had her Grand Slam debut at the U.S. Open Championships.

One of the greatest-ever tennis players, Billie Jean King started out training on neighborhood tennis courts.

Plaque at U.S. Open Court of Champions at the Billie Jean King National Tennis Center, celebrating her amazing wins, 2013

During her professional tennis career, Billie was ranked world number one for several years. She won 39 Grand Slam titles, including 12 singles, 16 women's doubles, and 11 mixed doubles titles. Billie has been ranked the number-three greatest female athlete of the 20th century by *Sports Illustrated,* and by *Marie Claire* as one of the eight greatest women in sports history. In 1972, she became the first tennis player—and first woman—to receive the *Sports Illustrated* Sportsman of the Year (now "Sportsperson of the Year") Award.

BATTLE OF THE SEXES

In 1973, Billie Jean King took on the challenge known as the "Battle of the Sexes" against Bobby Riggs. Riggs felt that women's tennis was so inferior to men's that, even at 55 years old, he could beat the top female players. Billie took on the challenge and beat Riggs. It was a landmark match that immediately increased respect for women's tennis. She went on to campaign for equal recognition and equal prize money for men's and women's tennis. She is also the founder and first president of the Women's Tennis Association, World TeamTennis, and the Women's Sports Foundation. Billie was inducted into the International Tennis Hall of Fame in 1987.

International Tennis Hall of Fame, Newport, Rhode Island, U.S.A.

A COURAGEOUS CHAMPION OFF-COURT

In 1981, Billie came out as a lesbian. This made her the first prominent female athlete to do so, which took a lot of courage. She has since become an advocate for lesbian, gay, bisexual, and transgender rights and a champion of social justice and equality. Billie has been named one of the "100 most important Americans of the 20th century" by *Life* magazine. In 1999, she was awarded the Arthur Ashe Courage Award for her activism, an award presented annually to individuals whose contributions transcend sports. Billie was also the first female athlete to be awarded the Presidential Medal of Freedom by U.S. President Barack Obama. Recently, she was appointed the Global Mentor for Gender Equality by UNESCO. Billie continues to work tirelessly towards greater equality for all, both in and out of sports.

FABULOUS FIRSTS

- FIRST FEMALE ATHLETE TO BE AWARDED THE PRESIDENTIAL MEDAL OF FREEDOM
- FIRST TENNIS PLAYER TO BE NAMED SPORTS ILLUSTRATED'S SPORTSPERSON OF THE YEAR
- FIRST PROMINENT FEMALE ATHLETE TO COME OUT AS A LESBIAN
- FIRST AND ONLY WOMAN TO WIN 20 WIMBLEDON TENNIS TITLES

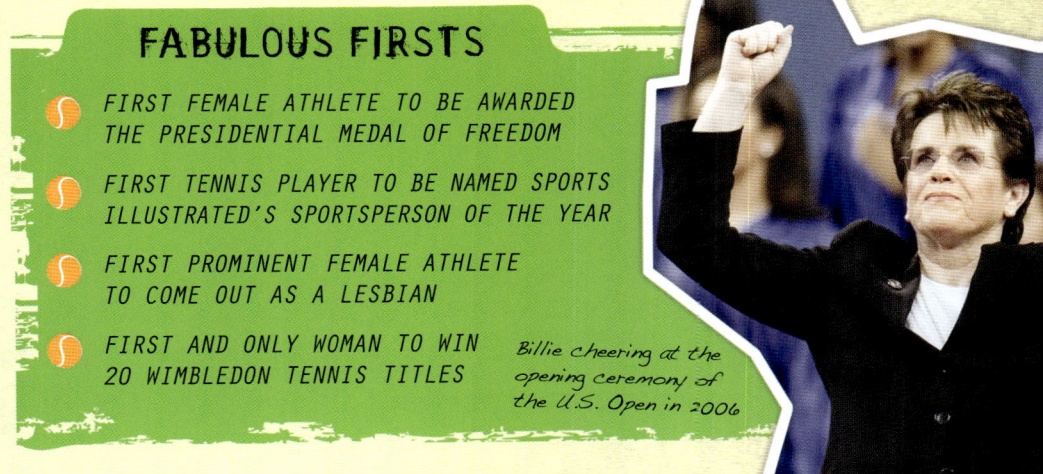

Billie cheering at the opening ceremony of the U.S. Open in 2006

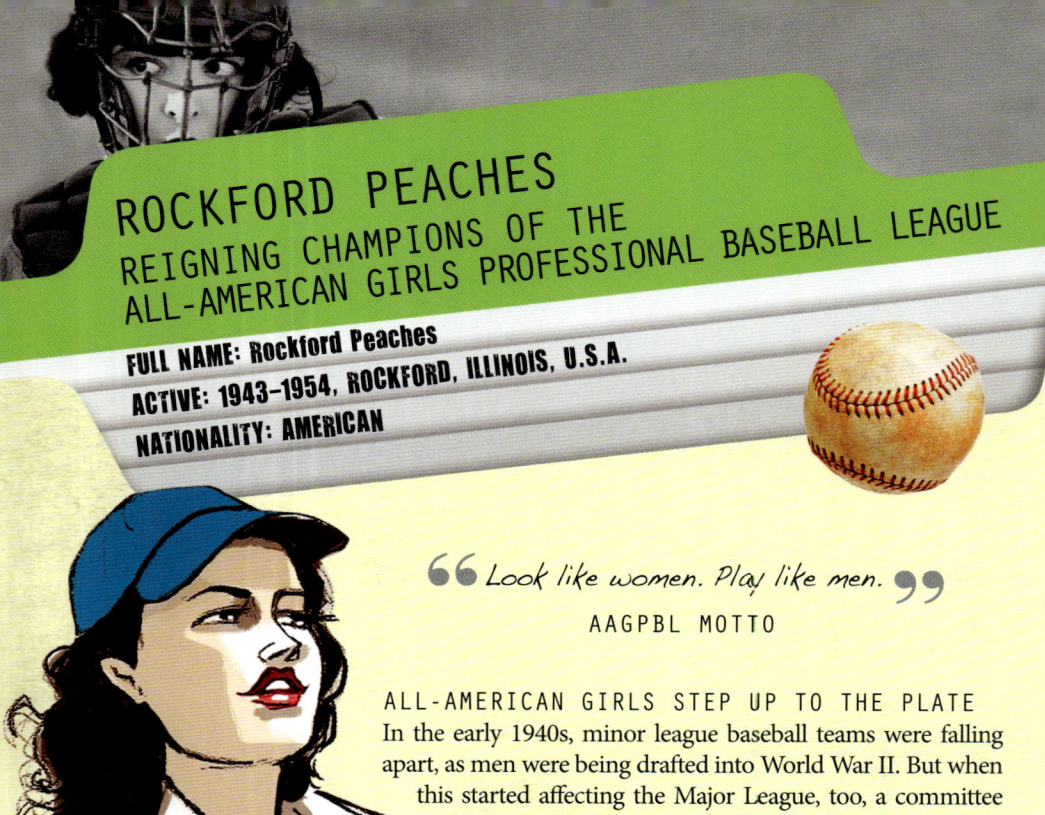

ROCKFORD PEACHES
REIGNING CHAMPIONS OF THE ALL-AMERICAN GIRLS PROFESSIONAL BASEBALL LEAGUE

FULL NAME: Rockford Peaches
ACTIVE: 1943–1954, ROCKFORD, ILLINOIS, U.S.A.
NATIONALITY: AMERICAN

> *Look like women. Play like men.*
> AAGPBL MOTTO

ALL-AMERICAN GIRLS STEP UP TO THE PLATE

In the early 1940s, minor league baseball teams were falling apart, as men were being drafted into World War II. But when this started affecting the Major League, too, a committee of businessmen knew they had to do something to keep fans in the bleachers. So in the spring of 1943, the All-American Girls Baseball League (AAGPBL) was born. The League ran only from 1943 to 1954, but during that time it gave 600 female athletes an unexpected sporting opportunity.

RULES OF THE GAME

The rules of the game were a cross between men's baseball and women's softball—but the women's league had one extra rule: femininity. After daily practices, players were required to attend "charm" classes. They also had to keep their hair long and uniform skirts short, and to wear make-up. Team numbers were small, which meant players often had to play with serious injuries, and because their legs were bare from wearing skirts, they had constant cuts and bruises from sliding into base. The league had one simple rule: "Look like women. Play like men."

Yankee Stadium: the Rockford Peaches were nicknamed the "New York Yankees of the All-American League."

A TEAM OF STARS

The Rockford Peaches, based in Rockford, Illinois, were one of four original teams in the AAGPBL—and one of only two who played for all 12 years of the league's existence. The team was nicknamed the "New York Yankees of the All-American League" by its first base"man," Dorothy "Kammie" Kamenshek, who was considered the best female baseball player of all time. The Peaches also included stellar batter and third base"man" Millie Warwick, one of the most feared batters in women's baseball history. Another star player was pitcher Olive Bend Little. Olive pitched the first-ever women's professional no-hitter; in all, she pitched four no-hitter games. The Rockford Peaches won the most play-offs of the entire AAGPBL's existence, winning in 1945, 1948, 1949, and 1950.

A LEAGUE OF THEIR OWN

The players worked hard, and the fans loved them. However, when the war ended, the focus moved back to men's sports and sadly the league was disbanded, soon to be forgotten. Decades passed before its players and teams finally got the recognition they deserved. In the 1980s, several female players were inducted into the National Women's Baseball Hall of Fame. In 1992, the story of the AAGPBL was made into a feature film called *A League of Their Own*, starring Geena Davis, Madonna, and Rosie O'Donnell.

PAT SUMMITT
MORE WINS THAN ANY OTHER COACH IN THE HISTORY OF COLLEGE SPORT

FULL NAME: Pat Head Summitt
BORN: JUNE 14, 1952, CLARKSVILLE, TENNESSEE, U.S.A.
NATIONALITY: AMERICAN

Pat Head Summit is given the Presidential Medal of Freedom by U.S. President Barack Obama.

BASKETBALL COACH OF THE CENTURY

Pat Summitt was the head coach of the University of Tennessee "Lady Volunteer" (women's) Basketball Team from 1974 to 2012. After 38 seasons in the role, she has more wins than any other coach in NCAA history, including both men's and women's teams. Not only was Pat an incredible coach, she also raised the profile of women's college basketball. Pat led her team to eight NCAA Championship victories and 32 combined Southeastern Conference titles. In 2000, she was named the Naismith Basketball Coach of the Century, and the *Sporting News* named her one of the 50 greatest coaches of all time. She is the only woman on the entire list.

"WE BACK PAT!"

In 2011, Pat bravely revealed that she has early onset dementia, of the Alzheimer's type. In spite of this news, she continued to be active in the 2011–12 basketball season. So loved is Pat Summitt that as soon as she revealed her illness, the "We Back Pat" campaign went viral, raising funds for and awareness of Alzheimer's. Pat retired from coaching in 2012, and on retirement was given the lifelong title of Women's Basketball Head Coach Emeritus. In addition to her phenomenal record as a coach, Pat has been given a number of awards for her courage and activism relating to Alzheimer's. *The Huffington Post* made Pat a 2011 Game Changer, and in 2012 she was awarded the Arthur Ashe Courage Award, while U.S. President Barack Obama awarded her the Presidential Medal of Freedom. In 2013, Pat was inducted into the International Basketball Federation (FIBA) Hall of Fame for her incredible contributions to basketball.

FABULOUS FIRSTS

COACH WITH THE MOST WINS EVER IN THE HISTORY OF COLLEGE SPORT

WOMEN IN TENNIS

From winning multiple Grand Slams and Olympic medals to fighting for equal pay—and from championing human rights to encouraging para-sports—these tennis superstars really are the queens of the court. Each and every one has had a profound and lasting influence on the sport of tennis and prompted generations of girls and boys to overcome their own individual obstacles and to pursue their sporting dreams.

CLOCKWISE FROM TOP LEFT:
MARTINA NAVRATILOVA, SERENA
WILLIAMS, BILLIE JEAN KING,
ESTHER VERGEER, AND VENUS
AND SERENA WILLIAMS

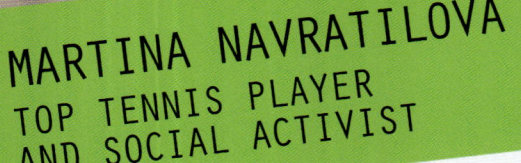

MARTINA NAVRATILOVA
TOP TENNIS PLAYER
AND SOCIAL ACTIVIST

FULL NAME: Martina Navratilova

BORN: OCTOBER 18, 1956, PRAGUE, CZECHOSLOVAKIA (NOW THE CZECH REPUBLIC)

NATIONALITY: CZECH, LATER AMERICAN

A FAMILY OF CHAMPIONS

Martina Navratilova came from a family of incredible tennis players: Martina's mother was an accomplished tennis player and gymnast, and her grandmother ranked as the number-two female tennis player in Czechoslovakia. Martina started playing the sport at the age of four, and at seven, she took up the sport seriously. In 1972, at the age of 15, Martina won the Czechoslovakia National Tennis Championship.

NEW HOME: NEW OPPORTUNITIES

Young Martina believed that staying in her home country of Czechoslovakia, under Soviet control, would limit her professional chances. So in 1975, at the age of 18, Martina defected to the United States. That choice cut her off from her family for several years—but it also opened up a range of opportunities. That same year, she turned professional. Martina won her first major singles title at Wimbledon, in 1978, against Chris Evert.

Grand Slam champion Martina Navratilova during a women's champions doubles' match at the 2014 U.S. Open

Martina is known for her aggressive playing style and for her extensive training techniques, in the gym and on the basketball court. Tennis legend Billie Jean King has described Martina as the "greatest singles, doubles, and mixed doubles player who's ever lived." She was the world number one for 332 weeks in singles, and a record 237 weeks in doubles. This makes her the only tennis player in history to have held the top spot in both singles and doubles for over 200 weeks. She is considered the greatest female tennis player for the years 1965 to 2005—longer than most athletes' entire careers. She retired, as a Grand Slam champion, at the age of 49.

CARING CAMPAIGNER

In 1981, Martina was accidentally "outed" as gay. Since then, she has been an outspoken advocate for gay rights, and in 2000 she received the National Equality Award from the Human Rights Campaign. An advocate and social campaigner, Martina is a vegetarian and cares passionately about animal rights. She also campaigns for freedom of speech and greater opportunities for young people, both on and off the court.

AMAZING ACHIEVEMENTS

- FIRST (AND ONLY) TENNIS PLAYER TO BE RANKED WORLD NUMBER ONE IN SINGLES AND DOUBLES FOR OVER 200 WEEKS
- CONSIDERED TO BE THE GREATEST FEMALE TENNIS PLAYER

Martina Navratilova in 2015

NANCY LIEBERMAN
FIRST WOMAN TO PLAY IN AND COACH PROFESSIONAL MEN'S BASKETBALL

FULL NAME: Nancy Lieberman
BORN: JULY 1, 1958, BROOKLYN, NEW YORK, U.S.A.
NATIONALITY: AMERICAN

Logo of the Women's
National Basketball
Association, the WNBA

THAT'S "LADY MAGIC" TO YOU

Nicknamed "Lady Magic," Nancy Lieberman is regarded as one of the greatest figures in women's basketball and a pioneer in women's sports. Young Nancy played basketball with the boys; she didn't play on a girls' team until she was a high-school sophomore. While still in high school, she was picked to play for the U.S.A's National Team. She played in the World Championships and Pan-American Games, where she won a gold medal. She was three years younger than her next-youngest teammate. In 1976, Nancy was part of the first-ever Women's Olympic Basketball Team. They won a team silver, and Nancy became the youngest Olympic basketball player to win a medal. She played college basketball for Old Dominion University, where she was a two-time National Player of the Year—all on a full scholarship.

Basketball star
Nancy Lieberman

A LONG AND DISTINGUISHED CAREER

During her career, Nancy played for several teams and leagues, including the Dallas Diamonds (in the Women's Pro Basketball League). In the men's leagues, she played for Springfield Fame and the Long Island Knights (in the United States Basketball League) and for the Washington Generals. In 1986, she became the only woman in history to play on a professional men's team. When the Women's National Basketball Association (WNBA) was formed in 1997, Nancy played for the Phoenix Mercury. At the age of 39, she was the oldest WNBA player of all time. In 2008, she broke her own record, playing one game for the Detroit Shock at the age of 50.

COACH AND LEADER

In addition to being a respected player and TV broadcaster, Nancy was a head coach for the Detroit Shock, as well as the coach of the Texas Legends. This made her the first woman to coach a professional men's basketball team, in 2009.

Nancy was inducted into the Naismith Memorial Basketball Hall of Fame in 1996 and the Women's Basketball Hall of Fame in 1999. In addition, Nancy is the first woman to be inducted into the New York City Basketball Hall of Fame. In 2015, she received the WBCNL Women's Professional Basketball "Trailblazer" Award. She has also set up a series of charities working with children to realize their dreams through sport and education. Nancy is currently the assistant coach for the Sacramento Kings— only the second woman in history to join the coaching staff of an NBA team.

AMAZING ACHIEVEMENTS

- 🏀 PLAYED IN THE FIRST-EVER U.S. OLYMPIC WOMEN'S BASKETBALL TEAM
- 🏀 FIRST WOMAN TO PLAY IN AND COACH PROFESSIONAL MEN'S BASKETBALL
- 🏀 OLDEST WNBA PLAYER IN HISTORY
- 🏀 FIRST WOMAN TO BE INDUCTED INTO THE NEW YORK CITY BASKETBALL HALL OF FAME

LYNETTE WOODARD
FIRST FEMALE MEMBER OF THE HARLEM GLOBETROTTERS

FULL NAME: Lynette Woodard
BORN: AUGUST 12, 1959, WICHITA, KANSAS, U.S.A.
NATIONALITY: AMERICAN

Globe, the Harlem Globetrotters' mascot, performs for the crowds before a game in Sacramento, California, in 2012.

FROM FAMILY GAMES TO THE HARLEM GLOBETROTTERS

Lynette Woodard's impressive sporting history spans the globe. Rumor has it she learned to score by shooting with a stuffed sock and playing with her brother and her cousin (who would later go on to join the Harlem Globetrotters). During her four college basketball years with the University of Kansas, she scored an amazing total of 3,649 points. Immediately after college, Lynette was signed to an Italian team, UFO Schio (Vicenza). She then captained Team U.S.A. at the 1984 Los Angeles Olympic Games, where her team won gold. Lynette also won medals in a number of World Cups and Pan-American Games.

In 1985, she made history when she became the first woman in history to play for the Harlem Globetrotters. The tryouts were tough, but Lynette proved her incredible ability, sharing equal court time with the male players for the next two years. Next, she moved to Japan to play for a league there. In 1997, she returned to the U.S.A. and competed in the newly founded Women's National Basketball Association (WNBA) for the Cleveland Rockers, before switching to the Detroit Shock the following year. In 1999, Lynette retired from playing and moved into coaching, returning to the University of Kansas.

FABULOUS FIRSTS

- FIRST WOMAN TO PLAY FOR THE HARLEM GLOBETROTTERS
- INDUCTEE INTO TEN DIFFERENT HALLS OF FAME

SLAM DUNK!

TEN-TIME HALL OF FAMER

Overall, Lynette has been inducted into ten different halls of fame, including the Naismith Memorial Basketball Hall of Fame (2002), the Women's Basketball Hall of fame (2005), and the African-American Sports Hall of Fame (2006). She was awarded the Harlem Globetrotters "Legends" award in 1996. In 2015, Lynette received the WBCNL Women's Professional Basketball "Trailblazer" Award. The award recognizes influential people in the world of women's basketball, helping to inspire a younger generation of female athletes and coaches.

In 1985, Lynette made history (and achieved her childhood dream) when she became the first female Harlem Globetrotter. The Globetrotters earned their Hollywood Walk of Fame star in 2015.

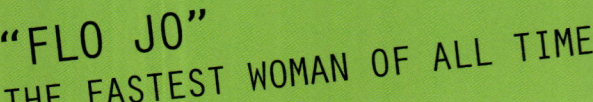

"FLO JO"
THE FASTEST WOMAN OF ALL TIME

FULL NAME: Florence "Flo Jo" Griffith Joyner
BORN: DECEMBER 21, 1959, LOS ANGELES, CALIFORNIA, U.S.A.
Died: September 21, 1998, MISSION VIEJO, CALIFORNIA, U.S.A.
NATIONALITY: AMERICAN

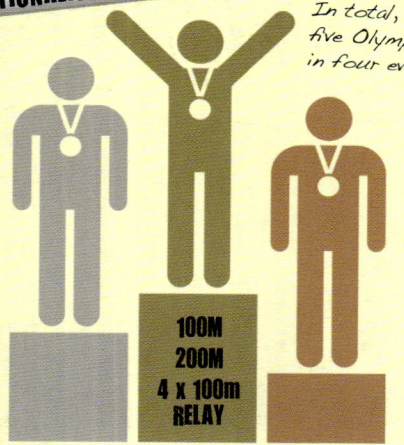

In total, Flo Jo won five Olympic medals in four events.

100M
200M
4 x 100m
RELAY

SUPER STYLE AND SUPERIOR SPEED

"Flo Jo" was something of a superwoman. She is considered the fastest woman of all time, based on records she set in 1988 for the 100 meters and 200 meters that remain unbroken today. Throughout her short career, Flo Jo repeatedly broke her own world records. During the late 1980s, she became popular for her incredible speed, as well as her personal style. Her husband was the triple-jumper Al Joyner, and her sister-in-law was the heptathlete and long jumper Jackie Joyner-Kersee.

Based on a record she set in 1988, Flo Jo is considered the fastest woman of all time. The record remains unbroken today.

OLYMPIC GLORY

In total, Flo Jo won five Olympic medals in four events. At the 1984 Olympics in Los Angeles, she won silver—but it was for her flashy outfits, long hair, and elaborate fingernails that she gained even more attention. At the 1987 World Championships, Flo Jo won both gold and silver medals. During the 1988 Olympic Trials, Flo Jo stunned her co-runners when she unexpectedly set a world record—100 meters in 10.49 seconds. She went on to set two more world records, for the 200-meter sprint and 4 x 100-meter relay, in which she won three golds and a silver. Shortly after, she retired from competition. In 1996, she attempted a comeback, but injury got in the way.

MULTI-TALENTED STAR

Flo Jo was a woman of many talents. In addition to her speed on the track, she designed basketball uniforms (Indiana Pacers, NBA), acted in the soap opera *Santa Barbara*, and was an artist and painter, wife and mother. Controversy surrounds allegations of possible drug use by Flo Jo. However, the International Olympic Committee is clear they have never found any evidence. Tragically, she died in her sleep from a seizure, at the young age of 38.

NADIA COMANECI
THE FIRST GYMNAST EVER AWARDED A PERFECT 10.0

FULL NAME: Nadia Comaneci

BORN: NOVEMBER 12, 1961, ONEȘTI, ROMANIA

NATIONALITY: ROMANIAN, LATER AMERICAN

WORLDWIDE SENSATION

Even after more than 40 years, Nadia Comaneci's 1976 Olympic performance on the uneven bars still looks amazing. (Check it out on the Olympic website: olympic.org/videos/first-perfect-ten-nadia-comaneci.) She was only 14 at the time, but her place in history was set as the first gymnast ever to be awarded a perfect 10.0.

At the age of six, Nadia joined a local gymnastics class. She recalls having tons of energy and always jumping on the couch and table, so her mom hoped gymnastics would tire her out. Little did her mom know, this little step would set her on an Olympic path. Nadia entered several competitions over the next eight years, during which she won both national and European championships.

TOO PERFECT FOR THE SCOREBOARDS!

At the 1976 Olympics in Montreal, Canada, Nadia was a skinny, shy 14-year-old from a small town in Romania, with a white leotard and a ponytail. When she stepped up to the uneven parallel bars, no one could have expected what would happen next. Nadia performed an incredible routine that earned her a score of 10.0. It was the first time

FABULOUS FIRSTS

FIRST GYMNAST TO BE AWARDED
A PERFECT SCORE

FIRST PERSON TO BE AWARDED THE
OLYMPIC HONOR MORE THAN ONCE

YOUNGEST ALL-ROUND OLYMPIC
GOLD MEDALLIST

Nadia Comaneci in 2014

ever an Olympic gymnast had earned a perfect score, and no one thought it possible. As a result, the scoreboard couldn't even display it properly and the judges had to hold up their fingers to show "10"! The entire audience of 18,000 broke out in applause, including her fellow competitors. During the 1976 Olympics, Nadia earned seven perfect 10s and five medals (three gold, one silver, and one bronze). Nadia became the youngest-ever all-round Olympic gold medallist in history. She found herself on magazine covers all around the world, including *Sports Illustrated* and *Time*, which called her simply "perfect." At the 1980 Olympics in Moscow, she went on to win two more golds and two more silvers. In total, Nadia won nine Olympic medals and has become one of the best-known gymnasts in the world. She retired from competition in 1984 and has worked as a coach. Nadia's performances redefined gymnastics and women's Olympic sports, popularizing both.

A MOVE TO THE U.S.A.

At the time of Nadia's early successes, Romania was governed by a harsh ruler named Nicolae Ceausescu. Nadia, and a number of other prominent athletes and celebrities, did not feel they had enough freedom to pursue their dreams under Ceausescu. It was a dangerous journey, but in 1989, Nadia defected to the U.S.A. She now lives in Oklahoma and continues to work in gymnastics. Nadia is on the international board of directors for the Special Olympics and runs a number of gymnastics academies and companies with her husband (Bart Connor, another Olympic gold medal-winning gymnast). In 1984 and 2004, Nadia received the Olympic Honor. This award is the highest given by the International Olympic Committee. Nadia is the only person to have received this honor twice.

JACKIE JOYNER-KERSEE
VOTED THE GREATEST FEMALE ATHLETE OF THE 20TH CENTURY

FULL NAME: Jackie Joyner-Kersee
BORN: MARCH 3, 1962, EAST ST. LOUIS, ILLINOIS, U.S.A.
NATIONALITY: AMERICAN

TV INSPIRATION

Sporty from a young age, Jackie was very talented in everything from basketball to volleyball, track to long jump. She was inspired to take up track and field after seeing a made-for-TV movie about another record-breaking woman from this chapter, Babe Didrikson Zaharias (*see pages 230–231*). Jackie continued in basketball and track and field throughout high school and college. She had severe asthma, a condition that causes difficulty breathing. She did not let this stand in her way. She managed to control the illness while continuing to train.

SIX-TIME OLYMPIAN

In 1981, at the age of 19, Jackie started training for the Olympics. In particular, she wanted to compete in the heptathlon—an Olympic event made up of seven separate events, including the 200-m run, 800-m run, and 100-m hurdles. At the 1984 Olympics in Los Angeles, Jackie won a silver medal in the event. At the 1988 Olympics in Seoul, she won heptathlon gold. She won a gold medal at the 1988 Olympics and a bronze medal at the 1992 Barcelona Olympics, both for the long jump. In her last Olympic Games—in 1996 in Atlanta, Georgia—Jackie won a bronze medal in the long jump. Jackie is ranked among the greatest-ever all-time athletes in both the heptathlon and the long jump. Overall, she won six medals at four different Olympic Games.

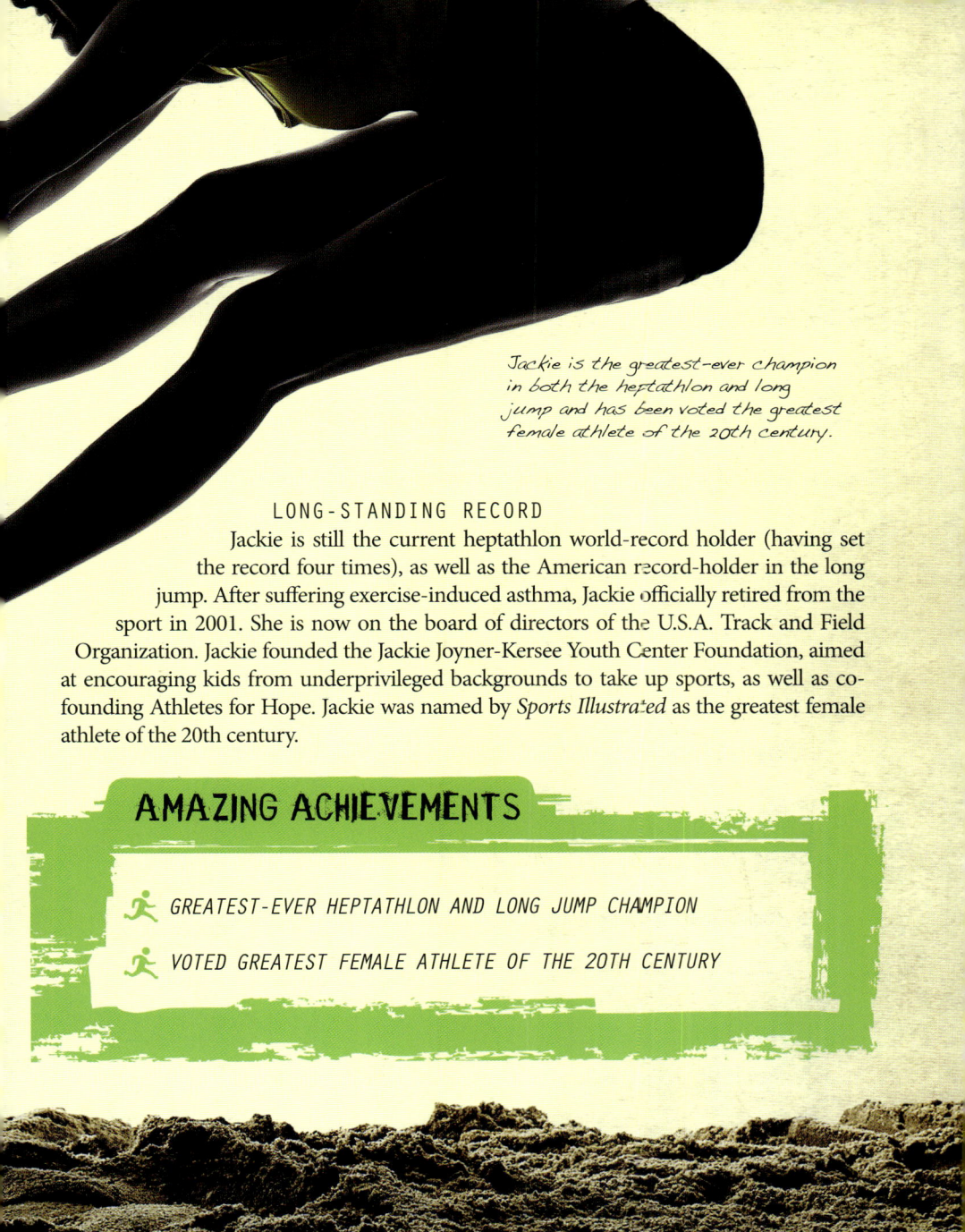

Jackie is the greatest-ever champion in both the heptathlon and long jump and has been voted the greatest female athlete of the 20th century.

LONG-STANDING RECORD

Jackie is still the current heptathlon world-record holder (having set the record four times), as well as the American record-holder in the long jump. After suffering exercise-induced asthma, Jackie officially retired from the sport in 2001. She is now on the board of directors of the U.S.A. Track and Field Organization. Jackie founded the Jackie Joyner-Kersee Youth Center Foundation, aimed at encouraging kids from underprivileged backgrounds to take up sports, as well as co-founding Athletes for Hope. Jackie was named by *Sports Illustrated* as the greatest female athlete of the 20th century.

AMAZING ACHIEVEMENTS

GREATEST-EVER HEPTATHLON AND LONG JUMP CHAMPION

VOTED GREATEST FEMALE ATHLETE OF THE 20TH CENTURY

NAWAL EL MOUTAWAKEL
PIONEER FOR MUSLIM AND ARABIC ATHLETES

FULL NAME: Nawal El Moutawakel
BORN: APRIL 15, 1962, CASABLANCA, MOROCCO
NATIONALITY: MOROCCAN

FIRST MOROCCAN WOMAN TO WIN GOLD

Nawal El Moutawakel came from a large family, in which everyone played sports. Nawal's parents made sure their sons and daughters were treated equally. Nawal began running for fun, but she soon found that she loved the competition. She won a number of Arabic, African, and World Championships before setting her sights on the Olympics. At the 1984 Summer Olympics in Los Angeles, Nawal won a gold medal in the 400-m hurdles event—the first time it was ever held for women. This made her the first Moroccan and first African Muslim woman to become an Olympic gold medallist. Before Nawal's win, many people believed that women, and specifically Muslim women, could not do well in sports. It just hadn't been done before. But Nawal's gold medal proved people wrong. She is now a role model for women around the world.

SPORTS CAN IMPACT LIFE FOREVER

Since her win, Nawal has become a member of the International Olympic Committee (IOC) and has held government positions for youth and sports. In 1993, Nawal started a five-kilometer run for women in Casablanca, Morocco, that now attracts 30,000 female participants, with the aim of encouraging sports and community. "I wanted to bring women outside to feel the power of sports together. It's like a mini-revolution," she said of the event. In these roles, she has worked to increase women's opportunities in sports and to improve girls' self-esteem and confidence through athletics.

BONNIE BLAIR
TOP SPEED SKATER AND ONE OF THE MOST DECORATED OLYMPIANS EVER

FULL NAME: BONNIE BLAIR

BORN: MARCH 18, 1964, CORNWALL, NEW YORK, U.S.A.

NATIONALITY: AMERICAN

Top speed skater Bonnie Blair, shown here in 2010

SPEED-SKATING SENSATION

Bonnie's family was dedicated to speed skating even before she was born. She was the youngest of six children, and, fortunately, Bonnie loved the sport, too. She practiced hard and showed a lot of skill. After high school, she joined the U.S. speed skating team, and in 1984 skated at her first Olympic Games. At the 1988 Olympics in Calgary, Canada, Bonnie won a gold and a bronze medal, and even set a world record. She went on to compete in four Olympic Games, winning five golds and one bronze overall.

In 2004, Bonnie was inducted into the United States Olympic Hall of Fame. At the time, she was the most decorated American athlete in Winter Olympic history—and she still remains so to this day. Bonnie was certainly the top speed skater of her era, for which she was voted the number-seven female athlete of the 20th century by *Sports Illustrated*.

TRISCHA ZORN
MOST SUCCESSFUL ATHLETE IN PARALYMPIC HISTORY

FULL NAME: Trischa Zorn
BORN: JUNE 1, 1964, ORANGE, CALIFORNIA, U.S.A.
NATIONALITY: AMERICAN

RECORDS ARE MEANT TO BE BROKEN

Trischa Zorn is a phenomenal athlete. Born completely blind, Trischa took up swimming at the age of ten. At only 16, she won seven gold medals at her first Paralympic Games, while also setting three world records. She swims in a variety of categories: backstroke, individual medley, breaststroke, medley relay, and free relay. She has competed at the Paralympic Games seven times (1980, 1984, 1988, 1992, 1996, 2000, and 2004) and won 55 medals (41 gold, 9 silver, and 5 bronze). This makes Trischa by far the most successful athlete ever in the history of the Paralympics. In 2012, she was inducted into the Paralympic Hall of Fame.

Trischa is now an elementary teacher for children with special needs, as well as being an attorney with a special interest in helping wounded veterans into sports. She may have retired from competition, but this has not stopped Trischa's hard work in encouraging people of all ages to see the amazing power of sports.

AMAZING ACHIEVEMENTS

 MOST SUCCESSFUL PARALYMPIC ATHLETE TO DATE

JOSEFA IDEM
ATHLETE WITH THE MOST OLYMPIC APPEARANCES IN HISTORY

FULL NAME: Josefa Idem
BORN: SEPTEMBER 23, 1964, GOCH, WEST GERMANY (NOW GERMANY)
NATIONALITY: GERMAN, LATER ITALIAN

Sprint canoeist Josefa Idem (shown both above and below in 2008) has participated in eight Olympic Games.

POWERFUL PADDLER

Josefa's sprint canoe medal record is truly astounding. In World Championships alone, she has won 22 medals (between 1989 and 2009), five of those gold. But it is for her Olympic record that Josefa is best known. Competing at eight Games, from 1984 to 2012, Josefa is the athlete with the most Olympic appearances in history. She represented West Germany in her first two Games and Italy in the following six. (Josefa was born in Germany but became an Italian citizen by marriage.) She has won five Olympic medals (one gold, two silver, and two bronze). Even after four decades of competitive sport, Josefa continued to train for four hours a day. Impressively, at her seventh Olympic appearance, at Beijing 2008, she won her fifth medal: a silver. In 2013, Josefa retired from competitive sports and moved into politics. Josefa plans to be at the Olympic Games in Rio in 2016—this time as a journalist.

KRISTINE LILLY
MOST CAPPED SOCCER PLAYER IN THE HISTORY OF THE SPORT

FULL NAME: Kristine Lilly
BORN: JULY 22, 1971, NEW YORK CITY, U.S.A.
NATIONALITY: AMERICAN

PETITE SPORTS STAR

Kristine Lilly is an American soccer player considered one of the best of all time. At only 5 foot, 4 inches, Kristine is not tall, but this gives her speed and agility—perfect for her positions as forward and midfielder. As a teenager, Kristine played for the North Carolina Tar Heels. At the same time, she started playing for the U.S. national team, which she represented from 1987 to 2010. During that time, she played in 352 international games (also known as winning 352 "caps"), the most games played by a single player in soccer history—either men or women. Kristine has played for a range of teams in the U.S.A. and Sweden. She also competed as the only woman in the all-male professional indoor league, for the Washington Warthogs. Kristine took part in five FIFA Women's World Cups (the only athlete to do so), as well as eight World Cup and Olympic tournaments.

In 2001, the Women's Soccer Association (WUSA) was formed—the world's first women's professional soccer league. Kristine became team captain and a founding member of the Boston Breakers. The association disbanded after two years, and Women's Professional Soccer (WPS) took its place; Kristine continued to be a star of the league. In total, Kristine scored 130 goals, second only to her teammate Mia Hamm in U.S. soccer. In 2012, Kristine was inducted into the U.S. Olympic Hall of Fame and in 2014 into the U.S. Soccer Hall of Fame.

AMAZING ACHIEVEMENTS

MOST CAPPED PLAYER IN SOCCER

MIA HAMM
ONE OF THE GREATEST SOCCER PLAYERS OF ALL TIME AND TOP SCORER

FULL NAME: Mia Hamm
BORN: MARCH 17, 1972, SELMA, ALABAMA, U.S.A.
NATIONALITY: AMERICAN

THE ORIGINAL SUPERSTAR OF WOMEN'S SOCCER

Considered the best female soccer player in history—and one of the greatest soccer players of all time—Mia Hamm is truly an incredible athlete. Mia played as a forward, great at both scoring and assisting her teammates. She is known for her excellent control of the ball, as well as for her impressive footwork and stamina.

Mia always enjoyed soccer, and at the age of 15 she became the youngest soccer player signed to the national team. At the age of 19, Mia set another record: she became the youngest team member in history to win a World Cup. She played for Team U.S.A. at two Olympic Games in 1996 and 2004, winning gold medals both times. Until 2013, Mia held the record for the most international goals scored by both men and women in the history of soccer, with 151 goals.

This wonder woman has been inducted into the National Soccer Hall of Fame and the World Football Hall of Fame—the first woman ever to be inducted there. Mia has won a number of awards over the years, including Female Athlete of the Year and Soccer Player of the Year, and is one of FIFA's 125 Greatest Living Soccer Players.

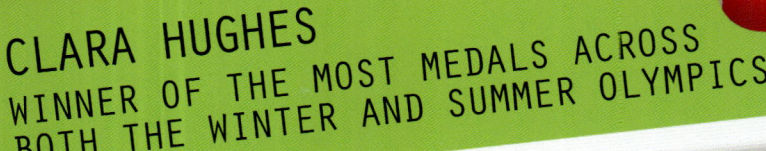

CLARA HUGHES
WINNER OF THE MOST MEDALS ACROSS BOTH THE WINTER AND SUMMER OLYMPICS

FULL NAME: Clara Hughes

BORN: SEPTEMBER 27, 1972, WINNIPEG, CANADA

NATIONALITY: CANADIAN

ALL-SEASON ATHELETE

Clara Hughes is one of only five athletes, male or female, to have won medals in both the Winter and Summer Olympic Games. An excellent cyclist and speed skater, Clara has represented Canada in four separate Olympics (one Summer and three Winter). She achieved this in two quite different sports: speed skating and cycling. At the 1996 Summer Olympics in Atlanta, she won two bronze medals in individual road race cycling and individual time trial cycling. In 2002, at the Salt Lake City Winter Games, she won a bronze in the 5,000-m speed skating event. At 2006's Winter Olympics in Turin, she won both a silver medal (in the speed skating team pursuit) and a gold medal (in 5,000-m speed skating). Finally, in 2010, she won another bronze medal at Vancouver's Winter Olympics, in the 5,000-m speed skating. In 2006, she received the International Olympic Committee's Sport and Community Trophy. In 2010, Clara received a star on the Canadian Walk of Fame and was inducted into Canada's Sports Hall of Fame.

Official flag of the Summer Olympics

Christa Luding-Rothenburger (born 1959, East Germany) is another of the select group of athletes who have won medals at both the Winter and Summer Olympic Games. In 1984, at the Winter Games in Sarajevo, Christa won a gold medal in the 500-m speed skating. At the Winter Games in Calgary, in 1988, she won a silver medal in the same event, as well as gold in the 1,000-m. That same year at the Summer Olympics in Seoul, she won a silver medal in match sprint cycling. Competing at 1992's Winter Games in Albertville, Christa won a bronze medal for the 500-m speed skating. Christa is the only athlete ever to win medals at both the Summer and Winter Olympic Games in the same year.

The Olympic Rings displayed on ice for the Winter Games

Lauryn Williams (born 1983, U.S.A.) is the newest addition to this elite list. She has also won medals across two different sports. At the Summer Games in Athens in 2014, she won a silver on the athletics track (in the 100-m sprint), followed by a gold at London's 2012 Games (for the 4 x 100-m relay). Two years later, at Sochi's 2014 Winter Games, Lauryn won a silver medal for a very different sport—the two-woman bobsleigh!

REGINA HALMICH
MOST SUCCESSFUL FEMALE BOXER OF ALL TIME

FULL NAME: Regina Halmich

BORN: NOVEMBER 22, 1976, KARLSRUHE, WEST GERMANY (NOW GERMANY)

NATIONALITY: GERMAN

Boxing and kickboxing champion Regina Halmich in 2014. A successful boxer, she has also developed her own line of cosmetics.

PACKING A PUNCH

Standing at only 5 foot, 3 inches, and weighing just 112 pounds, Regina Halmich is anything but a pushover. Originally a kickboxing champion, Regina switched to boxing and made her professional debut in 1994, at the age of 18. As a professional boxer, she has competed across a range of divisions, including Jr. Flyweight, Flyweight, Jr. Bantamweight, Bantamweight, and Featherweight.

Regina's boxing record stands at a hugely impressive 54 wins, 1 loss, and 1 draw, making her the most successful female boxer of all time. She is regarded as the pioneer of women's boxing, which she helped popularize across Europe and beyond. Regina's final televised fight, in 2007, has the highest-grossing female boxing (pay-per-view) match ever shown on T.V. Outside of the ring, Regina is a businesswoman with a wide range of businesses and interests, including her own line of cosmetics. She is now an ambassador to the German Children's Fund, working to promote the rights of children and young people.

ELLEN MACARTHUR
FASTEST PERSON TO SAIL SOLO, NONSTOP, AROUND THE WORLD

FULL NAME: Ellen MacArthur
BORN: JULY 8, 1976, DERBYSHIRE, ENGLAND, U.K.
NATIONALITY: BRITISH

Dame Ellen MacArthur was born in Derbyshire—a landlocked part of England. From her earliest memories, sailing played a major part. When she was a child, she saved her allowance for three years in order to buy her first boat: an eight-foot dinghy she named *Threp'ny Bit*. When she was 17, she bought her first full-size boat, a corribee, and named it *Iduna*. In 1995, she sailed this boat, singlehandedly, on a circumnavigation of Great Britain. Two years later, at 21 years old, she finished 17th in the Mini Transat solo transatlantic race. The following year, Ellen was named the Royal Yachting Association's Yachtsman of the Year. In 2005, aged 28, Ellen broke world sailing records. She became the fastest person to singlehandedly circumnavigate the world, nonstop. Ellen has since been given a Member of the Order of the British Empire (MBE) by the Queen of the United Kingdom for her services to sports—the youngest-ever recipient of this award. In 2009, Ellen retired from competitive racing. She now concentrates on environmental campaigning and has set up the Ellen MacArthur Foundation charity.

Ellen repeatedly broke sailing records, including on a yacht like this one pictured.

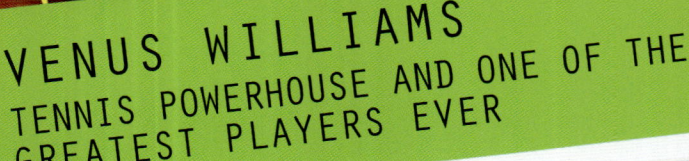

VENUS WILLIAMS
TENNIS POWERHOUSE AND ONE OF THE GREATEST PLAYERS EVER

FULL NAME: Venus Williams
BORN: JUNE 17, 1980, LYNWOOD, CALIFORNIA, U.S.A.
NATIONALITY: AMERICAN

A TENNIS FAMILY

Venus Williams was born into a family with a lot of ambition—and love. That ambition meant Venus started playing tennis when she was still a toddler, alongside her younger sister Serena. Coached by her mother and father for most of her life, Venus would practice four to five hours a day. She started playing professionally when she was only 14.

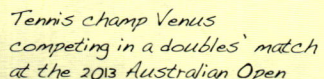

Tennis champ Venus competing in a doubles' match at the 2013 Australian Open

FABULOUS FIRSTS

- *ALONGSIDE SERENA, WINNER OF MOST OLYMPIC GOLD MEDALS IN TENNIS*

- *FIRST WOMAN TO WIN PRIZE MONEY EQUAL TO THAT OF THE MALE PLAYERS*

- *CO-FIRST AFRICAN-AMERICAN WOMAN TO OWN AN NFL FRANCHISE*

Venus Williams in 2005

THE INCREDIBLE WILLIAMS SISTERS

The Williams sisters are credited with raising the popularity of women's tennis and bringing in a "power era" to the sport. Venus has been ranked world number one in women's singles on three separate occasions. She has won 22 overall Grand Slam titles and five Wimbledon singles titles. She has competed in three Olympic Games (in 2000, 2008, and 2012), winning four gold medals in singles and doubles. Venus and her sister Serena have both won more Olympic gold medals than any other tennis player, male or female. Venus is known for her powerful playing style, which she best demonstrates on grass courts. She holds the record for the fastest serve in a number of Grand Slam tournaments, topping 129mph.

FIGHTING FOR EQUALITY

Off court, Venus has led the fight for equal prize money in men's and women's tennis (inspired by the work of another woman in this section, Billie Jean King). In 2007, her hard work paid off when the organizers of Wimbledon and the French Open announced they would pay equal prizes. Venus was the first woman to benefit from this at Wimbledon 2007. That same year, the United Nations Scientific and Cultural Organization (UNESCO) gave her the title of UNESCO Promoter of Gender Equality. In addition to tennis, Venus is a certified interior decorator and trained fashion designer. In 2008, Venus and Serena Williams also became the first African-American women to own an NFL franchise, when they became co-owners of the Miami Dolphins. In 2011, Venus was diagnosed with a condition that affects her immune system and leaves her tired and out of breath. However, in the usual can-do Williams' attitude, Venus has fought this new opponent and is keeping up her tremendous game.

ESTHER VERGEER
ATHLETE WITH THE LONGEST WINNING STREAK IN THE WORLD

FULL NAME: Esther Vergeer
BORN: JULY 18, 1981, WOERDEN, THE NETHERLANDS
NATIONALITY: DUTCH

A DECADE AT THE TOP

Esther Vergeer was the number-one wheelchair tennis player for over a decade. She has been described by tennis champion Roger Federer as "an astonishing athlete." But that kind of success doesn't come easy; Esther had to work for it. And work hard, she did.

FROM INJURY TO EXCELLENCE

At the age of six, Esther suffered a range of unusual symptoms after a swimming lesson. These would later develop into headaches, pain, and strokes. As a result, Esther needed several operations to her brain and spine. When she was eight, one such operation saved her life—but it also left her paralyzed. As part of young Esther's rehabilitation, she learned to play tennis, volleyball, and basketball in a wheelchair. Esther became so good at these sports that she played basketball at club level for several years, before joining the Dutch national wheelchair team. She eventually decided to pursue tennis instead. Esther went on to compete in—and win—a range of tennis opens and masters, as well as the Paralympic Games. At the Games, she has won seven golds in doubles and singles and one silver in doubles. Esther was also part of the Dutch team that won 14 World Team Cups.

With the world's longest winning streak, Esther powerfully returns a volley during a final at the U.S. Open in 2011.

Esther has played for the Dutch team in the Paralympic Games, in which she has won seven golds and one silver.

Wheelchair tennis champion Esther Vergeer attends the opening ceremony of the U.S. Open, in New York, in 2010.

WORLD'S LONGEST WINNING STREAK

Esther was the number-one wheelchair tennis player from 1999 until her retirement in 2013. Over the course of her career, she won 700 matches and lost just 25. A true superwoman, she is the professional athlete with the longest winning streak in the world: 10 years and 470 games undefeated. Esther retired from competition at the top of her game, in 2013. She now plays basketball again and works to promote more integrated tennis tournaments (tournaments where able-bodied tennis and wheelchair tennis are part of the same program). She has also started the Esther Vergeer Foundation, which encourages children to take up sports and spreads awareness of para-sport worldwide. With Esther's track record, no one doubts there will be more achievements to come.

Esther works hard to encourage more children to participate in sports. Here, she attends Arthur Ashe Kids' Day in New York, in 2010.

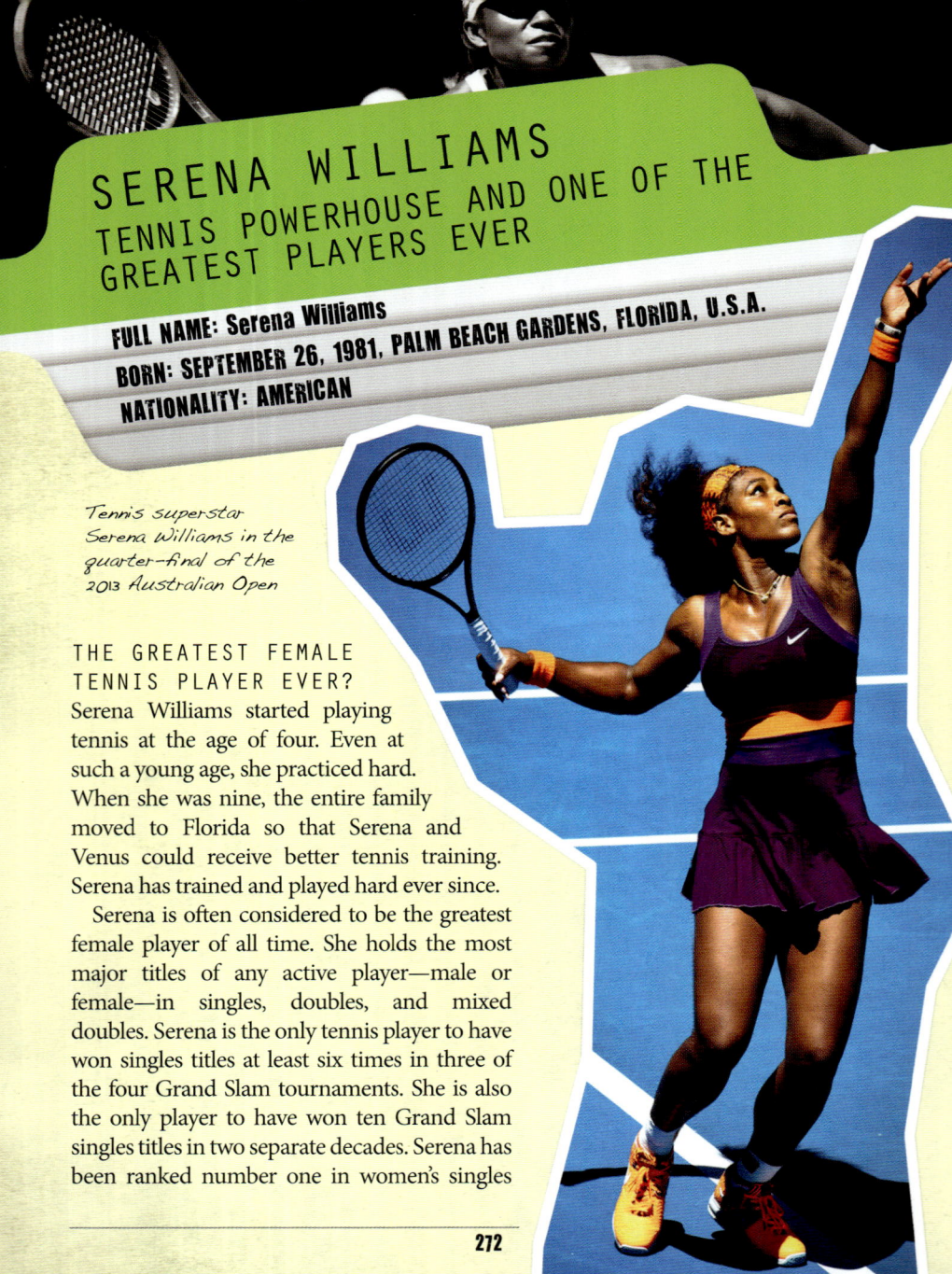

SERENA WILLIAMS
TENNIS POWERHOUSE AND ONE OF THE GREATEST PLAYERS EVER

FULL NAME: Serena Williams
BORN: SEPTEMBER 26, 1981, PALM BEACH GARDENS, FLORIDA, U.S.A.
NATIONALITY: AMERICAN

Tennis superstar Serena Williams in the quarter-final of the 2013 Australian Open

THE GREATEST FEMALE TENNIS PLAYER EVER?

Serena Williams started playing tennis at the age of four. Even at such a young age, she practiced hard. When she was nine, the entire family moved to Florida so that Serena and Venus could receive better tennis training. Serena has trained and played hard ever since.

Serena is often considered to be the greatest female player of all time. She holds the most major titles of any active player—male or female—in singles, doubles, and mixed doubles. Serena is the only tennis player to have won singles titles at least six times in three of the four Grand Slam tournaments. She is also the only player to have won ten Grand Slam singles titles in two separate decades. Serena has been ranked number one in women's singles

AMAZING ACHIEVEMENTS

- HOLDER OF THE MOST MAJOR TITLES OF ANY ACTIVE TENNIS PLAYER

- ALONGSIDE VENUS, WINNER OF MOST OLYMPIC GOLD MEDALS IN TENNIS

- CO-FIRST AFRICAN-AMERICAN WOMAN TO OWN AN NFL FRANCHISE

Official flag of the Wimbledon championships

tennis six times. In addition to an amazing number of Grand Slam wins, Serena has competed in three separate Olympics (in 2000, 2008, and 2012), winning four gold medals for both doubles and singles—an all-time record shared with her sister, Venus. The year 2014 was a good one, as Serena won four Grand Slams: Wimbledon, the French Open, the Australian Open, and the U.S. Open—this achievement is known as the "Serena slam." In 2015, Serena was named Sportsperson of the Year by *Sports Illustrated*.

INCREDIBLE POWER AND STYLE

Serena is known as a strong player with a powerful forehand shot. Her playing style is aggressive and accurate, while her serve is considered the greatest in women's tennis history. In addition to her impressive playing, Serena is also known for her unique outfits on the court. Serena loves fashion and is a certified nail technician and clothing designer. Off court, she has set up a number of organizations to support education and justice, and to end community violence. Serena has also served as a UNICEF Global Ambassador.

DANICA PATRICK
RACING PIONEER

FULL NAME: Danica Patrick

BORN: MARCH 25, 1982, BELOIT, WISCONSIN, U.S.A.

NATIONALITY: AMERICAN

Danica Patrick signals to fans at the Atlanta Motor Speedway in 2012.

> *I've never asked for special treatment along the way. And I'm never going to hide the fact that I'm a girl, ever.*
>
> DANICA PATRICK

SPEED DEMON IN A GO-KART

Danica was born and raised in Illinois, where she began competing in go-karts at a young age. From 1992 to 1997, Danica won a number of regional karting titles and scooped the World Karting Association Grand National Championship three times as a teenager (in 1994, 1996, and 1997). Soon after, young Danica changed course—and location. She decided to compete in European road racing.

FIRST WOMAN ON THE PODIUM

At only 5 foot, 1 inch tall, Danica is petite, but she has never let her size or gender get in the way of her ambition. She quickly gained a lot of attention, especially when she came in second at the Formula Ford Festival in England— the highest-ever finish for an American. Over the next couple of years, Danica became the first woman in series history to finish on the podium when she moved up to the Toyota Atlantic Series. She went on to set numerous records during her Indianapolis 500 debut, earning rave reviews for her road-handling and winning the title Rookie of the Year. Danica has regularly been named Most Popular Driver and her top place at Indy 500 was an impressive third—the highest position ever for a female driver. In 2008, Danica won the Indy Japan 300. In addition to IndyCar, Danica also races in the NASCAR series. As part of NASCAR, in 2013, Danica lead the Daytona 500 race and held the top spot—becoming one of only 14 drivers ever to have led both the Daytona 500 and Indianapolis 500.

RACING IN A MAN'S WORLD

Danica has done well in each form of racing she has tried (kart racing, IndyCar, and NASCAR), breaking into an overwhelmingly male-dominated sport with impressive results. Danica remains the most successful woman in the history of American open-wheel racing.

Danica has competed in both IndyCar open-wheel racing (far left) and NASCAR (below).

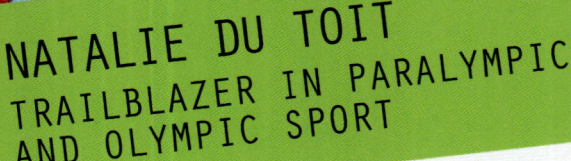

NATALIE DU TOIT
TRAILBLAZER IN PARALYMPIC AND OLYMPIC SPORT

FULL NAME: Natalie du Toit
BORN: JANUARY 29, 1984, CAPE TOWN, SOUTH AFRICA
NATIONALITY: SOUTH AFRICAN

A DETERMINED SWIMMER

Natalie Du Toit was an enthusiastic swimmer from a young age. At only 14 years old, she entered her first international competition: the 1998 Commonwealth Games. Three years later, as Natalie was riding her scooter after swimming practice, she was hit by a car. The injury was so bad that doctors had to amputate her left leg at the knee. It was believed she would never swim again, but Natalie proved everyone wrong. Within three months, before she could even walk again, Natalie was back in the pool. The very next year, Natalie was competing at the Commonwealth Games once again. As if that weren't impressive enough, she won both the multi-disability 50-m freestyle and the multi-disability 100-m freestyle in record time, as well as qualifying for the 800-m able-bodied freestyle final. This was the first time a disabled athlete had ever qualified for the final of an able-bodied event.

MAKING HISTORY IN THE POOL

Over the next several years, Natalie won many championships and repeatedly made history. At the end of the 2012 Paralympic Games, Natalie retired, but during her incredible career she won 13 Paralympic golds and 12 World Championship golds. She is ranked as one of the fastest distance swimmers in the world. She is a trailblazer in both Paralympic and Olympic sports, becoming the first amputee ever to qualify for the Olympic Games in 2008. Natalie remains the only athlete in history to have carried her country's flag at the opening ceremony of both the Olympic and Paralympic Games, which she did for South Africa in 2008.

ZAHRA NEMATI
FIRST IRANIAN WOMAN TO WIN A MEDAL AT THE OLYMPIC OR PARALYMPIC GAMES

FULL NAME: Zahra Nemati
BORN: APRIL 30, 1985, KERMAN, IRAN
NATIONALITY: IRANIAN

Iranian
flag

ARCHERY ACE IN SIX MONTHS

Sporty from the age of five, Zahra gained a black belt in Taekwondo as a teenager. When she was 19, a car accident left her paralyzed from a spinal injury. But she didn't let this stand in her way. Zahra went on to college, where she took up archery. Only six months after picking up a bow for the first time, Zahra competed in the National Championships alongside able-bodied archers. She finished in third place. As a result, she was asked to join the National Archery Team—and she has won a medal in every championship she has competed in since.

INSPIRATIONAL ROLE MODEL

During her short time as an archer, Zahra has broken the world record in four separate distances. At the 2012 Summer Paralympics in London, she set a Paralympic record and won an individual gold medal, as well as a team bronze. Zahra became the first Iranian woman ever to make it to the podium in either the Olympic or Paralympic Games. In doing so, she has become a role model for women and people with disabilities across the Muslim world and beyond. As a result of her determination, she has helped to change the way athletes with disabilities are perceived. Zahra won Sport Accord's 2013 Spirit of Sport Individual Award. When she retires from archery, Zahra plans to take up fishing.

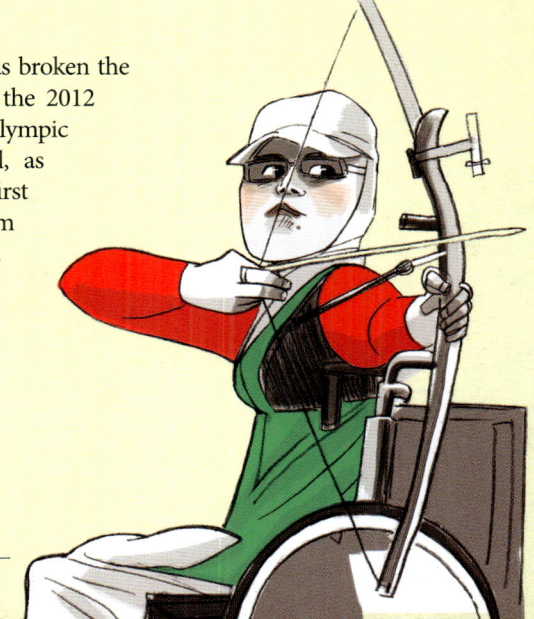

Add your own great women here

EPILOGUE: BONUS ENTRIES!

And just when you thought you were done, here are a few more amazing women to inspire you! As mentioned in the Introduction, there simply is not enough space to include every incredible individual in the pages of this book. However, by popular demand, I have been able to add a few more. While these entries are found at the back of the book, they are certainly no less important. I hope you will enjoy reading these remarkable bonus entries!

More!

More!

More!

More!

More!

More!

More!

More!

More!

More!

More!

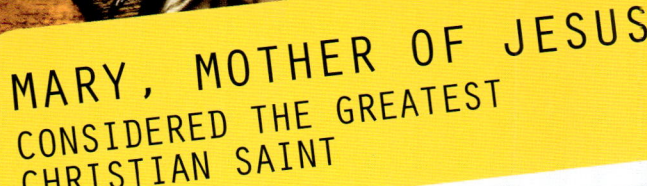

MARY, MOTHER OF JESUS
CONSIDERED THE GREATEST CHRISTIAN SAINT

FULL NAME: Mary of Nazareth, Mother of Jesus
BORN: C. 18 B.C., NAZARETH, NOW ISRAEL
DIED: C. A.C. 41
NATIONALITY: GALILEAN

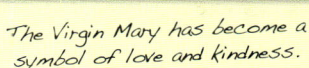

The Virgin Mary has become a symbol of love and kindness.

MOTHER MARY

Mary, Mother of Jesus is a woman of many names: the Blessed Virgin Mary, the Madonna, Saint Mary, and Mary of Nazareth. She is one of the most significant individuals within the Christian faith, revered as highly as God and Jesus.

Mary is the subject of many stories in the Bible, as well as the Qur'an (where she is known as Maryam). She also appears in literature, paintings, and music across the Western world. She is often depicted as calm, angelic, young, and beautiful, wearing robes of blue and red and with a halo over her head.

THE HOLY FAMILY

The story goes that while she was still a young teenager, Mary was visited by the Archangel Gabriel. In a scene known as the "Annunciation," he told Mary that she was pregnant with the son of God (known as the "Messiah"). Mary was very religious and took the word as truth. At the time, she was engaged to a man named Joseph, and later the two married. After the birth of Jesus in Bethlehem, they raised him as Joseph's own. The Virgin Mary, Saint Joseph, and Jesus have become known as the Holy Family. Jesus went on to share the teachings of God, perform miracles, and love those deemed unlovable in Roman society. He was later crucified (killed by being nailed to a cross) for his beliefs. Mary is known as the "first believer" of Jesus, and of Christianity. During all of this, Mary was a devoted mother to Jesus and a strong supporter of and sharer in his faith, constantly at his side. When Mary died, it is believed that her whole body rose into Heaven, to be rejoined with her soul, and to sit once more alongside her son, Jesus Christ.

Mary has been honored since the early days of Christianity. Many believers across all Christian denominations consider her to be the greatest of all the Christian saints. Mary plays a hugely important role in the lives of many Christians, as she is seen as the most devoted, selfless, and caring of the saints.

HARRIET BEECHER STOWE
ANTI-SLAVERY WRITER WHO TRIGGERED THE U.S. CIVIL WAR

FULL NAME: Harriet Elisabeth Beecher Stowe
BORN: JUNE 14, 1811, LITCHFIELD, CONNECTICUT, U.S.A.
DIED: JULY 1, 1896, HARTFORD, CONNECTICUT, U.S.A.
NATIONALITY: AMERICAN

> 66 *I would write something that would make this whole nation feel what an accursed thing slavery is.* 99
>
> HARRIET BEECHER STOWE

A hugely important author, Harriet Beecher Stowe could just as easily have found herself in the Arts & Literature chapter. However, her writing—paired with her strong beliefs and activism—played a huge part in changing the politics and social landscape of 19th-century America.

Portrait of Harriet Beecher Stowe (date unknown)

CHANGING SOCIETY

Harriet came from a family of 11 children. Impressively, each one went on to shape the world in a number of different ways: some as ministers, others as pioneers of education, and another as an advocate for women's right to vote. Harriet believed her writing could make the biggest impact on society. She wrote more than 30 books in her lifetime, as well as essays, poems, and articles, on everything from religion to biography, homemaking to childrearing. But it was her best-selling anti-slavery novel, *Uncle Tom's Cabin*, that made her permanent mark in history books around the world.

An anti-slavery (abolitionist) newspaper, called *National Era*, commissioned Harriet to write a story about slavery. It was to appear in three instalments, and the first instalment was published on June 5, 1851. Harriet went on to write 40 in total, based on powerful first-hand accounts of real families. The book became *Uncle Tom's Cabin*. It would quickly become a bestseller in the U.S.A. (selling 10,000 copies in its first week), Britain, Asia, and Europe and was translated into 60 languages. It is even thought to be the second best-selling book of the 19th century, second only to the Bible. The book made a very factual and heartfelt case about the injustices of slavery, changing the view of many Americans. It made the argument for why the country should end slavery and move toward equality for all. It was an important trigger for the start of the U.S. Civil War, with a goal of ending the practice of owning people as property.

THE BOOK THAT STARTED THIS GREAT WAR

The U.S.A. was deeply divided at the time over the rights and wrongs of slavery. Many in the North wanted an end to slavery but did not fully understand the horrors still occurring in the South. Meanwhile, many Southerners continued to own slaves and often failed to see them as people. Abraham Lincoln was president at a very difficult time, being pressured by both sides. However, he agreed that slavery was wrong and the powerful account of *Uncle Tom's Cabin* helped spur him to action. After the war began, Harriet traveled to Washington, D.C., to meet with President Lincoln. In a popular, but undocumented, anecdote, Lincoln said to Harriet, "So you are the little woman who wrote the book that started this great war."

For the next 40 years, Harriet continued the struggle for civil rights and went on to write several further books of fiction and nonfiction. *Uncle Tom's Cabin* remains her most influential book. It has been turned into plays, movies, and graphic novels, and "Uncle Tom" has become American slang for racism.

This 1865 painting by Gustav Bartsch shows President Lincoln visiting Union troops during the Civil War, in Virginia, U.S.A.

HARRIET TUBMAN
THE MOST FAMOUS "CONDUCTOR" OF THE UNDERGROUND RAILROAD

FULL NAME: Araminta Harriet Ross Tubman
BORN: C. MARCH 1822, DORCHESTER COUNTY, MARYLAND, U.S.A.
DIED: MARCH 10, 1913, AUBURN, NEW YORK, U.S.A
NATIONALITY: AMERICAN

U.S. postage stamp, circa 1978, honoring "General Tubman"

A FAMILY DIVIDED

Araminta "Minty" Ross was one of nine children born to enslaved parents. Her family was split up when three of her sisters were sold to another plantation. But when another child, a son, was about to be up for purchase, Araminta's mother successfully fought the sale. It was an important example to her young daughter. Life for slaves involved back-breaking manual labor and physical violence. For young Araminta, it was no different. She was often beaten, and one particular blow to the head (for not helping to restrain an escaped slave) caused a skull fracture, leading to seizures and headaches for the rest of her life.

Many families in the early 1800s included both free people and slaves. Araminta's father was technically freed from slavery aged 45, but there were not many options available to him, so he continued working for his previous owners. Her mother and siblings should also have been allowed to go free, but their owners refused, leaving the family trapped in slavery.

GENERAL TUBMAN

In 1844, Araminta married a free black man named John Tubman. Around the same time, she changed her first name to Harriet. Little is known of John, and he does not appear to feature later in her life. In 1849, Harriet's owner died, and she decided to take advantage of the opportunity for escape. On September 17, she left Maryland with two of her brothers. A reward was offered for their return, and the brothers decided to go back to the plantation. Harriet continued on alone, traveling 90 miles to Pennsylvania. Pennsylvania was a "free state," and Harriet later recalled looking at her hands after crossing the border, to check that she was the same person. Her escape followed the route of the Underground Railroad, a network of safe houses and secret routes supported by abolitionists and former slaves.

Harriet was finally free. However, she could not feel free while others were enslaved, so she made it her life mission to rescue family and non-family alike. Nicknamed "Moses" and "General Tubman" for her incredible leadership, Harriet was able to help around 300 slaves to freedom (including her parents and siblings), by making 19 separate life-risking trips. This put a massive bounty on her head. In 1850, the Fugitive Slave Law was passed, which stated that slaves who escaped from the South could be captured in the North and returned. Both former slaves and free black people were enslaved in the South. Harriet reacted by rerouting the secret Underground Railroad to Canada, where there was no slavery. Harriet became the most celebrated conductor of the Underground Railroad, famously saying she had "never lost a single passenger."

THE FIVE-FOOT GIANTESS OF ABOLITION

In 1861, the U.S. Civil War broke out, with differing North/South attitudes to slavery at its core. Harriet supported the Union (North) as a cook, nurse, scout, and spy. She led an armed expedition, becoming the first woman to do so in the war, freeing 700 slaves in South Carolina.

After the war, Harriet spent her final years on a small property in New York with family and friends. Despite having little herself, she continued to help others and became a supporter of women's suffrage. She donated land to a local church, which later became the Harriet Tubman Home for the Aged in 1908. This is where she would spend her final days.

Harriet was well known by fellow civil rights activists during her lifetime. However, it was after she died that her incredible actions became more widely known. Harriet is now an American icon, famed for her bravery and selflessness. In April of 2016, the U.S. Treasury announced that Harriet Tubman's portrait would be featured on the $20 bill to be launched in 2020 (significantly replacing war hero Andrew Jackson, who himself owned slaves). She will be the first woman to appear on U.S. bills.

This Harriet Tubman statue was erected in Harlem, New York, in 2008.

ELEANOR ROOSEVELT
HUMANITARIAN AND
"FIRST LADY OF THE WORLD"

FULL NAME: Anna Eleanor Roosevelt
BORN: OCTOBER 11, 1884, NEW YORK CITY, NEW YORK, U.S.A.
DIED: NOVEMBER 7, 1962, NEW YORK CITY, NEW YORK, U.S.A.
NATIONALITY: AMERICAN

Eleanor Roosevelt on a visit to the Galapagos Islands, March 21, 1944

Eleanor Roosevelt is remembered as the longest-serving First Lady of the U.S.A., as well as one of the most outspoken ever in the White House. However, that single role does not define this great woman, who is also renowned for her experience as an activist, diplomat, and UN spokeswoman.

Born into the Roosevelt empire, Eleanor had a very privileged and political upbringing. Her uncle was Theodore Roosevelt, future president of the U.S.A., and she would go on to marry her distant cousin, future president Franklin Delano Roosevelt. However, by the time she was ten years old, she had lost both of her parents and turned into a shy, withdrawn child. As a teenager, she was educated in England, and this experience helped build her confidence and independence. Eleanor's chosen career was as a social worker, which would serve her well in later life. In 1905, she married Franklin, and the couple had six children. Franklin was a senator, and Eleanor was active in the American Red Cross (see Clara Barton, pages 172–173) during World War I.

A POLITICS OF CARING

In 1921, Franklin contracted polio, which left his legs paralyzed. Eleanor encouraged him to remain in political service. She threw her energy into helping with his career and, in 1933, Franklin became U.S. President. Franklin and Eleanor did not always see eye to eye, but they were an excellent team. Eleanor was no wallflower and made her voice heard, ultimately changing the role of First Lady from hostess to politician. She spoke passionately about women's rights, human rights, racial discrimination, welfare, workers' rights, and children's issues. She worked with the Women's Trade Union League to end child labor and to set up a minimum wage. She was active in the civil rights movement, insisting on equal rights for all, regardless of race, and she broke tradition by inviting several African-Americans to the White House for social and political causes during her time.

While not everyone liked the idea of a First Lady with a voice, many regarded her as a leader of women's rights and civil rights. She had her own newspaper column and was a pioneer in her engagement with the media over political issues. As the policy of presidential terms was different then, F.D.R. (as Franklin came to be known) spent four terms in office (1933 to 1945, spanning both the Great Depression and World War II). This made Eleanor the longest-serving First Lady of the U.S.A. For her compassion and activism, she was nicknamed "First Lady of the World."

The statue of Eleanor at the FDR Memorial in Washington, D.C. honors her contributions as both First Lady and UN delegate.

A PLACE AT THE UN TABLE

When Franklin died in 1945, Harry Truman took over the Oval Office. Eleanor briefly considered withdrawing from politics, but Truman quickly appointed Eleanor as a delegate to the United Nations—a post she held from 1945 to 1953. During this time, as chair of the UN's Human Rights Commission, she made what is now considered her greatest achievement, co-writing the Universal Declaration of Human Rights. But it didn't end there. In 1961, President John F. Kennedy appointed the 77-year-old Eleanor once more to the UN, followed by the National Advisory Committee of the Peace Corp. She also became chair of the President's Commission on the Status of Women.

Eleanor Roosevelt was a great many things: mother, wife, caregiver, First Lady, diplomat, activist, and feminist. But at the heart of everything she did, she was a great humanitarian with overwhelming sensitivity toward those around her. She sought political and social change and continued to strive to make the world a better place until the very end of her life. Eleanor set the stage for the strong First Ladies who followed in her footsteps, and Michelle Obama lists Eleanor as one of her idols.

SEA CHANGE:
THE WAVES OF FEMINISM

Feminism has evolved through several different stages, each of which has different values and figureheads. These have been classified into simple "waves," with prominent thinkers connected to each, as outlined below.

First-wave feminism occurred during the early 1700s and 1800s, concentrating on legal and cultural issues, such as property laws and women's voting rights. Mary Wollstonecraft and Olive Schreiner were part of this wave.

Second-wave feminism found its voice in the mid-20th century, kick-started in the U.S.A. This was the time that feminism began to really gain steam. The activists of this wave focused on issues such as equality in the workplace and at home, sexuality, and violence against women. Several prominent feminists are connected to this wave, including the authors Simone De Beauvoir, Betty Friedan, Gloria Steinem, and Germaine Greer.

Third-wave feminism does not sit within a clearly set timeframe, although it started in around the early 1990s. This stage of feminism was a backlash against the previous wave, and it aimed to include a more diverse group of women in the struggle for women's rights. Feminists of this group believe in the importance of women's choices in all matters, with an emphasis on social and political issues. The Riot grrrl punk movement is part of third-wave feminism.

Fourth-wave feminism is still up for debate, but its earliest mention was in 2008. This wave utilizes social media and technology in its pursuit of greater social change around gender equality and social justice, working alongside other social justice movements.

IMPORTANT FEMINIST ICONS

Mary Wollstonecraft
(1759–1797, U.K.)
Mary was a writer, philosopher, and women's rights campaigner. She remains best known for her book *A Vindication on the Rights of Woman* (1792), arguing that men and women should be treated as equal. Mary is regarded as one of the founding feminist philosophers.

Betty Friedan
(1921–2006, U.S.A.)
Betty was an author and activist. Her 1963 book, *The Feminine Mystique*, is credited with sparking U.S. feminism in the 1900s. She was the founder of the National Organization of Women (NOW).

Simone De Beauvoir (1908–1986, France)
Simone was a philosopher and writer. Her most famous book, *The Second Sex* (1949), remains a pivotal text in contemporary feminism, critiquing the oppression of women throughout history.

Gloria Steinem (born 1934, U.S.A.)
Gloria is an enduring feminist icon, as well as an author and social activist. She was the co-founder of the feminist *Ms* magazine and a leader of the women's liberation movement from the 1960s.

Germaine Greer (born 1939, Australia)
Germaine is an author and major "radical" feminist voice of the mid-20th century. She is the author of *The Female Eunuch* (1970), which deconstructed the various stereotypes associated with femininity.

Conclusion

You've made it to the end—but don't forget to go back and add your own "greats" at the back of each chapter! Hopefully, through reading this book, you've come across beloved figures you already admired, some you recognized but were able to learn more about, as well as others who were completely new to you. But in all, I hope you've found yourself entertained and motivated by the incredible things achieved by the wonderful women and glorious girls in this book—inspired to create, invent, train, and act, to make your own mark on the world.

In researching these entries, I loved learning new facts about women I admired, such as actress Hedy Lamarr's role as an inventor, as well as about those I'd never come across before, such as Somali queen Arawelo and food "inventor" Ruth Graves Wakefield. However, the part I loved most was uncovering the spider's web of connections that exists between seemingly disparate people throughout history. As you'll have noticed, time and again, individual entries cross-reference to other women in this book. These include Beyoncé supporting the Girl Scouts' campaigns, Justice Ruth Bader Ginsburg working as director of the ACLU (co-founded by Helen Keller), paleoanthropologist Mary Leakey hiring Jane Goodall to work on her first chimpanzee field project, and Jackie Joyner-Kersee being inspired to take up sports after seeing Babe Zaharias' story on TV. Of all of these, however, my favorite is

the connection I found most unexpected. That was when, in 1955, screen goddess Marilyn Monroe quietly used her star status to get jazz singer Ella Fitzgerald booked at a whites-only music venue, simultaneously propelling Ella's career and triggering widespread desegregation in venues across the U.S.A.

On a personal note, I was delighted to learn that the models for both of the original *Rosie the Riveter* illustrations (Geraldine Hoff Doyle for J. Howard Miller's "Westinghouse poster," and Mary Doyle for Norman Rockwell's *Saturday Evening Post* cover) were both women with my last name, Doyle. I love the fact that my namesakes helped create one of the ultimate and most enduring symbols of feminism, still widely recognized today. I'd like to think I have a little bit of their spirited blood in my own Doyle veins.

This book is meant to be read, discussed, shared, and read again. Each woman featured has a story to tell. I hope you will use it as a stepping-stone to learning more about these incredible women—and as a reminder to read their novels, discover their theorems, listen to their music, and (if you're up to the challenge) to better their records.

Bibliography

Agence-France-Presse. (AFP). (21 April, 2016).
"'Honey, we're better than the Supremes': Sudan's girl band going strong 45-years on."
Online at http://www.theguardian.com/world/2016/apr/21/sudans-girlband-the-nightingales-world-tour-sudanese-supremes (accessed 14/06/2016).

Albers Foundation. (n.d.). "Josef & Anni Albers."
Online at http://www.albersfoundation.org/artists/biographies/ (accessed 14/06/2016).

All-American Girls' Professional Baseball League, The. Official Website.
Online at http://www.aagpbl.org (accessed 14/06/2016).

America's Navy. (n.d.). "USS Hopper (DDG 70). "Amazing Grace.""
Online at http://www.public.navy.mil/surfor/ddg70/Pages/namesake.aspx (accessed 14/06/2016).

American Film Institute. (2016). "AFI's 50 Greatest American Screen Legends."
Online at http://www.afi.com/100years/stars.aspx (accessed 14/06/2016).

amightygirl@amightygirl. Online at https://twitter.com/amightygirl (accessed 14/06/2016).

Ankeny, Jason. (n.d.). "Sister Rosetta Tharpe." All Music.com.
Online at http://www.allmusic.com/artist/sister-rosetta-tharpe-mn0000013511/biography (accessed 14/06/2016).

annefrank.com. http://annefrank.com/about-anne-frank/who-is-anne/ (accessed 15/06/2016).

anniebonnypirate.com. (n.d.). "Ching Shih Pirate Biography and Facts."
http://www.annebonnypirate.com/famous-female-pirates/ching-shih/ (accessed 14/06/2016).

audreyhepburn.com.
http://www.audreyhepburn.com/menu/index.php?idMenu=55 (accessed 14/06/2016).

BBC History. (2014). "Aphra Behn (1640-1689)."
Online at http://www.bbc.co.uk/history/historic_figures/behn_aphra.shtml (accessed 14/06/2016).

BBC History. (2014). "Boudicca. (died c.AD 60)."
Online at http://www.bbc.co.uk/history/historic_figures/boudicca.shtml (accessed 14/06/2016).

BBC History. (2014). "Catherine the Great. (1729-1796)."
Online at http://www.bbc.co.uk/history/historic_figures/catherine_the_great.shtml (accessed 14/06/2016).

BBC History. (2014). "Mary Anning."
Online at http://www.bbc.co.uk/schools/primaryhistory/famouspeople/mary_anning/ (accessed 14/06/2016).

BBC News. (14 September, 2015). "Ada Lovelace: Letters shed light on tech visionary." Online at http://www.bbc.co.uk/news/science-environment-34243042 (accessed 14/06/2016).

BBC News. (23 June, 2011). "Harry Potter series to be sold as e-books." Online at http://www.bbc.co.uk/news/entertainment-arts-13889578 (accessed 14/06/2016).

BBC Science & Nature. (17 September, 2014). "The Mona Lisa (La Gioconda)." Online at http://www.bbc.co.uk/science/leonardo/gallery/monalisa.shtml (accessed 14/06/2016).

BBC Sport (12 February, 2013). "Esther Vergeer quits wheelchair tennis after perfect decade." Online at http://www.bbc.co.uk/sport/disability-sport/21426554 (accessed 14/06/2016).

Bennett, Kitty. (16 July, 2010). "Nadia Comaneci." AARP Bulletin. Online at http://www.aarp.org/politics-society/history/info-07-2010/where_are_they_now_nadia_comaneci.html (accessed 14/06/2016).

Biharprabha/BP Staff. (7 April, 2014). "The Biography of Dorothy Mary Hodgkin." Online at http://news.biharprabha.com/2014/04/the-biography-of-dorothy-mary-hodgkin/ (accessed 14/06/2016).

billieholiday.com. http://www.billieholiday.com/ (accessed 14/06/2016).

Biography.com Editors (n.d.). "Ada Lovelace Biography." Online at http://www.biography.com/people/ada-lovelace-20825323 (accessed 14/06/2016).

Biography.com Editors (n.d.). "Anna Wintour Biography." Online at http://www.biography.com/people/anna-wintour-214147 (accessed 14/06/2016).

Biography.com Editors (n.d.). "Annie Jump Cannon Biography." Online at http://www.biography.com/people/annie-jump-cannon-9236960# (accessed 14/06/2016).

Biography.com Editors (n.d.). "Artemisia Gentileschi Biography." Online at http://www.biography.com/people/artemisia-gentileschi-9308725 (accessed 14/06/2016).

Biography.com Editors (n.d.). "Aung San Suu Kyi Biography." Online at http://www.biography.com/people/aung-san-suu-kyi-9192617#arrest-and-election (accessed 14/06/2016).

Biography.com Editors (n.d.). "Beatrix Potter Biography." Online at http://www.biography.com/people/beatrix-potter-9445208 (accessed 14/06/2016).

Biography.com Editors (n.d.). "Billy Holiday Biography" Online at http://www.biography.com/people/billie-holiday-9341902#early-life (accessed 14/06/2016).

Biography.com Editors. (n.d.). "Bonnie Blair Biography." Online at http://www.biography.com/people/bonnie-blair-9926791#later-years (accessed 14/06/2016).

Biography.com Editors (n.d.). "Cleopatra VII Biography."
Online at http://www.biography.com/people/cleopatra-vii-9250984 (accessed 14/06/2016).

Biography.com Editors (n.d.). "Dorothea Lange Biography."
Online at http://www.biography.com/people/dorothea-lange-9372993# (accessed 14/06/2016).

Biography.com Editors (n.d.). "Édith Piaf Biography."
Online at http://www.biography.com/people/edith-piaf-9439893 (accessed 14/06/2016).

Biography.com Editors (n.d.). "Eleanor Roosevelt Biography."
Online at http://www.biography.com/people/eleanor-roosevelt-9463366#. (accessed 14/06/2016).

Biography.com Editors (n.d.). "Elizabeth Cady Stanton Biography."
Online at http://www.biography.com/people/elizabeth-cady-stanton-9492182# (accessed 14/06/2016).

Biography.com Editors (n.d.). "Ella Fitzgerald Biography."
Online at http://www.biography.com/people/ella-fitzgerald-9296210 (accessed 14/06/2016).

Biography.com Editors (n.d.). "Emmy Noether Biography."
Online at http://www.biography.com/people/emmy-noether-39432

Biography.com Editors (n.d.). "Eva Perón Biography."
Online at http://www.biography.com/people/eva-per%C3%B3n-9437976#first-lady-of-argentina (accessed 14/06/2016).

Biography.com Editors (n.d.). "Ginger Rogers Biography."
Online at http://www.biography.com/people/ginger-rogers-9462173#early-life (accessed 14/06/2016).

Biography.com Editors (n.d.). "Harriet Beecher Stowe Biography."
Online at http://www.biography.com/people/harriet-beecher-stowe-9496479# (accessed 14/06/2016).

Biography.com Editors (n.d.). "Harriet Tubman Biography."
Online at http://www.biography.com/people/harriet-tubman-9511430# (accessed 14/06/2016).

Biography.com Editors (n.d.). "Helen Keller Biography."
Online at http://www.biography.com/people/helen-keller (accessed 14/06/2016).

Biography.com Editors (n.d.). "Hillary Clinton Biography."
Online at http://www.biography.com/people/hillary-clinton-9251306# (accessed 14/06/2016).

Biography.com Editors (n.d.). "J.K. Rowling Biography."
Online at http://www.biography.com/people/jk-rowling-40998 (accessed 14/06/2016).

Biography.com Editors. (n.d.). "Jackie Joyner-Kersee Biography."
Online at http://www.biography.com/people/jackie-joyner-kersee-9358710#olympic-star
(accessed 14/06/2016).

Biography.com Editors (n.d.). "Joan of Arc Biography."
Online at http://www.biography.com/people/joan-of-arc-9354756# (accessed 14/06/2016).

Biography.com Editors (n.d.). "Lucy Stone Biography."
Online at http://www.biography.com/people/lucy-stone-9495976# (accessed 14/06/2016).

Biography.com Editors (n.d.). "Lynette Woodard Biography."
Online at http://www.biography.com/people/lynette-woodard-533268 (accessed 14/06/2016).

Biography.com Editors (n.d.). "Ma Rainey Biography."
Online at http://www.biography.com/people/ma-rainey-9542413 (accessed 14/06/2016).

Biography.com Editors (n.d.). "Maria Callas Biography."
Online at http://www.biography.com/people/maria-callas-9235435 (accessed 14/06/2016).

Biography.com Editors (n.d.). "Marie Curie Biography."
Online at http://www.biography.com/people/marie-curie-9263538 (accessed 14/06/2016).

Biography.com Editors (n.d.). "Marilyn Monroe Biography."
Online at http://www.biography.com/people/marilyn-monroe-9412123#synopsis (accessed 14/06/2016).

Biography.com Editors (n.d.). "Martina Navratilova Biography."
Online at http://www.biography.com/people/martina-navratilova-9420862 (accessed 14/06/2016).

Biography.com Editors (n.d.). "Mary Leakey Biography."
Online at http://www.biography.com/people/mary-leakey-9376051 (accessed 14/06/2016).

Biography.com Editors (n.d.). "Meryl Streep Biography."
Online at http://www.biography.com/people/meryl-streep-9497266# (accessed 14/06/2016).

Biography.com Editors. (n.d.). "Mia Hamm Biography."
Online at http://www.biography.com/people/mia-hamm-16472547 (accessed 14/06/2016).

Biography.com Editors (n.d.). "Mother Teresa Biography."
Online at http://www.biography.com/people/mother-teresa-9504160. (accessed 14/06/2016).

hy.com Editors (n.d.). "Nellie Bly Biography."
Online at http://www.biography.com/people/nellie-bly-9216680# (accessed 14/06/2016).

Biography.com Editors (n.d.). "Oprah Winfrey Biography."
Online at http://www.biography.com/people/oprah-winfrey-9534419#! (accessed 14/06/2016).

Biography.com Editors (n.d.). "Phyllis Diller Biography."
Online at http://www.biography.com/people/phyllis-diller-9542308 (accessed 14/06/2016).

Biography.com Editors (n.d.). "Rachel Carson Biography."
Online at http://www.biography.com/people/rachel-carson-9239741# (accessed 14/06/2016).

Biography.com Editors (n.d.). "Ruth Bader Ginsburg Biography."
Online at http://www.biography.com/people/ruth-bader-ginsburg-9312041

Biography.com Editors (n.d.). "Sandra Day O'Connor Biography."
Online at http://www.biography.com/people/sandra-day-oconnor-9426834 (accessed 14/06/2016).

Biography.com Editors (n.d.). "Sarah Boone Biography."
Online at http://www.biography.com/people/sarah-boone-21329877 (accessed 14/06/2016).

Biography.com Editors (n.d.). "Sister Rosetta Tharpe Biography."
Online at http://www.biography.com/people/sister-rosetta-tharpe-17172332 (accessed 14/06/2016).

Biography.com Editors (n.d.). "Sojourner Truth Biography."
Online at http://www.biography.com/people/sojourner-truth-9511284# (accessed 14/06/2016).

Biography.com Editors (n.d.). "Sor Juana Inés de la Cruz Biography."
Online at http://www.biography.com/people/sor-juana-in%C3%A9s-de-la-cruz-38178 (accessed 14/06/2016).

Biography.com Editors (n.d.). "Temple Grandin Biography."
Online at http://www.biography.com/people/temple-grandin-38062# (accessed 14/06/2016).

Biography.com Editors (n.d.). "Virginia Woolf BiographyBiography."
Online at http://www.biography.com/people/virginia-woolf-9536773#early-life (accessed 14/06/2016).

black-inventor.com. (2008). "Dr. Shirley Ann Jackson."
http://www.black-inventor.com/Dr-Shirley-Jackson.asp (accessed 14/06/16).

British Golf Museum. (n.d.). FAQs. Online at http://www.britishgolfmuseum.co.uk/faqs/ (accessed 14/06/2016).

British Monarchy. (n.d.).
Online at http://www.royal.gov.uk/historyofthemonarchy/scottish%20monarchs(400ad-1603)/thestewarts/maryqueenofscots.aspx (accessed 14/06/2016).

Brown, Chip. (July, 2011). "The Search for Cleopatra." National Geographic.
Online at http://ngm.nationalgeographic.com/2011/07/cleopatra/brown-text (accessed 14/06/2016).

Burke, Monte. (26 August, 2010) "How The Chicago Bears Fumbled Away A Fortune." Forbes Magazine.
Online at http://www.forbes.com/forbes/2010/0913/nfl-values-10-bears-chicago-football-money-midgets-midway.html (accessed 14/06/2016).

Calmes, Jackie, (20 April, 2016). "Harriet Tubman Ousts Andrew Jackson in Change for a $20." New York Times.
Online at http://www.nytimes.com/2016/04/21/us/women-currency-treasury-harriet-tubman.html (accessed 14/06/2016).

Cartwright, Mark. (30 September, 2012). "Nike. Definition." Ancient History Encyclopedia.
Online at http://www.ancient.eu/nike/ (accessed 14/06/2016).

Chappo, Ashley. (4 June, 2015). "The Stunning Story of the Woman Who Is the World's Most Popular Artist." Observer.
Online at http://observer.com/2015/04/the-stunning-story-of-the-woman-who-is-the-worlds-most-popular-artist/ (accessed 14/06/2016).

Churchwell, Sarah. (5 September, 2009). "Breakfast at Tiffany's: When Audrey Hepburn won Marilyn Monroe's role." The Guardian.
Online at http://www.theguardian.com/books/2009/sep/05/breakfast-at-tiffanys-audrey-hepburn (accessed 14/06/2016).

Corbin, Brett. (12 September, 2010). "Wheelchair Champ Has Rivals, but no Equals." The New York Times.
Online at http://www.nytimes.com/2010/09/12/sports/tennis/12wheelchair.html?ref=handicapped (accessed 14/06/2016).

danicapatrick.com. http://www.danicapatrick.com/ (accessed 14/06/2016).

Davies, Gareth A. (26 December, 2007). "Nawal El Moutawakel is still a running light." Telegraph.co.uk.
Online at http://www.telegraph.co.uk/sport/othersports/athletics/2329449/Nawal-El-Moutawakel-is-still-a-running-light.html (accessed 14/06/2016).

deliaderbyshire.org. http://delia-derbyshire.org/ (accessed 14/06/2016)

Digplanet. (n.d.). "Nise de Silveira."
Online at http://www.digplanet.com/wiki/Nise_da_Silveira (accessed 14/06/2016).

dollyparton.com. http://dollyparton.com/about-dolly-parton (accessed 14/06/2016).

Duguid, Sarah. (9 June, 2012). "Nawal el-Moutawakel, Morocco." Financial Times Magazine.
Online at http://www.ft.com/cms/s/2/2aa7c59a-adfb-11e1-bb8e-00144feabdc0.html (accessed 15/06/16).

Dunn, Daisy. (12 November, 2010). "Harry Potter by Numbers." Telegraph.co.uk.
Online at http://www.telegraph.co.uk/culture/harry-potter/8126514/Harry-Potter-by-numbers.html

Dunne, Eleanor. (4 September, 2013). "Seven Wonders: How Coco Chanel Changed The Course of Women's Fashion." Wonderland Magazine.
Online at http://www.wonderlandmagazine.com/2013/09/seven-wonders-how-coco-chanel-changed-the-course-of-womens-fashion/ (accessed 14/06/16).

eleanorroosevelt.org. http://www.eleanorroosevelt.org/ (accessed 14/06/16).

ellafitzgerald.com. http://www.ellafitzgerald.com/about/index.html (accessed 14/06/16).

Encyclopedia Britannica Online. (n.d.). "Boudicca."
http://www.britannica.com/biography/Boudicca (accessed 14/06/16).

Encyclopedia Britannica Online. (n.d.). "Chien-Shiung Wu."
http://www.britannica.com/biography/Chien-Shiung-Wu (accessed 14/06/16).

Encyclopedia Britannica Online. (n.d.). "Cleopatra. Queen of Egypt."
http://www.britannica.com/biography/Cleopatra-queen-of-Egypt (accessed 14/06/16).

Encyclopedia Britannica Online. (n.d.). "Dame Margot Fonteyn."
http://www.britannica.com/biography/Margot-Fonteyn (accessed 14/06/16).

Encyclopedia Britannica Online. (n.d.). "Dorothea Lange."
http://www.britannica.com/biography/Dorothea-Lange (accessed 14/06/16).

Encyclopedia Britannica Online. (n.d.). "Dorothy Kamenshek."
http://www.britannica.com/biography/Dorothy-Kamenshek (accessed 14/06/16).

Encyclopedia Britannica Online. (n.d.). "Hypatia."
http://www.britannica.com/biography/Hypatia (accessed 14/06/16).

Encyclopedia Britannica Online. (n.d.). "Margaret Bourke-White."
http://www.britannica.com/biography/Margaret-Bourke-White (accessed 14/06/16).

Encyclopedia Britannica Online. (n.d.). "Marie-Catherine Le Jumel de Barneville, countess d'Aulnoy."
http://www.britannica.com/biography/Marie-Catherine-Le-Jumel-de-Barneville-Countess-dAulnoy. (accessed 14/06/16).

Encyclopedia Britannica Online. (n.d.). "Maria Gaetana Agnesi."
http://www.britannica.com/biography/Maria-Gaetana-Agnesi (accessed 14/06/16).

Encyclopedia Britannica Online. (2016). "Mary, Mother of Jesus."
http://www.britannica.com/biography/Mary-mother-of-Jesus (accessed 14/06/16).

Encyclopedia Britannica Online. (n.d.). "Mona Lisa (da Vinci)."
http://www.britannica.com/topic/Mona-Lisa-painting (accessed 14/06/16).

Encyclopedia Britannica Online. (n.d.). "Murasaki Shikibu."
http://www.britannica.com/biography/Shikibu-Murasaki (accessed 14/06/16).

Encyclopedia Britannica Online. (n.d.). "Olive Schreiner."
http://www.britannica.com/biography/Olive-Schreiner (accessed 14/06/16).

Encyclopedia Britannica Online. (n.d.). "Shirley Chisholm."
http://www.britannica.com/biography/Shirley-Chisholm (accessed 14/06/16).

Encyclopedia Britannica Online. (n.d.). "Virginia Woolf."
http://www.britannica.com/biography/Virginia-Woolf (accessed 14/06/16).

engineergirl.org. "Martha J. Coston."
http://www.engineergirl.org/Engineers/HistoricalEngineers/4395.aspx (accessed 14/06/16).

Ericson, Raymond. (September 17, 1977). "Maria Callas, 53, Is Dead of Heart Attack in Paris."
The New York Times.
Online at http://www.nytimes.com/learning/general/onthisday/bday/1202.html
(accessed 14/06/16).

Evelyn Glennie Biography (March, 2015).
Online at https://www.evelyn.co.uk/biography/ (accessed 14/06/16).

florencegriffithjoyner.com http://www.florencegriffithjoyner.com/ (accessed 14/06/16).

Garber, Megan. (15 July, 2013). "Night Witches: The Female Fighter Pilots of World War II." The Atlantic.
Online at http://www.theatlantic.com/technology/archive/2013/07/night-witches-the-female-fight-
er-pilots-of-world-war-ii/277779/ (accessed 14/06/16).

georgiaokeeffe.net. http://www.georgiaokeeffe.net/ (accessed 14/06/16).

gibson.com (23, April, 2007). "SisterW Rosetta Tharpe: The Untold Story."
http://www.gibson.com/News-Lifestyle/Features/en-us/Sister-Rosetta-Tharpe--The-Untold-Story.
aspx (accessed 14/06/16).

girlscouts.org. https://www.girlscouts.org/
(accessed 14/06/16).

Goodly, Simon. (6 June, 2013). "Dagenham sewing machinists recall strike that changed women's lives." The Guardian.
Online at http://www.theguardian.com/politics/2013/jun/06/dagenham-sewing-machinists-strike (accessed 14/06/16).

Google Patents. "Muffler US 1473235 A."
Online at http://www.google.com/patents/US1473235 (accessed 14/06/16).

Guardian Staff. (12, May, 2014). "Dorothy Hodgkin: The only British woman to win a Nobel science prize gets a doodle." The Guardian.
Online at https://www.theguardian.com/technology/2014/may/12/google-doodle-honours-bio-chemist-dorothy-hodgkin (accessed 14/06/16).

Guinness World Records. (n.d.). "Best-selling female recording artist."
Online at http://www.guinnessworldrecords.com/world-records/best-selling-female-recording-artist (accessed 14/06/16).

Guinness World Records. (n.d.). "Oldest Person Ever."
Online at http://www.guinnessworldrecords.com/world-records/oldest-person/ (accessed 14/06/16).

Haden-Guest, Anthony. (15 November, 2008). "New York art sales: 'I Knew it was too good to last.'
The Guardian. Online at http://www.theguardian.com/artanddesign/2008/nov/15/artmarkets

Hansen, Liane, (July 18, 2010). "Mary, Queen of Scots, Mother of Golf." NPR.
Online at http://www.npr.org/templates/story/story.php?storyId=128600389 (accessed 14/06/16).

harlemglobetrotters.com (2015). "Lynette Woodard."
http://www.harlemglobetrotters.com/harlem-globetrotter-legend/lynette-woodard (accessed 14/06/16).

harrietbeecherstowecenter.org. https://www.harrietbeecherstowecenter.org/hbs/ (accessed 14/06/16).

harriet-tubman.org. http://www.harriet-tubman.org/ (accessed 14/06/16).

Hastings, Christopher. (14 June, 2008). "Anna Wintour awarded OBE." The Telegraph.
Online at http://fashion.telegraph.co.uk/news-features/TMG3364968/Anna-Wintour-awarded-OBE.html (accessed 14/06/16).

Heroes Centre. (2012). "Charlotte Cooper Sterry – All time tennis legend."
Online at http://www.heroescentre.co.uk/hall-of-fame/sport/sport-charlotte-cooper-sterry/w (accessed 14/06/16).

hillaryclinton.com. https://www.hillaryclinton.com/ (accessed 14/06/16).

History.co.uk Staff. (n.d.). "Biographies. Amy Johnson." http://www.history.co.uk/biographies/amy-johnson (accessed 14/06/16).

History.co.uk Staff. (n.d.). "Biographies. Catherine The Great." http://history.co.uk/biographies/catherine-the-great (accessed 14/06/16).

History.co.uk Staff. (n.d.). "Biographies. Evita." http://www.history.co.uk/biographies/evita (accessed 14/06/16).

History.com Staff. (2009). "Hatshepsut." http://www.history.com/topics/ancient-history/hatshepsut (accessed 14/06/16).

History.com Staff. (2009). "Joan of Arc." http://www.history.com/topics/saint-joan-of-arc (accessed 14/06/16).

History.com Staff. (2009). "Margaret Thatcher." http://www.history.com/topics/british-history/margaret-thatcher (accessed 14/06/16).

History.com Staff. (2009). "Sandra Day O'Connor." http://www.history.com/topics/sandra-day-oconnor (accessed 14/06/16).

History.com Staff. (2010). "Susan B. Anthony." http://www.history.com/topics/womens-history/susan-b-anthony (accessed 14/06/16).

Hodgson, Brian. (7 July, 2001). "Delia Derbyshire." The Guardian. Online at http://www.theguardian.com/news/2001/jul/07/guardianobituaries1 (accessed 14/06/16).

Holloway, Marguerite. (16 December, 1996). "Mary Leakey: Unearthing History." Scientific American. Online at http://www.scientificamerican.com/article/mary-leakey-unearthing-hi/ (accessed 14/06/16).

Holt, S. & Hussain, L. (20 February, 2015). "What the invincible sportswoman did next." CNN. Online at. http://edition.cnn.com/2015/02/17/tennis/the-career-of-invincible-esther-vergeer/ (accessed 15/06/16).

Huey, Steve. (n.d.). "Édith Piaf Biography." All Music.com. Online at http://www.allmusic.com/artist/%C3%A9dith-piaf-mn0000150629/biography (accessed 14/06/16).

Imagination Library. "Dolly Parton." Online at https://usa.imaginationlibrary.com/news_and_media.php#.Vyjm528VHuo (accessed 14/06/16).

IMDb. "Madonna." http://www.imdb.com/name/nm0000187/ (accessed 14/06/16).

IMDb. "Meryl Streep." http://www.imdb.com/name/nm0000658/bio?ref_=nm_ov_bio_sm (accessed 14/06/16).

IPC (8 March, 2013). "Top 10 women in Paralympic sport."
Online at http://www.paralympic.org/news/top-10-women-paralympic-sport (accessed 14/06/16).

Jacobs, Laura. (11 February, 2014). "Sonja Henie's Ice Age." Vanity Fair.
Online at http://www.vanityfair.com/hollywood/2014/02/sonja-henie-ice-skating-queen (accessed 14/06/16).

Jankowski, Lauren. (27 August, 2015). "Aphra Behn." About.com.
Online at http://womenshistory.about.com/od/behnaphra/a/Aphra-Behn.htm accessed 14/06/16).

J.K. Rowling.com. http://www.jkrowling.com/en_GB/#/about-jk-rowling. (accessed 14/06/16).

Josephine Baker, Official Website.
http://www.cmgww.com/stars/baker/about/biography.html (accessed 14/06/16).

J. Paul Getty Museum, The. "Julia Margaret Cameron." (n.d.).
http://www.getty.edu/art/collection/artists/1990/julia-margaret-cameron-british-born-in-dia-1815-1879/ (accessed 14/06/16).

Kettler, Sara. (n.d.). "Emmeline Pankhurst Biography."
Online at http://www.biography.com/people/emmeline-pankhurst-9432764 (accessed 14/06/16).

Kiger, Nick. (August 30, 2012). "Trischa Zorn inducted into Paralympic Hall of Fame." TeamUSA.org.
http://www.teamusa.org/US-Paralympics/Features/2012/August/30/Trischa-Zorn-inducted-into-Paralympic-Hall-of-Fame (accessed 14/06/16).

Kristine Lilly, Official Website. http://kristinelilly13.com/ (accessed 14/06/16).

Kruhly, Madeleine. (15 July, 2011). "Harry Potter, Inc: How the Boy Wizard Created a $21 Billion Business." The Atlantic.
Online at http://www.theatlantic.com/business/archive/2011/07/harry-potter-inc-how-the-boy-wizard-created-a-21-billion-business/241948/ (accessed 14/06/16).

Lamont, Tom. (6 December, 2014). "Dolly Parton: 'There's more to me than the big hair and the phoney stuff.'" The Guardian.
Online at http://www.theguardian.com/music/2014/dec/06/dolly-parton-more-to-me-than-big-hair-phoney-stuff

Langley, William. (13 October, 2013). "Edith Piaf: Mistress of heartbreak and pain who had a few regrets after all." Telegraph.co.uk.
Online at http://www.telegraph.co.uk/culture/10374637/Edith-Piaf-Mistress-of-heartbreak-and-pain-who-had-a-few-regrets-after-all.html (accessed 14/06/16).

Lewis, Jone Johnson. (26 March, 2016). "Cleopatra, Last Pharaoh of Egypt." About.com.
Online at http://womenshistory.about.com/od/cleopatra/a/cleopatra.htm (accessed 14/06/16).

Lewis, Jone Johnson. (2015). "Emmy Noether." About.com.
Online at http://womenshistory.about.com/od/sciencemath1/fl/Emmy-Noether.htm (accessed 14/06/16).

Lewis, Jone Johnson. (4 May, 2016). "Josephine Baker." About.com.
Online at http://womenshistory.about.com/od/bakerjosephine/p/joseph_ne_baker.htm (accessed 14/06/16).

Lewis, Jone Johnson. (n.d.). "Margaret Bourke-White." About.com.
Online at http://womenshistory.about.com/od/margaretbourkewhite/a/Margaret-Bourke-White.htm (accessed 14/06/16).

Lewis, Jone Johnson. (n.d.). "Maria Agnesi." About.com.
Online at http://womenshistory.about.com/od/sciencemath1/a/maria_agnesi.htm (accessed 14/06/16).

Lewis, Jone Johnson. (18 February, 2016). "Nellie Bly." About.com.
Online at http://womenshistory.about.com/od/blynellie/p/Nellie-Bly.htm (accessed 14/06/16).

Lifetimetv (n.d.). "Coco Chanel Biography."
Online at http://www.lifetimetv.co.uk/biography/biography-coco-chanel (accessed 14/06/16).

Louvre. "Mona Lisa – Portrait of Lisa Gherardini, wife of Francesco del Giocondo."
Online at http://www.louvre.fr/en/oeuvre-notices/mona-lisa-%E2%80%93-portrait-lisa-gherardini-wife-francesco-del-giocondo (accessed 14/06/16).

madonna.com. http://www.madonna.com/ (accessed 14/06/16).

Maranzani, Barbara. (2013). "Bertha Benz Hits the Road." History.com.
Online at http://www.history.com/news/bertha-benz-hits-the-road-125-years-ago (accessed 14/06/16).

margaretthatcher.org. http://www.margaretthatcher.org/essential/biography.asp (accessed 14/06/16).

"Marie Curie – Biographical." Nobelprize.org. Nobel Media AB 2014.
Online at http://www.nobelprize.org/nobel_prizes/physics/laureates/1903/marie-curie-bio.html (accessed 14/06/16).

marilynmonroe.com. 14/06/2016. http://marilynmonroe.com/about/ (accessed 14/06/16).

Mello, Luiz Carlos. (November, 2006). "Nise de Silveira and the Artists of Engenho de Dentro." Review Literature and Arts of the Americas Issue 72(2):270-276. https://www.researchgate.net/publication/233103051_Nise_da_Silveira_and_the_Artists_of_Engenho_de_Dentro (accessed 14/06/16).

mercedes-benz.com. "Bertha Benz." https://www.mercedes-benz.com/en/mercedes-benz/classic/history/bertha-benz-2/ (accessed 14/06/16).

mistycopeland.com. http://mistycopeland.com/ (accessed 14/06/16).

motherteresa.org. http://www.motherteresa.org/layout.html (accessed 14/06/16).

nancylieberman.com. http://www.nancylieberman.com/ (accessed 14/06/16).

Napikowski, Linda. (n.d.). "The Dagenham Women's Strike of 1968." About.com. Online at http://womenshistory.about.com/od/feminism/a/Dagenham-Womens-Strike.htm (accessed 14/06/16).

National Trust. (n.d.). "The Life of Beatrix Potter." Online at http://www.nationaltrust.org.uk/beatrix-potter-gallery-and-hawkshead/features/the-life-of-beatrix-potter (accessed 14/06/16).

National Women's History Museum (n.d.). "Dr. Chien-Shiung Wu (1912-1997)." Online at http://www.nwhm.org/education-resources/biography/biographies/chien-shiung-wu/ (accessed 14/06/16).

National Women's History Museum. (n.d.). "Sojourner Truth. (1797-1883)" Online at https://www.nwhm.org/education-resources/biography/biographies/sojourner-truth/ (accessed 14/06/16).

New Zealand History (Updated 17 July, 2014). "New Zealand women and the vote." Online at http://www.nzhistory.net.nz/politics/womens-suffrage (accessed 14/06/16).

okeeffemusem.org. https://www.okeeffemuseum.org/about-georgia-okeeffe/ (accessed 14/06/16).

olympic.org. (n.d.). "Charlotte Cooper." http://www.olympic.org/charlotte-cooper (accessed 14/06/16).

olympic.org. (n.d.). "Josefa Idem." http://www.olympic.org/josefa-idem (accessed 14/06/16).

olympic.org. (n.d.). "Ms Nawal El Moutawakel." http://www.olympic.org/ms-nawal-el-moutawakel (accessed 14/06/16).

olympic.org. (n.d.). "Nadia Comaneci." http://www.olympic.org/videos/first-perfect-ten-nadia-comaneci (accessed 14/06/16).

Oulton, Randal. (3 August, 2010; revised 8 December, 2010). "Ruth Wakefield." CooksInfo.com. Online at http://www.cooksinfo.com/ruth-wakefield (accessed 14/06/16).

Pawtucket, Morris. (n.d.). "Top 10 Most Famous Photographers Of All Time." Picture Correct.com. Online at http://www.picturecorrect.com/tips/top-10-most-famous-photographers-of-all-time/ (accessed 14/06/16).

PBS American Masters. (28 April, 2006) "Georgia O'Keeffe. About the Painter" Online at http://www.pbs.org/wnet/americanmasters/georgia-okeeffe-about-the-painter/55/

Poetry Foundation. (n.d.). "Sappho." Online at http://www.poetryfoundation.org/poems-and poets/poets/detail/sappho (accessed 14/06/16).

rachelcarson.org. http://rachelcarson.org/ (accessed 14/06/16).

Ray, Rachel. (26 February, 2012). "Daytona 500: Racing Superstar Danica Patrick commits career to America's NASCAR." Telegraph.co.uk. Online at http://www.telegraph.co.uk/sport/motorsport/indycar/9106630/Daytona-500-Racing-superstar-Danica-Patrick-commits-career-to-Americas-NASCAR.html (accessed 14/06/16).

reginahalmich.org. http://www.regina-halmich.org/(accessed 14/06/16)

rejectedprincesses.com. (n.d.). "Ching Shih (1775-1844)." http://www.rejectedprincesses.com/princesses/ching-shih (accessed 14/06/16).

RNIB (2014). "Who was Helen Keller?". http://help.rnib.org.uk/help/daily-living/helen-keller (accessed 14/06/16).

Schudel, Matt. (22 May, 2010) "Dorothy "Dottie" Kamenshek dead; women's professional baseball player." Washington Post. Online at http://www.washingtonpost.com/wp-dyn/content/article/2010/05/21/AR2010052104773.html

Scotsman, The (25 September, 2004). "Variations on the Dr Who theme." Online at http://www.scotsman.com/lifestyle/variations-on-the-dr-who-theme-1-555717

serenawilliams.com. http://serenawilliams.com/about/ (accessed 14/06/16).

Sischy, Ingrid. (8 June, 1998). "The Designer COCO CHANEL." Time. Online at http://content.time.com/time/magazine/article/0,9171,988494,00.html (accessed 14/06/16).

Smith, Monica M. (26 March, 2015). "The Woman Inventor Behind "Monopoly." Smithsonian National Museum of American History. Online at http://invention.si.edu/woman-inventor-behind-monopoly (accessed 14/06/16).

sojournertruth.com. (n.d.). "Sojourner Truth." http://www.sojournertruth.com/ (accessed 14/06/16).

Supreme Court Historical Society, The. (n.d.). "Justice Ruth Bader Ginsburg." supremecourthistory.org. (accessed 14/06/16).

susanbanthonyhouse.org. https://susanbanthonyhouse.org/her-story/biography.php (accessed 14/06/16).

Tate Modern. "Yayoi Kusama." http://www.tate.org.uk/whats-on/tate-modern/exhibition/yayoi-kusama (accessed 14/06/16).

TCM. Turner Classic Movies.com (n.d.). "Katharine Hepburn." http://www.tcm.com/tcmdb/person/85052%7C92357/Katharine-Hepburn/ (accessed 14/06/16).

TED.com. "Sylvia Earle." http://www.ted.com/speakers/sylvia_earle (accessed 14/06/16).

templegrandin.com. http://templegrandin.com/(accessed 14/06/16).

Tennessee Athletics. (n.d.). "Women's Basketball. Pat Summitt." Online at http://www.utsports.com/sports/w-baskbl/mtt/summitt_pat00.html (accessed 14/06/16).

Time Out. (n.d.)."Top 20 women photographers." Online at http://www.timeout.com/newyork/art/top-20-women-photographers (accessed 14/06/16).

Topend Sports. (n.d.). "Oldest and Youngest Olympians (Summer Games)." Online at http://www.topendsports.com/events/summer/oldest-youngest.htm.

Topend Sports. (n.d.). "Sports Illustrated Top 100 Female Athletes. (2000)." Online at http://www.topendsports.com/world/lists/greatest-all-time/women-si100.htm (accessed 14/06/16).

TopFor. "Top 10 Inventions by Women that Changed the World." Online at http://top10for.com/top-10-inventions-women-changed-world/ (accessed 14/06/16).

Unicef. (19 June, 2003). "Audrey Hepburn." Online at http://www.unicef.org/people/people_audrey_hepburn.html (accessed 14/06/16).

venuswilliams.com. http://venuswilliams.com/venus/ (accessed 14/06/16).

Victoria and Albert Museum. 'Beatrix Potter." (n.d.). Online at http://www.vam.ac.uk/page/b/beatrix-potter/ (accessed 14/06/16).

Victoria and Albert Museum. 'Julia Margaret Cameron." (n.d.). Online at http://www.vam.ac.uk/page/j/julia-margaret-cameron/ (accessed 14/06/16).

Glossary

Abolitionist
A person who fights to get rid of a law or practice that they feel is harmful. This commonly referred to the abolition of slavery in the U.S.A.

Activist/Advocate
A person who speaks out for and defends what they feel is right.

Civil Rights
Rights of liberty and equality for every individual in society, regardless of race, gender, age, ability, and more.

Feminism
A belief system and social movement that supports equal rights for women to those of men.

Humanitarian/Philanthropist
A person who actively supports social welfare and works to improve the lives of others. Philanthropy may also include financial support.

Segregation
The practice of separating things or people, according to their characteristics. This practice was used in the past to separate people according to race, such as in the American South.

Suffrage/Suffragette/Suffragist
Suffrage is the right to vote. The suffragettes (a term more commonly used in the U.K.) and suffragists (U.S.) are both terms for individuals who fought for women's right to vote.

Index

Image credits

All illustrations by Chuck Gonzales

Cover images: Rosa Parks—ALAMY; Frida Kahlo—ALAMY; Malala Yousafzai—Shutterstock; Beyoncé—Shutterstock

Chapter One: Arts & literature, Page 19 tr, Behn Oroonoko title page—United States public domain; 20 tr, D'Aulnoy—United States public domain; Page 24 tr Julia Margaret Cameron—Henry Herschel Hay Cameron; 27 tr Beatrix Potter—Charles G.Y. King; 30 bl Coco Chane—Time/Getty; 39 tl Dorothea Lange—FSA photo by Rondal Partridge via Library of Congress; 39 bl Lee Miller—David E. Scherman; 58 tr Ella Fitzgerald—William P. Gottlieb; 84 Evelyn Glennie Horniman—Caroline Purday; 85 Evelyn Glennie, snare drum and bowtie—Philipp Rathmer/Brigitte; 88 tl Mary Wollstonecraft; Chapter Two: Politics & world-building: 132 Rosa Parks; Chapter Three: Science & innovation: 159 Maria Gaetana Agnesi—United States public domain; 165 tr Ada Lovelace computation of Bernoulli numbers—Ada Lovelace; 166 tr Maria Mitchell—H. Dassell; 167 tr Maria Mitchell's telescope—Dpbsmith; 177 tr Annie Jump Cannon—Smithsonian Institution from United States; 180 tr Emmy Noether—Unknown; 185 tr Emmy Noether—U.S. federal government; 185 tr Chien-Shiung Wu—Smithsonian Institution Archives; 193 bl Emmy Noether—Unknown; 199 br Maria Telkes—New York World-Telegram and the Sun staff photographer; Chapter Four: Sports & endurance: 220 Eliza Pollock—Courtesy of the Chicago Historical Society; 220 Hilda Hewlett—Unknown; 222 Ladies Championship card—Unknown; 223 South End Lawn Tennis Club—Unknown; 235 tl Hilda Hewlett—Unknown; Epilogue: Eleanor Roosevelt in Galapagos Island—U.S. National Archives and Records Administration.
All other images Shutterstock

ABOUT THE AUTHOR

Caitlin Doyle is an author, editor, creative writing teacher, and social activist with a postgraduate degree in women's studies. Caitlin has written and edited a number of books for adults and children for over almost 20 years. Her titles include *Outrageously Adorable Dog Knits* and *Why I Love Bedtime*, among others. Caitlin is tremendously proud of her latest title, *Girls Can Do Anything*, a book she has dreamed of publishing for ten years. Originally from Detroit, Michigan, U.S.A. (by way of St. Andrews, Scotland, and Dublin, Ireland), Caitlin now lives in London, England. Her writing muse, Ivy the Pug, snored loyally by her side during the writing of every page of this book.

ABOUT THE ILLUSTRATOR

Chuck Gonzales works in both the adult and children's sectors, creating characters, environments, and masterful likenesses for books, advertising, animation, and editorial markets . . . always with at least a hint of humor. Some of his clients include: The *New York Times*, MetLife, ESPN, Fortune, *New York* Magazine, Nickelodeon, Disney, Chronicle Books, HarperCollins, Penguin, and Scholastic. He lives and works in Providence, Rhode Island, U.S.A.

Acknowledgements

Ten years ago, I started planning this book in my head. I never knew if it would see the light of day—or the ink of a printing press, for that matter. I'm over the moon that it has, and I would like to take this opportunity to thank the people who have helped me make *Girls Can Do Anything* a reality. As a reader, you may not be aware of how many people are involved to make a book actually happen, from editor to proofreader, designer to illustrator, production to sales, and everyone in between.

I am grateful to my lovely illustrator, Chuck Gonzales, who was passionate about this book from its very first mention. A big thank you goes to my designer, Pete Clayman, who worked tirelessly and enthusiastically at all hours to create the beautiful book now in your hands. Thanks to Catherine Brereton and Simon Holland (and his fellow production baby), the hard-working editorial team behind the text. And thank you to Firefly Books, and Mary Thompson at HarperCollins, for making it a reality. Thank you to my family and friends for their support, input, and enthusiasm, including Mom, Dad, Megh, Steve, Pete, Stew, and each and every friend who shared ideas along the way—and a particular thank you goes to Will for his patience as "Girls CDA" took up my every spare waking (and non-waking!) moment, as the Fates threw everything they could at 2016. I owe a very big thank you (and a handful of treats) to my devoted writing companion, Ivy the Pug, who snored beside me, in sisterly solidarity, with each page I wrote.

Finally—and most crucially—I'm grateful to the women included in this book for achieving such incredible things and for being such amazing individuals, often in the face of extreme hardship and prejudice. You are my heroes.

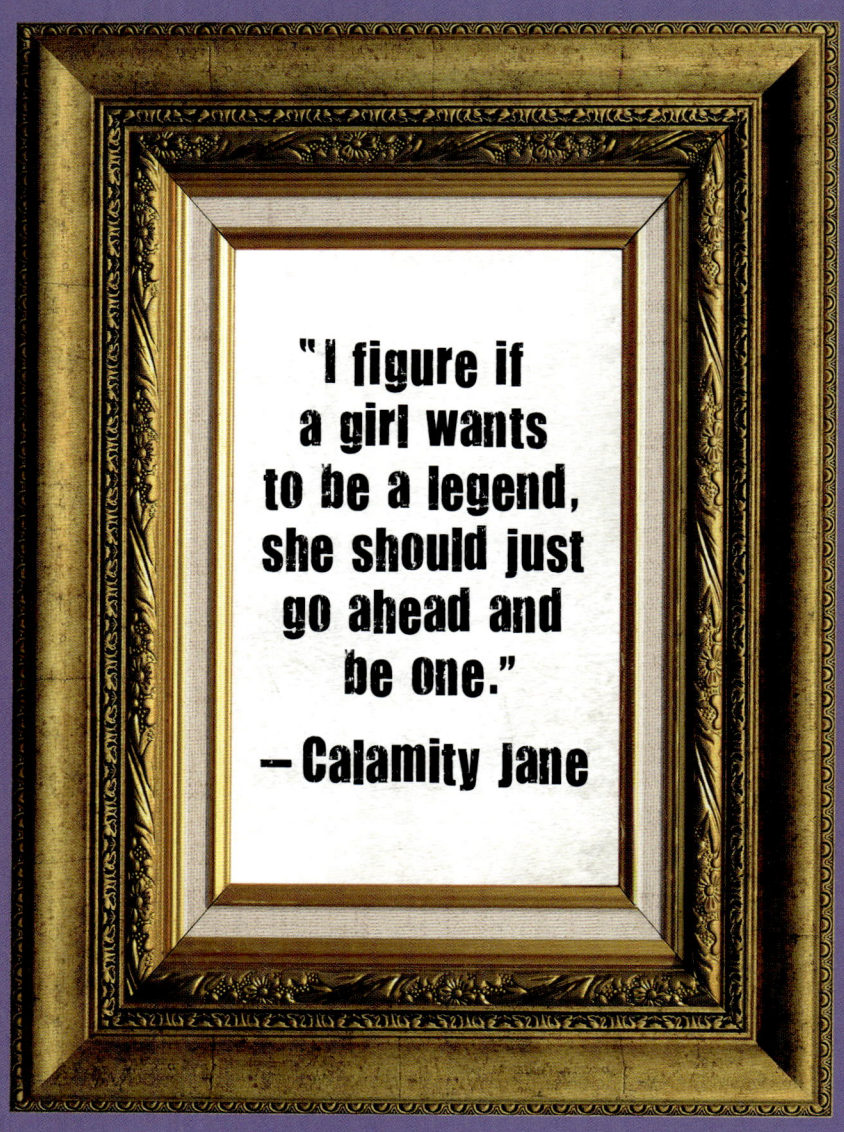

"I figure if
a girl wants
to be a legend,
she should just
go ahead and
be one."

— Calamity Jane